Youth and Politics in Japan

Youth and Politics in Japan

Joseph A. Massey
Dartmouth College

Lexington Books
D.C. Heath and Company
Lexington, Massachusetts
Toronto   London

Library of Congress Cataloging in Publication Data

Massey, Joseph A
  Youth and politics in Japan.

  Bibliography: p.
  Includes index.
  1. Youth—Japan—Political activity. 2. Political socialization. 3. Japan—
Politics and government—1945- I. Title.
HQ799.J3M374   301.5'92'0952   75-21304
ISBN 0-669-00163-5

Copyright © 1976 by D.C. Heath and Company.

Published simultaneously in Canada.

Printed in the United States of America.

International Standard Book Number: 0-669-00163-5

Library of Congress Catalog Card Number: 75-21304

Liz, kimi no tame ni . . .

Contents

List of Figures   xi

List of Tables   xiii

Preface   xvii

Chapter 1   **Political Socialization in a New Democracy**   1

Political Socialization and Political
   Regimes: The Case of Japan   1
The Theoretical Context   2
The Political Culture of Democracy:
   The Formal Ideal   8
Two Political Countercultures:
   Tradition and Structural Opposition   9
Research Design and Methodology   15
The Structure of the Analysis   17

Chapter 2   **The Missing Leader: Japanese Youths' View of Political Authority**   21

Introduction   21
The Emperor: Peripheral Monarch   23
The Prime Minister: Distant and
   Impersonal Leader   27
The Spillover of Affect: Support for
   Institutions among Teenagers and
   Parents   38
The Missing Leader and the Missing
   Hero: Some Speculations on the
   Role of History   44
Conclusion   47

Chapter 3   Symbols of Consensus: Democracy
             and Peace   51

             Introduction   51
             The Meaning of Democracy   52
             The Value of Democracy   55
             Consensus versus Majority Rule   56
             Democracy, Peace, and National
                 Identity   64
             Conclusion   68

Chapter 4   Symbols of Dissensus: The Growth
             of Partisanship   73

             Introduction   73
             Parties and Ideologies: The Nature
                 of Political Confrontation   75
             The Extent of Party Identification   77
             The Inheritance of Partisanship:
                 The Family as Source   80
             Social Determinants of Partisanship:
                 Urban-Rural Residence and
                 Socioeconomic Status   90
             The Cognitive and Affective Content
                 of Partisanship   94
             Conclusion   95

Chapter 5   Symbols of Dissensus: The Emergence
             of Ideology   101

             Introduction   101
             Cognitive and Perceptual Aspects
                 of Ideology   104
             Affective Responses to Capitalism,
                 Socialism, and Other Symbols   108
             Constraint and Causal Reasoning:
                 Ideology as a Style of Thought   111
             Ideology and Partisanship   116
             Conclusion   122

Chapter 6   **The Political Self: Social and**
                   Psychological Influences   125

                   Introduction   125
                   Intervening Psychocultural Influences
                     on the Political Self: Ego-Autonomy
                     and Social Trust   127
                   The Dependent Variables: The Teenager's
                     Political Self   131
                   Conclusion   149

Chapter 7   **Sources of the Political Self:**
                   The Role of the Family   155

                   Introduction   155
                   The Family in the Wider Nexus of
                     Socializing Influences   158
                   Fathers versus Mothers as Political
                     Role Models   161
                   Parent-Child Agreement on Political
                     Orientations   164
                   Affection, Authority, and Family
                     Political Influence   170
                   "The Family Writ Large":
                     Generalization from the
                     Family to the Polity   174
                   Conclusion   177

Chapter 8   **Summary and Conclusions**   183

                   The Findings   183
                   Some Remaining Questions   189
                   Political Socialization and the
                     Future of Japanese Political Culture   190

                   Appendixes   193

Appendix A   Methodological Postscript   195

Appendix B   Student and Parent Questionnaires   201

x

Bibliography   211

Index   227

About the Author   235

List of Figures

2-1   Mean Scores, by Grade, for Images of the
Prime Minister and Local Leader   33

6-1   Path Analysis Model of Japanese Teenagers'
Political Efficacy and Political Interest   141

6-2   Path Analysis Model of Japanese Teenagers'
Output Support   148

6-3   Path Analysis Model of Japanese Teenagers'
Input Support   148

List of Tables

1-1   Patterns of Political Orientations in the
       Formal Democratic Culture and the
       Traditional and Structural-Oppositional
       Countercultures in Japan   11

2-1   Perceptions of the Emperor's Importance   24

2-2   Younger Children's Attitudes toward the
       Prime Minister   28

2-3   Cross-National Comparison of Children's
       View of Political Leaders' Honesty   29

2-4   Adult Popular Support for Japanese and
       American Chief Executives   31

2-5   Comparison of Political Institutions'
       Concern for Ordinary People   38

2-6   Comparison of Political Institutions'
       Responsiveness   40

2-7   Comparison of Political Institutions'
       Inclusiveness   42

2-8   Corruption in the Government and Diet   43

2-9   Willingness to Abandon Popular Input into
       Politics   44

3-1   Preferred Method of Group Decision Making   58

3-2   Attitudes toward Majority Rule: The Large
       Minority   60

3-3   Attitudes toward Majority Rule: The Small
       Minority   62

3-4   Reactions to Pacifism and Democracy Compared   65

3-5   Peace versus Freedom   67

4-1   Cross-National Comparison of Party Identification
           among Japanese, American, and European Youth   80

4-2   Distribution of Party Support, by Age and
           Generation: Parents and Students Compared   82

4-3   Students' Party Identification, by Parents'
           Party Identification   85

4-4   Cross-National Comparison of Parent-Children
           Agreement in Party Identification   86

4-5   Party Identification of Students and Parents,
           by Urban-Rural Residents and Socioeconomic
           Status   92

4-6   Interaction of Urban-Rural Residence and
           Socioeconomic Status on Party Identification
           of Students and Parents   93

4-7   Accuracy of Children's Perceptions of Policies
           of the Two Major Parties (LDP and JSP)   95

5-1   Capitalism versus Democracy as Defining
           Characteristics of Japan   104

5-2   Meaning of Capitalism and Socialism: Correct
           and Incorrect Associations   106

5-3   Affective Reactions to Various "isms" of
           Students and Parents   108

5-4   Capitalism and Socialism Compared on Five
           Attributes   109

5-5   Correlations between Reactions to Capitalism,
           Socialism, and Communism   112

5-6   Correlation of Students' and Parents' Reactions
           to Capitalism and Socialism with Comparison
           of Values in Capitalist versus Socialist
           Countries   114

5-7	Attitudes toward the Relationship between Democracy and Capitalism and Socialism	116
5-8	Students' Party Support and Ideology	119
5-9	Partial and Conditional Gammas between Students' Party Support and Ideology Scale with Other Factors Controlled	120
6-1	Ego-Autonomy Scale Items with Responses, by Generation	129
6-2	Social Trust Scale Items and Responses, by Generation	130
6-3	Political Efficacy Scale Items and Responses, by Generation	132
6-4	Correlates of Teenagers' Political Efficacy	133
6-5	Political Interest Scale Items and Responses by Generation	136
6-6	Correlates of Teenagers' Political Interest	137
6-7	Matrix of Institutional Support Scale Correlations	143
6-8	Correlates of Teenagers' Input and Output Support	144
7-1	Teenagers' Perceptions of Political Aspects of Parents, Teachers, and Friends	158
7-2	Students' Perceptions of Parents' Political Interest	162
7-3	Parent-Student Agreement on Six Political Orientations	164
7-4	Parent-Student Agreement on Six Political Orientations, by Sex Both of Students and Parents	166

7-5   Parent-Student Agreement on Six Political Orientations, by Two Measures of Family Politicization   169

7-6   Family Efficacy: Students' and Parents' Replies to Two Items on the Child's Influence in the Family   172

7-7   Parent-Student Agreement on Six Political Orientations, by Two Measures of Family Interference with Students' Autonomy   174

7-8   Correlations of Students' Image of Prime Minister's Concern for the Ordinary People with Two Measures of Parental Concern for the Child   176

Preface

The research reported in this study took place during 1968 and 1969 at the height of a period of student unrest and violence in Japan. One college campus after another was shut down by disturbances, and the conflict even found its way to many high school campuses. The turmoil soon reached the University of Tokyo, where I was affiliated with the program in Sociology of the Faculty of Arts; I thus had a close-up view of the character of political alienation among an important segment of Japanese youth. It was against the background of this turmoil, and in part as an attempt to place the alienation of the student activists into a framework within which its significance could be evaluated relative to the broader patterns of political values and beliefs of young Japanese as a whole, that I conducted this study of the political learning process among Japanese teenagers.

Throughout the study I have followed the Japanese practice in writing Japanese names—that is, family name precedes surname. In the case of American authors of Japanese ancestry, however, the name is given in the Western style. I should also note that for the sake of simplicity I have omitted marking long vowels in Japanese words.

It is one of the great joys of scholarship that carrying out a large-scale study inevitably requires the assistance and support of many kind people. I have accumulated a debt of gratitude to numerous colleagues and friends, both Japanese and American, that I can acknowledge but never hope to repay.

Throughout every stage in the process of research and writing I have been uniquely fortunate to have had the counsel and wisdom of Fred Greenstein—teacher, adviser, friend—without whom this study would have been impossible. His thorough reading of the entire manuscript and detailed suggestions for improvements are responsible for much of what is of value in the pages that follow.

To Chitoshi Yanaga, who introduced me to the joys and woes of the study of Japanese politics and who gave unceasingly of his guidance and encouragement, I am likewise profoundly indebted. Lewis Austen and Peter Busch have read the entire manuscript and contributed their insights and suggestions. Howard Erdman's comments on part of the manuscript have likewise been most helpful. I also benefited in diverse ways from the assistance of other American colleagues too numerous to mention here by name.

In Japan, I was the beneficiary of a veritable cornucopia of kindness. Professor Watanuki Joji was instrumental in an enormous number of ways in making this study possible, beginning with sponsoring my affiliation with the program in Sociology at Tokyo University.

I am likewise deeply indebted to a fellow student of political socialization in Japan, Professor Okamura Tadao, for his great generosity in sharing his knowledge and scholarly resources in the area of our shared interest. Both Professors Watanuki and Okamura afforded me the privilege of participating in their seminars at Tokyo University and International Christian University, respectively, as a result of which I not only learned a great deal about Japanese culture and politics but also met and made friends with students and other young scholars with interests similar to my own, who also helped me in many ways.

Professor Sato Nobuo of Utsunomiya University and his wife, Katsuko, a fellow member of Professor Watanuki's seminar, were of tremendous help in establishing contact with the schools in Tochigi prefecture where I carried out the survey. I am also grateful to Professor Matsubara Haruo of Tokyo University for his help in this regard as in many others. Professor Suzuki Hiro of Tokyo University of Education kindly shared with me some of his vast knowledge of Japanese student politics.

An important part of the validity of the findings reported here depends on the validity of the questionnaire. I was fortunate to have had the help of a large number of friends and colleagues in the drafting and polishing of the questionnaire. Professors Watanuki and Okamura played an especially important role here, as did the students in their seminars. I should mention in particular the help of Iwase Yori in this regard.

The great practical difficulties that beset a large-scale research project such as this one could not have been overcome without the efficient and unflagging help of my assistants. Yasue Akio, in particular, played a vital role, assisting both in the administration of the questionnaires and in the individual interviews. Sakogawa Yoshikazu and Mimoto Hiroko also contributed invaluable help in both the survey and the interviews. Maki Atsuko spent long hours transcribing the taped interviews. Takeuchi Etsuko took charge of the enormous task of coding the responses from the questionnaires, in which she was ably assisted by Inui Setsuko, Ishii Nobuko, Komatsu Hiroe, Munemasa Yasuko, Nagase Kumiko, Sato Yukimi, Shiokawa Yumi, Ueno Naoko, Umezu Machiko, Yagi Tsutako, Yoshii Setsuko, and Yoshiaki Mayumi. Sato Fumiko did the exacting job of keypunching the more than six thousand IBM cards with speed, accuracy, and good spirits.

No group of people has been more important to this study than the teachers and principals of the schools who permitted me into their classrooms, and the children and the parents who are themselves the subjects of this study. I am especially grateful to Ishigooka Jiro sensei of Bunkyo-Ku Dai-Roku Chugakko in Tokyo who gave a great deal of his time and his generosity in innumerable ways to this foreign scholar. I hope that he and the other teachers to whom I owe so much will find this study of some interest and some use in their own continuing study of Japanese youth.

Funding for various phases of the study has come from a variety of sources. The Department of Political Science of Yale University provided support for the initial analysis of the data. The bulk of the computer analysis of the data was carried out using the superb facilities of the Kiewit Computation Center at Dartmouth with support for the analysis generously provided by the College. I am grateful to my colleague Dennis Sullivan for his help in getting the data on the computer and to John Cunningham, John Lyons, and especially John Fry for assistance in programming. Dartmouth has also borne part of the cost of the typing of the manuscript. Mrs. Donna Musgrove's patience and gusto in typing an early draft of the manuscript did as much for my spirits as for the physical progress of the book, and I am grateful on both counts.

Support of my field research in Japan, as well as during a period of some months prior to and following the field work, was provided by a grant from the Foreign Area Fellowship Program. Needless to say, the conclusions, opinions, and other statements herein are entirely my own responsibility not that of the Fellowship Program nor any other individual or institution.

I am indebted to the *American Political Science Review* for extending permission to reprint Chapter 2, which was originally published as an article in that journal.

Finally, nothing I can say can adequately express my appreciation and admiration for the countless ways and selfless spirit in which my wife, Elizabeth T. Massey, has helped in bringing this study to realization. She has contributed much to the substance of this study, from translating the transcript of the interviews into colloquial English, which made their analysis an infinitely easier task, to serving as a principal editor and critic of the manuscript. She has been a vital source of strength and encouragement as well as a sometime gadfly without whose gentle prodding the study might still be in the planning stage.

1

Political Socialization in a New Democracy

Political Socialization and Political Regimes: The Case of Japan

In much of politics, as in much of all else, the child is the father of the man. Political regimes rest not only on constitutional and philosophical foundations but on cultural and psychological ones as well. They are rooted not only in the history of the society but in the values and beliefs of its citizens and leaders. Those values and beliefs, which activate and legitimate the institutions of authority and the processes of participation, are formed and molded in a life-long process that begins long before political adulthood.

This book is a study of the emerging cultural and psychological foundations of politics in contemporary Japan, a study of the political values and beliefs of young people raised and socialized under Japan's new democratic regime. It examines how the individual in today's Japan acquires a political consciousness and a political identity in the journey through childhood and adolescence and how that identity compares with those acquired by his parents in their own socialization under the old regime and resocialization under the new one. It is, consequently, a study of political continuity and change in the oldest and stablest of the new democracies in the non-Western world.

It is paradoxical, though by no means surprising, that most of what we know about the development of regime support comes from research on the United States, where a democratic regime has long been established and where (at least until the mid-1960s basic orientations toward the institutions, norms, and values of political life have constituted a broad political cultural consensus in which ideological cleavage has been at a minimum. But in many contemporary political systems the regime is likely to have been only recently established, with still fragile roots in the political culture. New democracies, in particular, have proven to be especially fragile as postwar history has demonstrated with depressing regularity. Thus, a central question of comparative politics becomes how a new regime—especially a new democracy—develops strength and legitimacy in a political system torn between competing values and loyalties and conflicting traditions and ideologies.

Japan's democratic regime was imposed by a foreign military occupation less than three decades ago. The norms, values, and beliefs associated with that new regime run directly counter, in many cases, to those that Japanese born and educated before 1945 had learned to hold dear. In addition, ever since the

1

inception of the democratic regime, Japanese politics has been characterized by a profound cleavage along ideological lines. Confronting each other over a gulf of hostility and fundamental policy disagreement have been conservatives who have dominated the national government throughout the postwar period and progressives[a] who, while in a position of near-permanent opposition and frustrated in nearly all of their national policy objectives, have enjoyed the overwhelming support of the nation's intellectuals, journalists, and teachers. Japan is thus, from several perspectives, a model of the new democracy confronted with challenges from both past and present. Given the high mortality rate of the democracies established outside the West, especially in Asia where Japan now appears to be the sole democratic success, the reasons for that success inevitably incite inquiry.

The approach to that inquiry taken here is to examine the role played by the political socialization of today's Japanese adolescents in the development of a political culture supportive of the democratic regime. This study focuses on a range of political orientations associated with democratic politics and a democratic political culture, and it examines the competitive values and attitudes that arise from the coexistence of political countercultures on the right and the left and from past tradition and present ideological cleavage. The range of orientations over whose development the analysis extends includes: (1) support for the institutions of the democratic regime and for its legitimizing values and principles, decision processes and rules; (2) orientations that are linked to the creation of a political self-identity and center on identification with a political party and the acquisition of an ideology; and (3) attitudes encouraging involvement in the political process that are supported by feelings of political efficacy and political interest. The analysis also incorporates data on the teenagers' parents across the whole range of orientations studied in order to permit comparison of the prevailing patterns in both the current and the emerging political cultures.

The Theoretical Context

The proposition that political systems depend for support, at least in part, on mass psychological foundations created as the result of pre-adult socialization is a relatively recent basis for political research but derives from a long-established view with origins in the works of the classical commentators on politics—Plato and his successors.[1] Among the influential modern proponents of this view have been the writers of the "national character" school who occupy a special place in the history of both social theory generally and the study of Japanese culture in particular.[2]

---

[a]"Progressive" is used in this study as it is used in Japanese politics to refer to the "progressive camp"—that is, the Socialist and Communist Parties and associated groups on the left.

The first premise of the national character approach was that the learning that takes place in the experiences of early childhood and infancy is of primary and enduring importance in determining the personality of the individual and in structuring all his subsequent learning. The attitudes of the child toward his father and mother that result from those experiences will be the prototypes for his attitudes toward all people he encounters thereafter, particularly those who occupy positions of authority, such as his boss and even his political leaders.

A second major premise of the approach was that a common set of experiences with parents in early childhood produce in the members of a culture a common set of psychological structures ("national character"), the central needs and drives of which are reflected in the social and political institutions of the society.[3] Thus, in this perspective, the state is essentially "the family writ large," and the patterns of adult political attitudes and behavior that predominate in a society derive from its prevailing child-rearing practices. "Only by changing the patterns of social experience in infancy," said Douglas Haring, writing of Japanese character, "can a society undergo permanent reform either toward democracy or toward autocracy."[4]

The numerous national character analyses of imperial Japan written by Westerners in the 1940s played an important role in the intellectual climate surrounding the social and educational reforms imposed by the American Occupation in its program to democratize postwar Japanese society. Those analyses laid the blame for the antidemocratic aspects of the society before 1945—its authoritarian institutions and its overseas aggression—mainly and ultimately on the family. Some analysts pointed to the alleged paternal authoritarianism of the family as the prototype for political authoritarianism and militarism; others singled out the trauma supposedly suffered by the Japanese infant as a result of excessively early and harsh toilet training and weaning as the source of adult feelings of aggression and fear of authority.

Despite the insights this emphasis on the individual's early childhood experiences brought to the analyses of Japanese culture as well as the cultures of other societies, it has become apparent that the national character approach is replete with problems of evidence and inference. Critics have pointed out that the national character writers rarely if ever made any attempt to establish empirically just how dominant or modal the child-rearing practices they described were; nor did they often marshal data on the distribution of the asserted national characteristics themselves.[5] If the data were thus questionable, so too was the structure of inferences linking the family and other primary institutions with the disparate and much more complex institutions of the political system. Criticism has been particularly leveled at the simple analogy between family authority patterns and political authority patterns that so often lay at the heart of national character analyses.

Political scientists are among those who have been critical of the obvious and important theoretical and empirical inadequacies of the national character approach. At the same time, however, there has occurred a converging recognition in several major currents of political science theory and research of the necessity and significance of directing attention to the political learning that takes place prior to adulthood. These streams, which comprehend many of the central concerns of empirical theory in the study of politics, range from the level of "general theory" and the universal characteristics and requisites of all political systems to middle-level theories about the specific requirements of democratic systems and the contributions made thereto by childhood socialization and include theories about the individual psychological traits that are congruent with democratic "character." The conceptual framework of the present study incorporates related elements from theories on each of these levels.

At the first level, two of the most influential general theories of the political system in recent years have been those of Gabriel Almond[6] and David Easton.[7] Each theory, in seeking to specify and explain the universal attributes of political systems and their linkages to the wider social environment, has accorded a prominent role to the political socialization process. In Almond's theoretical scheme, political socialization is one of the requisite functions whose performance is necessary in any political system for that system to be capable of maintaining itself in operation. The function performed by the political socialization process is the transmission to the members of the system, from generation to generation, of a common store of psychological orientations toward politics. These orientations include beliefs and values about the manifold aspects of the political system, such as the system itself as a general object, the governmental (or output) institutions and the political (or input) institutions, and the self and others as actors in the political process. The prevailing patterns of such orientations in a society constitute its "political culture." This concept, which has come to have widespread currency in contemporary political analysis, plays a major role in this study since a central objective here is to determine the predominant patterns of the political values and beliefs of young Japanese and how they compare with those predominating among Japanese adults and among youngsters in other democracies as well.

One of the important continuities between the national character and political culture approaches is the emphasis placed on the individual's *politically relevant* learning experiences of childhood and adolescence. The political culturalists view the experiences of childhood and adolescence in family, school, job, church, and voluntary associations, and so forth as experiences with pre-political decisions on the basis of which the individual may generalize to the political sphere by expecting, for example, that he will (or will not) be able to participate in the making of decisions in the political system if he has (or has not) been able to participate in decisions in the family, job, and so on. That it is not assumed that such pre-political experiences will all themselves be modeled on what happens in the family and that those which happen later in the more formal, impersonal, and structured authority systems may override the impact on the behavior and attitudes of the individual when he attains political majority, are significant departures from the national character tradition.

The politically relevant self has also been the object of theories proposed by political scientists—most prominently Harold Lasswell and Robert Lane[8]—who have argued in effect that underlying and partly determining the political cultural orientations are psychological characteristics lying deeper within the psyche that constitute components of political character or personality. Among the characteristics of the democratic character or personality in these formulations, feelings of personal competence (or ego-strength) and of trust in people play central roles. Since subordination of the self to the group and consequent low ego-autonomy as well as in-groupism and nonsociability have been linked to traditional Japanese culture, the question of whether they persist in the contemporary culture is of obvious relevance to the present study. Moreover, the degree to which such "characterological" aspects of the self affect the formation in childhood and adolescence of the constituent orientations of the political self is an intriguing empirical question of political socialization theory, to which one part of the analysis here will address itself.

But while politically relevant aspects of the self continue to interest political scientists concerned with the psychological bases of politics, including those who are concerned with political culture, a major difference in the political culture approach from that of the national character approach is that it places great emphasis on *specifically political learning*. The attitudes and values of political man relate not simply to authority in some general sense, but to specific political figures, institutions, and processes. These attitudes he learns throughout his life, from childhood through adolescence, into adulthood. The political socialization process, as opposed to child rearing, imbues the individual with a many-faceted political self, so that by the time he enters into the adult political realm he comes equipped with political identifications, values, and beliefs that have potentially wide-ranging and important specific effects on his political behavior and thus link his pre-adult learning much more closely to the political system than do the experiences of toilet training or weaning.

The emphasis on the specifically political learning that takes place before adulthood is equally prominent in Easton's systems analysis theory of the polity.[9] Easton sees as the principal task of the political socialization process the creation of what he calls "diffuse support" for the political system. In order to persist, every political system must constantly secure the support of its members. One obvious way in which a system can elicit support is by producing outputs—decisions, policies, and so forth—that satisfy the demands made by the members. But not all decisions can satisfy all members all of the time. Thus, in order to keep dissatisfaction with specific outputs from turning into general rejection of the system itself, there must be a mechanism for creating a reservoir of goodwill among the membership that is not dependent on a quid pro quo demand satisfaction basis. This task Easton sees as being performed mainly by the socialization process, particularly that occurring in childhood and adolescence when the individual is inculcated with enduring generalized attachments to the political objects—the political community or nation, the political regime, and the authorities or government—that make up the system. Much of this diffuse support is generated through the attachments developed toward the first two objects: the patriotic sentiments that early on in childhood one is taught to feel with regard to the nation, and the related feelings of pride in the political heritage embodied in the regime. Not only do these elements of the political system act to attract and build up diffuse support but that support may then spill over into the individual's orientations toward the authorities so that when, as an adult, he encounters a governmental decision counter to his interests or desires, he may nevertheless continue to support the decision makers.

Since a principal objective of this study is to determine the degree of support among Japanese youths for the present democratic regime, this study borrows from the Eastonian scheme both the concept of "diffuse support" as just defined and that of the "political regime." As used by Easton and in this study, the political regime refers broadly to the constitutional order of the polity: the values upon which it is founded; the norms specifying the procedures and rules of the game for the making of decisions and for participation in the political process; and the structures of authority.[10] Thus, major emphasis will be placed in this study on delineating Japanese youths' feelings about (1) such democratic values and principles as liberty, equality, and popular sovereignty; (2) democratic rules of the game, especially majority rule; and (3) the institutions of contemporary politics—that is, the prime minister, government, and Diet in the output sphere of governmental authority and the political parties, elections, and associated elements of the input process linked to popular participation.

The political process, as both Almond's and Easton's theoretical frameworks reflect, is concerned both with authority and with participation. The distinction between the output institutions and processes (those involved with authority and the making of decisions) and the input institutions and processes (those involved with participation and the making of demands) is of particular salience to the study of political socialization since an output component and an input component each play a major role in two influential theories of the socialization sources of political legitimacy and stability, especially in democracies.

The first theory has to do with attitudes toward political authority figures as sources of regime support. One of the most widely noted findings on the early empirical research on the political socialization of American children, corroborated in later studies of English and other European children as well, was that from early in childhood they exhibited unexpectedly high levels of positive affect toward the national political leader—in the American case, the president; in the British, the queen. These attachments were so positive and so widespread that they appeared to constitute an important, potentially enduring, basis of support in leadership charisma for the political systems in those countries.[11] The once overarching role of the emperor in Japan as the institutional charismatic source of legitimacy for an authoritarian regime makes the role played by affection for the leader in Japanese youths' support for the democratic regime today of special significance. Hence, considerable attention is devoted in this study to investigating the feelings Japanese youth exhibit toward political leaders—especially the prime minister now that the emperor's role has become so restricted—and to comparing their feelings with those of American and other foreign children, with those of the older generation within their own country, and with their own attitudes toward other aspects of the political regime.

The childhood sources of support for the political regime in America and England include not only such attachments to authority, however, but attachments to an important component of the input side of the regime as well—the political parties. Already by the early years of elementary school, researchers have found, nearly as many American and British children identify themselves as Democrats or Republicans, Conservatives or Labourites, as adults in the two nations do.[12] The widespread existence among the American and British electorates of such party identifications, formed early in childhood as one of the prime political legacies of the family, has been cited as a major reason for the stability of party competition in the two systems and hence of an important element of their democratic regimes. The chronic instability of French politics in the Fourth Republic, in contrast, has been attributed to the absence of such extensive and durable party attachments there, as the result of the absence of parental transmission of partisanship in the French family.[13] The short history of the postwar Japanese parties and the asserted personalism of popular electoral attitudes in Japan are among a number of factors that would appear to diminish the likelihood that Japanese youngsters would form extensive ties to the parties from childhood as well as the likelihood that the family plays a leading role in the transmission of such ties. But these are empirical questions of central importance here, and the analysis of both the partisan identifications of Japanese teenagers and the role played by parents in the creation of those identifications (and in the creation of a wide range of other political orientations) constitutes a major concern of the book.

Americans and Britons, then, are linked by their childhood political socialization to both the authoritative and the participatory elements of their democratic regimes. Their attachments thus develop a kind of positive symmetry of support for the regime. In Japan, prior to the establishment of the democracy, regime support was founded almost exclusively on the attachments created toward authority. In the present, as we shall discover, very nearly the opposite appears to be the case. A profound division and asymmetry between attitudes toward politics-as-authority and politics-as-participation characterizes one of the prevailing bases of support for the democratic regime as well as a central component of the political culture being created in the contemporary political socialization process.

Our principal concern, here, then is with the development among Japanese youth of a political culture supportive of the democratic regime. What are the special characteristics of a democratic political culture and how do they coincide with, or diverge from, the other patterns of political culture current in contemporary Japan?

The Political Culture of Democracy:
The Formal Ideal

Democratic politics is of course popular politics. The very notion of the democratic polity is predicated upon the active participation of free and equal citizens in the political process. One of the great symbolic changes wrought in Japanese politics by the inception of the democratic regime was the replacement of the sovereign emperor with the sovereign people. The Occupation reformers who imposed popular sovereignty by fiat realized that it would require extensive changes in the patterns of popular attitudes and behavior if the new ideal was to be a meaningful guide to, and reflection of, the actual conduct of political life. They thus dictated extensive changes in the content of education and legislated changes in other aspects of social life—including the patterns of formal power and authority in the family—in an attempt to cultivate social and cultural supports for the new regime.[14] Those changes have endured, as have the institutions they were designed to support. A quarter century after regaining independence, Japan retains the formal structure of democratic government. Has she also developed a political culture of participation in the democratic political process?

The central premise in the concept of a participant democratic culture is that for democracy to flourish it requires a society in which a high proportion of the citizens are equipped with both cognitive and affective orientations that maximize their potential for effective participation in the political process.[15] The ideal democrat knows about the impact on his life of government at all levels—local, regional, and national. He knows what his rights are and what he is entitled to do in seeking to influence government as well as how to go about it. He participates in the political process: ideally on an active and positive basis by voting, campaigning for candidates, petitioning his representatives, discussing issues with friends and co-workers, and so forth; if not so actively, at least to the extent of feeling involved and interested in what happens in the political realm.[b] He feels capable of exerting an influence on what is at issue in the political

---

[b]How much participation is necessary or desirable in a democratic culture is a matter of some dispute. Almond and Verba have expressed concern that high levels of participation might lead to an undesirably excessive degree of politicization of the society. See Gabriel Almond and Sidney Verba, *The Civic Culture* (Princeton, N.J.: Princeton University Press, 1963), p. 494. Others have disagreed. See Carole Patman, *Participation and Democratic Theory* (Cambridge: Cambridge University Press, 1970), and Dennis F. Thompson, *The Democratic Citizen* (Cambridge: Cambridge University Press, 1970), for more recent discussions with a different emphasis.

process and on the decisions taken there. Those decisions, he accepts, should be governed by the principle of majority rule with respect for the basic rights of the minority. In the competition of political ideas and principles, he takes sides by becoming a partisan, a supporter of one or another of the political parties between whom the conflict of democratic politics is played out. But while that partisanship may engage his intense preferences, it does not involve intransigent enmity toward his opponents.

With respect to the institutions of the political system the democratic citizen is supportive but not awestruck. He takes a moderate patriotic pride in his nation and its political heritage and values—that is, pride in the very fact that it is a democracy. His support for government is based on a belief that its institutions are legitimate, that its rules and procedures for making decisions are fair and just, and that the men who occupy its offices are responsive and basically moral. But that support is qualified and conditional; it is based on a posture toward authority that is independent and critical rather than submissive and deferential.[c] After all, he feels, when the people are sovereign, leaders are their representatives not their rulers, and government officials are their civil servants not their superiors.

These then are some of the major elements of a widely held view of the political culture of democracy. There are of course no real-world societies populated exclusively with such ideal democrats. Real democracies have their share of the alienated and the authoritarian as well as the apathetic and the cynical. The democratic culture is an "ideal type"—a construct that is meant to serve as a norm against which the prevailing political cultural patterns can be measured and by which the relative levels of psychological and cultural support for democracy can be compared across societies and across generations.

Two Political Countercultures:
Tradition and Structural Opposition

It is one of the theses of this book that political socialization in contemporary Japan takes place in the context of political cultural competition and confrontation—that is, Japanese youth are influenced not only by the formal democratic culture but by two alternative models of political man and society, each with its own roots in Japanese political experience. The first model derives from the carryover into the present of patterns of value and behavior associated with political life before the introduction of democracy; the second, from a complex of perceptions and beliefs linked to the rejection of the capitalist socioeconomic

[c]The model of the democratic culture put forth by Almond and Verba, *The Civic Culture*, does not emphasize an independent attitude toward authority despite the importance of such an attitude in most democratic theory. On this point, see Robert A. Dahl, *Modern Political Analysis*, 2nd ed. (Englewood Cliffs, N.J.: Prentice-Hall, 1970), p. 94, and the works cited there.

order that has characterized political opposition throughout the postwar period. These two competing models, which have been termed in this study the traditional counterculture and the structural-oppositional counterculture,[d] each exert an impact on the political perceptions and values of Japanese youth, and together they interact to modify and adapt the democratic culture to the special requirements of Japanese society and politics. Moreover, although the specific details of each are individual to Japan, the broad outlines of both are common to many polities and constitute the principal sources of strain on new democratic regimes as well as some established ones. Thus, how the confrontation between these countercultures and the democratic culture works itself out in the political socialization of Japanese youth may offer an insight into how new democracies can achieve legitimacy and vitality in the face of contradictory crosscurrents of traditional and ideological opposition.

Table 1-1 presents a summary of some of the principal ways in which these two political countercultures differ from the democratic culture just described and from each other, as an overview to the discussion, which begins with the traditional counterculture.

The Traditional Political Counterculture: Past Cultural Patterns as Persisting Impediments to Democracy

Despite questions on the validity of the national character writers' claims that the political values and attitudes of pre-1945 Japan were founded in character as molded by culturally determined child-training practices, the values and attitudes themselves do appear to have constituted a major set of ingredients of the political culture that prevailed prior to the inception of the democratic regime. Indeed, it has been the various traditional values and beliefs that are most frequently identified as the prime obstacles to developing cultural roots for democracy in Japan.

In terms of specifically political orientations, the traditional political culture included allegiance to and adulation of the emperor and the belief that ultimate sovereignty derived from and rested with him rather than with the people. It was characterized by fervent nationalism and national pride and a chauvinism based on the very existence in Japan of the emperor. The norms of this ideology of the emperor system specified that the appropriate attitude of the common man toward the institutions of government was that of a "subject," which entailed

---

[d]The concept of structural opposition as used here has been borrowed from Robert A. Dahl, who uses it to describe political opposition in democratic polities that is based on rejection of either or both the political and socioeconomic regimes of the society, in contrast to simple opposition to either the political authorities or their policies. See his *Political Oppositions in Western Democracies* (New Haven, Conn.: Yale University Press, 1963), pp. 341-342.

Table 1-1

Patterns of Political Orientations in the Formal Democratic Culture and the Traditional and Structural-Oppositional Countercultures in Japan

Orientation Focus	Formal Democratic Culture	Traditional Counterculture	Structural-Oppositional Counterculture
System Affect	Patriotism, Pride in Institutions	Chauvinism, Centered on the Throne	Patriotism Equated with Chauvinism
System Definition	Democracy	Emperor System	Capitalism (neg.)
Role of the Emperor	Symbol	Sovereign	Symbol, Accepted by Some, Rejected by Others
Decision Principles	Majority Rule and Minority Rights	Unanimous Consensus without Dissent	Majority Rule Equals Majority Tyranny
Output Institutions (authorities)	Conditional Support	Obedience and Implicit Support	Mistrust and Hostility
Input Institutions and Processes	Support	Mistrust and Apathy	Conditional Support
Political Efficacy	High	Low	Variable
Political Interest	High	Low	High
Political Participation: Electoral	High	High	Variable
Extra-Electoral	High	Low	Variable

obedience and implicit trust and support of authority. Toward the nongovernmental institutions of politics, especially those concerned with the representation of opposition and dissent—political parties and partisan elections, for example—traditional Japanese political culture was suspicious. Indeed, one of the most prominent elements of this culture was a stress on harmony and consensus and a consequent intolerance of overt dissent. It was therefore antimajoritarian in nature, seeking rule not by the majority but by unanimity, and requiring the passive and silent acquiescence of the minority.

Interpretations of the carryover of the traditional culture into the present usually place emphasis on its broad negative impact on the self as an actor in the political process. The sense of submissiveness to authority conflicts with the sense of political efficacy and the assertiveness of one's rights that are ascribed to the democratic citizen. This sense of political powerlessness is further affected by the norm of subordination to the group—an emphasis on conformity and self-suppression that is at odds with the participant democrat's postulated character trait of autonomy and ego-strength. Moreover, in some though not all formulations, the traditional culture is alleged to include suspicion and mistrust of strangers as a result of the exclusive nature of group membership in which the individual supposedly belongs to a single, primary group that engages all his loyalties and nearly all his activities. Politics, then, is not for the common man; it is the arena of the powerful, populated by strangers out for their own interests. The ordinary man is well advised to concern himself with his own affairs and those of his family and leave politics to his leaders.

Nearly all observers argue that the traditional culture persists most strongly among those who live in the rural areas where the modernizing influences of postwar democratic society have been slowest to penetrate. Hence, the high levels of electoral participation found in the rural areas, it is argued, do not really reflect the democratic norm of spontaneous participation motivated by political interest; rather they are the product of both the mobilization of rural communities by local influentials or "bosses" and the social pressure to participate that is generated by the norm that values such participation in conjunction with the entire community as an expression of harmony and consensus.[16]

These, then, are the cultural and ideological supports of the *ancien regime* that students of contemporary Japan usually assert, to some greater or lesser degree, to be continuing impediments to the emergence of a democratic political culture. In focusing on the extent to which such orientations play a role in the political socialization of contemporary youth, the present study pays particular attention to both generational and urban-rural differences. Comparing the values of present-day youngsters with those of their parents is a constant feature of the analysis, while frequent comparisons between the orientations of urban and rural youngsters—and occasionally between those of urban and rural parents—are also made to test the assumption that rural Japan continues to be a stronghold of the traditional political culture.

The Structural-Oppositional Counterculture:
Ideological Conflict and Its Impact on Regime
Support and the Democratic Culture

While the traditional counterculture is the most frequently cited challenge to the contemporary democratic regime in Japan, there is another perhaps more explosive source of political cultural conflict—one with a different but potentially major impact on the political socialization of Japanese youth. Japanese politics is riven with an ideological split: the ruling conservatives have molded the capitalist economic system into an engine of economic growth, while the opposition has an intense antipathy toward that system based on socialist principles that derive in varying degree from the Marxist view of society and history.

The opposition challenges the established order along a broad spectrum. First, it calls into question the democraticness of Japan's present social and political system. Nearly all of the groups in the left opposition profess support for democracy. Indeed, even the Japan Communist Party makes extensive use of the term by labeling its youth organization (which controls most Japanese university student governments) the "Democratic Youth League" and by referring to itself and the other groups on the left as "the democratic forces." It is thus important to emphasize that while the rhetoric and symbolism of the opposition embraces democracy, that democracy is equated ultimately with a socialist political and economic order; from this point of view, a capitalist Japan cannot also be a genuinely democratic one.

Second, therefore, the members of the opposition, who range leftward from the socialists and communists to the most radical of student groups, cast themselves in the role of defenders of the democratic aspects of the present system—to protect the constitution and to defend freedom of thought and academic and educational liberty—against the predation of a government that while cloaked in the garb of democracy seeks to reimpose authoritarianism and militarism. Third, the opposition reserves the right to recourse by extraparliamentary action—including, for some, violence—against the use by the conservatives of parliamentary majority rule in matters of basic policy conflict between the two camps, which is seen as the "tyranny of the majority." In brief, the opposition calls into dispute the legitimacy of many of the bases of the social order and the political regime.

The Marxist-based, progressive critique of society and polity has been of great significance in the development of social and political thought in postwar Japan. It is accepted in part or in whole by most intellectuals and has monopolized respectable intellectual opposition to the conservatives. Two aspects of the spread of the ideology are worthy of special note. First is that some of the most basic concepts and terms of the ideology have become part of mass culture and are used by Marxist and non-Marxist alike. Especially prevalent is the use of the term "capitalist" to describe Japan. The defining characteristic of contemporary Japan that, as we shall see, comes first to mind for many adults and teenagers is not "democracy" but rather "capitalism," and this perspective, which derives from the conceptual framework of Marxism, has a decidedly different set of connotations and evaluations attached to it than those that accompany "democracy."

The second aspect of the spread of socialist ideology is its influence in education. Particularly important is the fact that the Japan Teachers Union, to which most public school teachers belong, has been one of the most enthusiastic supporters of the left and a militant foe of government educational policy. The union and the education ministry have been at bitter odds over the content of textbooks and of classroom instruction in the two subject fields most closely related to the political socialization process: the morals and social studies courses. The reinstitution of the teaching of morals in the curriculum by the ministry in 1958 was strenuously resisted by the union on the ground that the government would use the morals course to revive indoctrination in ultra-nationalism and other reactionary doctrines that had been the core of the pre-1945 ethics courses abolished by the Occupation. The continuing conflict over the teaching of social studies has centered around what texts should be used, whether the government's policy of permitting only approved texts to be used amounts to political censorship, and whether the primary objective should be to instill acceptance and support of Japan's polity and society or to develop a social "problem consciousness" that focuses on the flaws and inequities of the society.

While most of the principal characteristics of the traditional counterculture discussed earlier appear to be in conflict with the elements of democratic political culture, the oppositional counterculture includes both elements that are potentially facilitative of democracy as well as those that are contradictory. On the positive side, the progressive attitude may cause the individual to seek increased political information and knowledge, to be more deeply involved psychologically in political affairs, and to participate more widely and fully in political life. In addition, socialist ideology may increase the individual's social and political conscience, thereby making him less apathetic and less complacent about social, economic, and political ills and inequities. Finally, the socialist emphasis on the "undemocratic" behavior of the government may cause the individual to develop deep-rooted support for democratic principles, especially the protection of the rights of the minority and of the individual to oppose and dissent.

It is equally clear, however, that elements of the progressive counterculture might conflict with the formation of orientations that support democratic politics. The fact that the socioeconomic system is capitalist might outweigh the fact that its political institutions are democratic, leading the individual to emphasize his society's faults and to minimize or ignore its virtues; such dissatisfaction might spill over into a loss of faith in democratic processes and institutions. Indeed, in postwar Japan, such a loss of faith in the democratic regime is seen in most extreme fashion in the attitudes and behavior of the leftist student groups whose violent political activity has been among the most prominent manifestations of political alienation. In rejecting capitalist society as corrupt and oppressive, they also reject the democratic regime as a framework within which meaningful change can be achieved. Their intense interest in politics finds an outlet in anomic violence, not in participation in the democratic process. Although such radical extremists are few in number and not representative of young people generally, it is apparent that political and social alienation linked to rejection of capitalism have played, and continue to play, a major role in the politics of the wider student movement as well. Thus, one important focus of the present study is on the degree to which the opposition counterculture has become part of the more general political culture of Japanese youth.

Research Design and Methodology

The main source of data used in this study consists of the results of a set of survey questionnaires administered in the spring of 1969 to nearly 1,000 Japanese teenagers and their parents. Supplementing this data are several additional data sources: the transcripts of interviews conducted with some 40 of the teenagers from the survey sample and compositions written by 43 Tokyo eighth graders. Parts of the analysis also make use of the results of a 1968 nationwide survey of over 6,000 children in grades three through twelve that were kindly made available by Professor Okamura Tadao of Hosei University in Tokyo who conducted that survey.[e]

The instruments administered to the teenagers and their parents in the main survey were questionnaires of the pencil-and-paper, self-completion variety with fixed-choice items. Both the student and the parent versions of the questionnaire covered a wide range of topics and included both political items that probed values and attitudes toward the various institutions of politics, reactions toward ideological symbols, political interest and related aspects of the political self, as well as items that related to nonpolitical attitudes and to the family. Nearly all of the political items, and many of the nonpolitical ones as well, were identical in both versions to permit extensive comparison of parent-child correspondences. Many of the items, moreover, were chosen to facilitate cross-national comparison with the findings of previous studies on political socialization in the United States and elsewhere. English translations of both the student and the parent questionnaires, plus a discussion of their construction and pretesting, can be found in the appendix section of this volume.

The sample of teenagers consisted of 942 public school students in grades eight, ten, and twelve (second year in middle school, and first and third year in

---

[e]Although our two surveys were conducted independently, Prof. Okamura and I did consult with each other and participate in the construction and revision of each other's questionnaires. As a result of our parallel interest and of this partial collaboration, we decided to exchange data and to give one another the right to use those data in our respective countries. The author wishes to thank Prof. Okamura for granting permission to use the data from his survey in this book and to note that he bears no responsibility for the interpretations placed upon those data here. Prof. Okamura has published several articles in Japanese and one in English based on these data; see "The Child's Changing Image of the Prime Minister," *The Developing Economies* 6:4 (December 1968), pp. 566-86. In Japanese, see "Gendai ni okeru Seijiteki Shakaika" (Political Socialization in Contemporary Japan), *Nenpo Seijigaku*, 1970; "Seiji Ishiki no Kitei to shite no Soridaijinzo" (The Prime Minister's Image as the Foundation of Political Consciousness), in Taniuchi Ken, Ari Bakuji, Ide Yoshinori, and Nishio Masaru, eds., *Gendai Gyosei to Kanryosei* (Tokyo: Tokyo Daigaku Shuppankai, 1974); and "Seijiteki Shakaika ni okeru 'Minshushugi' to 'Heiwa'" ("Democracy" and "Peace" in Political Socialization), *Shakai Kagaku Janaru*, 1969.

high school, respectively). The ages of the students thus ranged from thirteen to eighteen. The schools in which the survey was conducted were located in central and suburban Tokyo and in two farming villages and two small cities in Tochigi prefecture, which is about 120 miles north of Tokyo. The schools were chosen to maximize the demographic representativeness of the sample, and the families in the sample do resemble families in the population at large in terms of urban-rural residence, occupational type, and educational level (of the father). Thus, the sample will be treated as generally representative of Japanese teenagers and parents, even though it was not drawn randomly.

The students themselves were surveyed in their classrooms during school hours by the author and a Japanese assistant. Each student's parents—both father and mother—were also surveyed by having the students take home (in sealed envelopes) two copies of the parent questionnaire and return them to the school when their parents had completed them. Completed questionnaires were returned by 1,637, or 86 percent, of the parents.

In addition to the questionnaire, personal interviews were also conducted with some 40 students. In these interviews, the same topics dealt with in the questionnaire were pursued in greater depth and detail in order to permit a freer and more spontaneous expression of the youngsters' own images and attitudes. These interviews, which proved to be a rich source of insight into the meanings and nuances that youngsters attach to the political phenomena they perceive as well as into the way they understood the questionnaire, are used extensively to illustrate and illuminate the points made on the basis of the questionnaire responses. Without the interviews, much of the data from the questionnaire would be readily susceptible to misinterpretation. However, the combination of the two sources of evidence provides a data base that is both more contextually reliable and more broadly useful in the analysis that follows than a single-strategy study relying either wholly on questionnaire data from a large sample or wholly on intensive interviews with a small number of respondents could have created.

One aspect of the research design requires special comment, namely, the ages of the youngsters studied. Adolescents—teenagers from thirteen to seventeen or eighteen—were chosen for several reasons. First, one important objective of the study is to assess the role of ideology, as it appears in the terminology that youngsters learn to use about politics and society and as an organizing framework for their political belief systems. Informal investigation of younger children indicated that prior to middle school, phrases and concepts such as "capitalism" "class," and the like, which are associated with ideological discourse among adults in Japan, do not appear with any significant degree of frequency in either the speech or the perceptions of Japanese youngsters. Both the growth of the cognitive capacity to deal with complex belief systems such as ideologies and the coming to consciousness of the social and political conflict that make ideologies meaningful take place most significantly in the years between thirteen and eighteen.

Second, another important objective of the study is to assay the influence of the family on the political development of the child. Studying adolescents permits us to investigate family influence on a broad range of specific political values and attitudes that would be beyond the ken of younger children or else would involve serious problems of comparability in devising questionnaire items meaningful to both parents and children. Pretesting of the questionnaire showed that thirteen year olds could be asked the same questions about politics as were asked of their parents. This would not have been feasible with younger children. Fortunately, Okamura's survey provided data on the attitudes of younger children in a number of areas that paralleled the interests of this study. Thus, focusing on adolescents maximized the information produced in the study survey while making use of his complementary data on the earlier stages of the political socialization process.

For further methodological details touching upon the sample, the construction and pretesting of the questionnaire, and interviewing procedures, the reader is referred to Appendix A. Appendix B includes English translations of both the student and parent questionnaires.

The Structure of the Analysis

The initial section of the analysis, Chapters 2 and 3, studies the overall distributive patterns of support for the elements of the democratic regime. Chapter 2 concentrates on the feelings of children and teenagers toward political institutions, with particular emphasis on the role of national political figures—especially the prime minister—as potential personal agents of regime legitimation. Chapter 3 turns to the meanings and values that young Japanese attach to democracy, its relationship with peace in their value systems, and how the democratic norm of majoritarianism interacts with the preference for consensus in their attitudes toward decisionmaking.

Chapters 4 and 5, which constitute the middle section of the book, are concerned with exploring how the lines of partisan and ideological cleavage emerge in the socialization process to affect the political identity that Japanese teenagers develop. Chapter 4 investigates the extent to which they form attachments to the political parties in comparison with American and European youngsters and with their parents; it also examines the role played by the family in the creation of those attachments and the degree to which partisanship is grounded in social cleavage. Chapter 5 considers the emergence of ideology in adolescence from three perspectives: that of the teenagers' conceptions of capitalism and socialism and their attitudes toward the two symbols; that of conceptual style, in which emphasis shifts to the degree to which their attitudes meet the criteria of consistency and causal reasoning; and that of the link between partisanship and ideology in both substance and style.

The final section of the analysis, Chapters 6 and 7, moves to an explicit consideration of the causal factors affecting the political orientations that the teenagers do develop. Chapter 6 draws together into multivariate path analysis models the basic social and personal characteristics of the teenagers, the "psychocultural" factors of ego-autonomy and social trust, and the cleavage factors of partisanship and ideology in accounting for differences in the teenagers' political efficacy, political interest, and support for input and output aspects of the regime. Chapter 7 presents an extensive analysis of the impact of the family on the political attitudes of the teenager. Included are the direct transmission of parental political orientations and indirect influence via the generalization of parental images onto political authority figures as well as the effect of family patterns of authority and affection on politically relevant aspects of the child's personality.

The concluding chapter summarizes the findings and attempts to distill from them the significance of the emerging political culture being created in the socialization process for the future of democratic politics in Japan.

Notes

1. On this point see Fred I. Greenstein, *Children and Politics* (New Haven, Conn.: Yale University Press, 1965), pp. 2-3.

2. An excellent discussion of the various modes of national character analysis and of the criticism directed against the approach can be found in H.C.T. Duijker and N.H. Frijda, *National Character and National Stereotypes* (Amsterdam: North Holland Publishing, 1960). On Japanese national character, the classic work is Ruth Benedict's famous book, *The Chrysanthemum and the Sword* (Boston: Houghton Mifflin, 1946). See also *inter alia* the various articles compiled in B.S. Silberman, ed., *Japanese Character and Culture* (Tucson: University of Arizona Press, 1962).

3. An elegant exposition and discussion of these postulates and their broader theoretical background is presented in Geoffrey Gorer, "Themes in Japanese Culture," in Silberman, *Japanese Culture and Character*, pp. 309-10.

4. Douglas G. Haring, "Aspects of Personal Character in Japan," reprinted in Douglas G. Haring, ed., *Personal Character and Cultural Milieu* (Syracuse, N.Y.: Syracuse University Press, 1956).

5. See Alex Inkeles, "National Character and Modern Political Systems," reprinted in Nelson Polsby et al., eds., *Politics and Social Life* (Boston: Houghton Mifflin, 1963), pp. 172-92, for a good example of the criticism raised against the approach on methodological and epistemological grounds. Later studies of national character, in which the premise of a single-character structure common to all members of a society was modified to one that recognized that a multiplicity of character or personality types was likely in a complex society, sought to establish empirical evidence as to the incidence of the various types in

a society and as to which variety, if any, could be determined to be the "modal personality" in that society. See Alex Inkeles and Daniel Levinson, "National Character: The Study of Modal Personality and Sociocultural Systems," in Gardner Lindzey, ed., *Handbook of Social Psychology*, vol. 2 (Cambridge, Mass.: Addison-Wesley Press, 1954), pp. 977-1020.

6. See Gabriel Almond and James Coleman, *The Politics of the Developing Areas* (Princeton, N.J.: Princeton University Press, 1960), and Gabriel Almond and Sidney Verba, *The Civic Culture* (Princeton, N.J.: Princeton University Press, 1963), for the original version of the theory and its application to democracy, respectively.

7. The most complete statement of Easton's theory is found in his *A Systems Analysis of Political Life* (New York: Wiley, 1965).

8. See Harold D. Lasswell, *The Political Writings of Harold D. Lasswell* (Glencoe, Ill.: Free Press, 1951), especially the chapter on "Democratic Character," and Robert E. Lane, *Political Ideology* (New York: Free Press, 1962).

9. See *A Systems Analysis of Political Life*, pp. 193 ff., and the first three chapters of David Easton and Jack Dennis, *Children in the Political System* (New York: McGraw-Hill, 1969).

10. See Easton, *A Systems Analysis of Political Life*, p. 193.

11. See Greenstein, *Children and Politics*; Easton and Dennis, *Children in the Political System*; and the various other works cited in the first five notes of Chapter 2.

12. See Greenstein, *Children and Politics*, pp. 71-72, and Jack Dennis and Donald McCrone, "Preadult Development of Political Party Identification in Western Democracies," *Comparative Political Studies* 3:2 (July 1970), 252.

13. See Philip Converse and Georges Dupeux, "Participation of the Electorate in France and the United States," in A. Campbell et al., *Elections and the Political Order* (New York: Wiley, 1966), pp. 269-91.

14. See Kazuo Kawai, *Japan's American Interlude* (Chicago: University of Chicago Press, 1960), for a Japanese perspective on the Occupation and its reforms.

15. Probably the most extensive and best known formulation of the democratic political culture is that set forth by Almond and Verba, *The Civic Culture*, on which much of the description here is based.

16. An excellent summary of the assumptions and hypotheses bearing on the nature of political participation in rural Japan may be found in Watanuki Joji, "Social Structure and Political Participation in Japan," report no. 32 (Iowa City: University of Iowa, Department of Political Science, Laboratory for Political Research, May 1970), pp. 2-3.

2 The Missing Leader: Japanese Youths' View of Political Authority

Introduction

The apparent vitality of Japan's democratic regime seems something of an anomaly. How does a regime imposed by the force of arms of a foreign occupation, which violates tradition and history on the one hand while frustrating contemporary opposition on the other, secure its future? Among the most influential current theories of the sources of political legitimacy is the benevolent leader thesis, for which Japan provides an interesting and appropriate test.

The pioneering work of Greenstein[1] and Easton and Hess[2] on the political socialization of American children established that they develop their allegiance to the American political system through a process in which the president plays a central and vital role. From early in his political socialization the child develops his first, deepest, and most enduring political orientation: an image of the president as wise, generous, powerful, and benign. This image of the "benevolent leader" dominates the cognitive and affective dimensions of the young child's political world. Moreover, it shares much of the character of the child's relationship with his parents and creates a link between the child and the leader that has a touch of the depth and strength of these basic human ties. This image thus serves as a major enduring source of support for the political system, onto which its affect overflows. While later research among children of an American rural subculture[3] and among black children[4] indicates that the benevolent leader syndrome is not a universal one, additional evidence from other nations including Great Britain and Holland[5] suggests that it is sufficiently common to be considered as a principal way in which contemporary political systems, including democracies, create generalized political allegiance on the part of children.

One particular variation on the benevolent leader theme is of special relevance to the question of how Japan's democratic regime secures its support. The evidence of the benevolent leader syndrome coupled with other aspects of political socialization processes, including such phenomena as American children's tendencies to confuse religious and political symbols and images, has led some scholars (notably Sidney Verba) to argue that political systems may secure legitimacy by functioning in effect as religions.[6] The role of the political leader becomes endowed with a sacred or religious quality and attachments to the system become couched in symbolism that both invokes and evokes religious imagery.

21

That such a process might be exceedingly effective in creating support for the regime has never been demonstrated more tellingly than in Japan in the period before 1945. The emperor was explicitly a sacred leader; and in various ways, including State Shinto, the regime saw to it that political allegiance took on the character of religious commitment. In a very real sense, Japan's postwar regime was founded in explicit repudiation of that equation of religion and politics. Thus, a major question confronting a study of the socialization sources of support for the contemporary regime is to determine to what extent support is dependent upon the creation of a new Japanese version of the benevolent leader and upon the inculcation of implicit and unquestioning trust in political authority.

The first objective here, therefore, is to focus on the empirical question of whether a benevolent leader exists in the political imagery of today's Japanese children. At the outset, the study concentrates on a comparative analysis of younger children's images of possible contenders for the role: the emperor, the prime minister (at the time of this study, Sato Eisaku[a]), and the local leader (mayor or governor). The principal focus, however, is on the prime minister as the most important national political figure. The analysis considers the role of children's conceptions of politics as a factor affecting the national leader's image and shows how that image is conditioned by certain important aspects of political reality, in particular the parliamentary political structure and the leadership style and personality of the national leader himself.

The second objective is to determine whether a spillover of affect from the national leader to other important institutions of the political system takes place in later childhood. Accordingly, in this chapter the attitudes of older youngsters, in their teens, toward the prime minister are compared with those toward other political institutions along several dimensions of political trust. The teenagers' attitudes are, in each case, also compared to those of their parents to assay the continuity or discontinuity of socialization.

Finally, some of the causes and consequences of the presence or absence of a benevolent leader in a political system are considered. Particular emphasis is placed on the historical roots of the benevolent leadership phenomenon that are to be found in most societies but are missing in Japan.

Much of the importance of the benevolent leader thesis derives from the generalization in the study of socialization that what is learned earliest is retained longest. It becomes essential, therefore, to determine whether such an image of the leader does indeed develop in early childhood. Thus, the first part of this chapter draws to a large extent upon data about Japanese grade school children's images of the emperor, prime minister, and local leader that were kindly made available by Professor Okamura Tadao of Hosei University from his

[a]Sato, the first Japanese to win the Nobel Peace Prize (in 1974, for his efforts toward nuclear nonproliferation and international reconciliation in the Pacific area) held office from 1964 to 1972. He died in 1975.

nationwide survey of over 6,000 children in grades three through twelve conducted in the fall of 1968.[7]

The Emperor: Peripheral Monarch

A principal and obvious difference between the American and Japanese political systems is the fact that the United States, as a presidential system, has the roles of head of government and head of state united in the office of the president, while in Japan the roles are divided between the emperor as head of state and the prime minister as head of government. There are thus two nationally prominent executive offices and figures. In an earlier time, there would have been little doubt about which of the two would be the more likely to inspire emotional attachment and respect on the part of Japanese, young and old alike.

Before defeat in the Pacific War so drastically changed the Japanese political system, the emperor's place was supreme, legally and constitutionally, spiritually and politically. He was very nearly the sole legitimate object of political affection and esteem. His portrayal as a father to whom all owed ultimate filial piety was part of a broader view of Japanese society as a "family-state" under his benevolent, patriarchal guidance. There is no doubt that ordinary people were profoundly attached to this father figure. American researchers studying the morale of the Japanese army found the soldiers' faith in the emperor to be so strong that any propaganda attack on him would only cause increased determination to fight and would thus risk prolonging the war. The researchers concluded that the emperor's place in the emotional and symbolic life of his subjects was so profound and central

. . . as to constitute a non-logical, cultural type of faith strongly reinforced in any one individual by the sheer pressure of the whole society. It would be impossible for one to reject it without stepping outside almost all the ideas and value systems that are Japanese.[8]

After the War, even though the Occupation heeded the advice not to attack or destroy the throne, it did make drastic changes in the throne's role in the new Japan. The emperor's spiritual status became that of mere mortal; his political status, under the new constitution, that of mere symbol.

What role, then, does the new emperor play in the images of government held by today's Japanese children? The significance of this question may best be understood by reference to some recent findings about English children's images of the queen. In several independent studies, researchers have found that the queen dominates the political imagery and perceptions of youngsters over a wide range of ages. At younger age levels, many English children believe that the queen is the most important person in England (and, for almost as many, the most important person in the world).[9] Fully 72 percent of working-class and 61 percent of middle-class eight and nine year olds in the same survey believed that "the Queen is more important than the Prime Minister in running Britain."[10] Even by age twelve, one-third of the working-class group continued to assert the queen's importance over the prime minister.[11] In another study, Greenstein found that 51 percent of English ten to twelve year olds responding said that the queen rules or governs while only 22 percent responded in those terms to a similar question about the prime minister, who was viewed primarily as her legislative helper.[12] Dennis and his associates obtained similar results. In short, the queen dominates young British children's images of government to a remarkable degree. In a similar item, Okamura asked a nationwide sample of children, "Who is the most important in running politics in today's Japan?" Table 2-1 summarizes the results for those in grades three to eight.

It is evident from the table that the lesson of popular sovereignty has been well learned. At all age levels except the three youngest, "each citizen" has a substantial lead over the other responses. This is a most interesting finding, for it has been said by many of the critics of the new regime that only imperial sovereignty suits the Japanese: "Popular sovereignty," says Kazuo Kawai, for example, "is completely alien to Japanese thought."[13] Ardath Burks concurs: "From the sheer historical point of view, some restoration of [imperial] theoretical authority, with popular controls . . . is almost inevitable."[14] But only among the third and fourth graders do we find a sizable proportion of children who conceive of the emperor as ruling as well as reigning, and in contrast to the British case, even among those youngest children the emperor runs second to the prime minister. By fifth grade, the emperor is picked less than any of the other responses including "each citizen." Although strict comparison

Table 2-1
Perceptions of the Emperor's Importance
(Percentages selecting each response by grade)

Grade	Emperor	Prime Minister	Dietmen	Each Citizen	Other and Don't Know	Total	(N)
3	21	32	12	7	28	100	(630)
4	21	32	19	13	15	100	(626)
5	11	25	24	23	17	100	(631)
6	4	20	11	55	10	100	(631)
7	5	16	12	55	12	100	(654)
8	3	15	22	50	10	100	(732)

Survey Item:
"Who is most important in running politics in today's Japan?"
Source: Okamura, 1968 Survey.

between the English and Japanese data is not possible because of differences in the items, it does seem clear that the absolute level of attributions of power to the monarch is substantially lower among even the youngest Japanese respondents than among their English counterparts.

If power and rule are missing from the Japanese child's image of the emperor, neither is his role as "symbol of the state" particularly prominent. Okamura also asked the children in his survey to choose the best symbol of Japan. The emperor was chosen by fewer than 10 percent of the children in any grade and trailed far behind the two favorite choices, the flag and Mt. Fuji, which together accounted for 65 percent or more of the responses of children in nearly every grade.[15]

It is clear that the emperor does not figure so centrally or importantly in the political life of the Japanese child as the queen does in that of the British child. This may deprive Japan of one of the leading benefits of monarchy: the promotion through the socialization process of a sense of identification with the regime that does not waver even when partisan opponents control the elected offices. Abrahamson and Inglehart, in a comparative study of the role of the monarch, point out that "the presence of a monarchy reduces the chances that an individual's first political perception is that government is in the hands of the 'bad guys.' "[16] They go on to note that the perception that government is controlled by the "bad guys" is likeliest to occur where partisan cleavage and hostility run deep. But for monarchy in Japan to bridge the partisan gulf, it would have to be the object of widespread affection among people of diverse political persuasions and not itself a source of partisan division. The symbolic emperor of postwar Japan gains acceptance and support from most adults, on the average about 70 percent, as public opinion polls over the past two decades have shown.[17] But for a minority, the present status of the emperor is a source of partisan and ideological conflict. On the one hand, a small number of conservatives wish the emperor restored to his former glory and authority; on the other, a few leftists would prefer that the throne be completely abolished. On the whole, however, the majority of the Japanese support the throne as it is, but with little apparent intensity. It is doubtful, therefore, that the emperor could serve as a focal point in the cementing of the individual's allegiance to the political system in the face of control of the government by the "bad guys."

This lack of intense emotional investment in the throne among Japanese adults is reflected in indifference and increasing ambivalence among the youngsters. In the mid-1950s Tokyo high school students were asked to choose among several alternatives to describe their feelings when they saw or heard the word "emperor." Positive responses far outdistanced negative ones: 52 percent chose "respect" or "affection" and only 8 percent "a foolish or unnecessary existence." But the low affective importance of the emperor to many youngsters was illustrated by the high proportion—38 percent— who found it hard to say what their feelings were since the emperor is "far removed from us."[18] About ten years later, in 1964, Titus and Yoshida and their associates found that feelings of emotional uninvolvement and indifference toward the emperor predominated over positive sentiments of affection, reverence, or adoration among both students at Tokyo's Meiji University (by 60 percent to 29 percent) and adults in their twenties in Kofu, a city near Tokyo (by 43 percent to 31 percent), and nearly equalled positive feelings among Kofu youngsters in their teens (34 percent to 39 percent).[19]

There are, of course, obvious and profound reasons why the present emperor is unable to play the role of benevolent leader. Because, historically, he is the very symbol of the old order that the new regime supplanted and because of his own retiring personality and unprepossessing manner, he is much less popularly visible than other monarchs, making few public appearances. Moreover, there is almost no color or pomp and ceremony—no horse guard, parades, nor crown and imperial regalia—remaining in the Imperial institution to delight the eyes and capture the affections of the young. Those days are gone, seemingly forever. Unable to perform the kind of broad-gauge legitimation of the regime that was once his most important political function, the emperor no longer stands at the symbolic and expressive center of the national political culture; he has faded into the periphery.

But before we dismiss the throne as a contender for the role of benevolent leader, we must recognize that it may emerge from its present eclipse with the accession of a new emperor. One of the most pointed of Titus and Yoshida's findings was that Japanese of all age levels would like to see the throne "popularized," with the emperor made more a part of popular life and less a distant and aloof figure.[20] A decade ago, the marriage of the crown prince to the beautiful daughter of a commoner caused an outpouring of enthusiasm from all segments of the people, especially the young. This leads us to ask whether the feelings of today's youth toward the crown prince foreshadow any future rekindling of popular affection for the throne. Once again, Okamura's 1968 survey provides data relevant to this additional aspect of the benevolent leader role in Japan. The children surveyed were asked to describe in their own words what sort of person the crown prince was. Roughly 60 percent of the youngest children chose terms of respect and goodwill, while almost none used negative or derogatory words or phrases. The positive sentiment decreased steadily with age, so that by twelfth grade only 24 percent mentioned respect or affection while another 24 percent used words of antipathy or disdain. Significantly, however, the largest proportion of the twelfth graders were noncommital: 13 percent made no comment, 14 percent said they didn't know much about the crown prince, and 25 percent made neutral or mixed comments.[21] This prevalence of high positive affect among the youngest children, turning to a noncommittal position among the high school seniors, may indicate that there are dormant resources of popular support and enthusiasm that a new and particularly a young emperor might be able to tap.

**The Prime Minister: Distant
and Impersonal Leader**

The change in the Japanese political regime that took place after 1945 removed the emperor from the role of benevolent leader. Does the prime minister fill the void? Let us look first at children's perceptions of his importance.

We saw above that comparison with the British case revealed the Japanese prime minister to be apparently more generally perceived by children as important in running politics than the emperor. This contrasted with the British case, where the prime minister was overshadowed by the queen. Additional data on American children's perceptions of the president's importance in politics help to put the Japanese prime minister's image into comparative perspective. A very sizable majority of the children surveyed by Hess and Torney (ranging from 86 percent of the second graders to 50 percent of the eighth graders) selected the president as "the one who does the most to run the country."[22] A second look at Table 2-1 reveals that the prime minister does not dominate Japanese children's perceptions nearly so one-sidedly. While the president's lead over Congress as most important drops to two-to-one only by eighth grade, the prime minister contends with the members of the Diet neck-and-neck from as early as the fifth grade. In comparative terms, the Japanese prime minister seems to fall between his British counterpart and the American president in the degree of his importance and dominance in children's imagery of government.

A second, and perhaps more important, question has to do with young children's affect toward the prime minister. Table 2-2 summarizes Okamura's findings. The most striking aspect of these figures is the high proportion of children who chose the neutral responses, especially on the liking and competence items. The prime minister would not appear to be a highly salient figure for young children, particularly as an object of affection and trust. For those to whom he is salient, moreover, the table shows that his image is strikingly more negative than positive, from almost the earliest grade levels. On none of the items do we find an outright majority of favorable responses at all grades, and only for his competence at his job (a point discussed below) do we find such a majority at most levels.

Consistent with findings about children's affect toward political figures in other societies, the figures in Table 2-2 show a marked tendency across all three items for positive feelings to decrease with age and for negative feelings to increase correspondingly. What is distinctive about the Japanese case is that the drop in supportive responses appears to happen earlier and to reach a substantially lower level by eighth grade than is true, for example, in the United States. Indeed, favorable replies among eighth graders to the liking and trust items were virtually nonexistent. Cross-national comparison helps to put these data into perspective and to point up the dramatically low level of Japanese children's affection for the prime minister. For example, Easton and Dennis report that in

Table 2-2
Younger Children's Attitudes toward the Prime Minister
(Percent positive, neutral, and negative responses by grade)

Grade	Competence[a]			Liking[b]			Honesty[c]		
	Pos	Neut	Neg	Pos	Neut	Neg	Pos	Neut	Neg
3	74	22	4	36	58	6	68	25	7
4	66	26	8	20	63	16	51	40	9
5	52	31	18	13	61	26	27	50	23
6	54	26	20	8	61	31	17	48	35
7	43	33	24	12	58	29	10	58	31
8	37	35	28	5	58	37	7	57	36

Survey Items:

	Positive Response	Neutral	Negative
[a]"Is the prime minister carrying out his responsibilities as prime minister?"	Very well; Well	Can't say; Don't know	Not very well; Hardly at all
[b]"Do you like the prime minister or dislike him?"	Like very much; Like	Can't say; Don't know	Dislike; Dislike very much
[c]"Is the prime minister honest or is he a liar?"	Very honest; Honest	Can't say; Don't know	Sometimes lies; Always lies

Note: *N*'s are as in Table 2-1.
Source: Okamura, 1968 Survey.

response to an item asking American children to choose whether they liked the president "more than anyone," "more than most," "more than some," "more than a few," or "less than anyone," 60 percent or more of the fourth through seventh graders and 56 percent of the eighth graders chose one of the three positive replies, while about a third of the fourth through seventh graders selected one of the two most positive. Only about 17 percent of any age level chose one of the two least favorable replies.[23]

The contrast between the American and Japanese findings is vivid. For example, 25 percent of the American eighth graders professed to like the president more than anyone or more than most, while only 5 percent of the Japanese eighth graders claimed to like the prime minister or to like him very much. Though the items used differ in wording, thereby making strict comparison impossible, independent evidence corroborates that many fewer Japanese than American children express a liking for their national leader. Japan was one of six nations included in a study of the socialization of primary school children into "compliance systems." With regard to liking for national leaders—in the Japanese case, the prime minister; in the American, the president—and belief that the national leader would help people who needed assistance, the proportion of youngsters giving positive responses to the identical items used was consistently lowest among the Japanese. The Japanese children were markedly less positive than their American, Indian, Italian, and Greek agemates. Only the Danish children approached their low levels of affect for the political authority figure.[24]

Turning to another dimension of affective evaluation—feelings about the truthfulness of the leader—we discover that here, too, Japanese children are more cynical than their agemates in other lands. Easton and Dennis asked American children, while Abrahamson and Inglehart asked Dutch and French children, about how often the leader (prime minister, president, or queen) keeps his or her promises. Okamura's item asked the children to say whether they thought the prime minister was honest or told lies. Though the differences in the items are thus sufficient for us to take note of them, it seems useful nonetheless to pursue the comparison, in view of the basic similarity in theme (Table 2-3).

Grade-by-grade comparisons between the United States and Japanese samples make the differences found in Table 2-3 even sharper. Favorable responses among American children ("always keeps promises" plus "usually keeps promises") *never* fall below 94 percent at any age level; as we saw in Table 2-2 favorable responses among Japanese children regarding the prime minister's honesty ("very honest" plus "honest") amounted to a majority only among the youngest children, and plummeted to merely 7 percent of the eighth graders, where fully 10 percent chose the most negative responses ("he always lies"). In

Table 2-3
Cross-National Comparison of Children's View of Political Leaders' Honesty
(Percent selecting most favorable response)

Age	U.S.A.[a] President	Netherlands[a] Queen	Netherlands[a] Premier	France[a] President	France[a] Premier	Japan[b] Prime Minister
8-11	42	65	36	48	36	15
12-14	23	71	33	30	16	1

Survey Items:

[a]"... always keeps promises."

[b]"... is very honest."

Source: For the United States, David Easton and Jack Dennis, *Children in the Political System* (New York: McGraw-Hill, 1969), Table 8-43, p. 180; for the Netherlands and France, Paul R. Abrahamson and Ronald Inglehart, "The Development of Systemic Support in Four Western Democracies," *Comparative Political Studies* 2 (1970), Table 4, p. 428; for Japan, Okamura, 1968 Survey.

an earlier study that asked small samples of both Japanese and American children identical questions about their respective leaders' honesty, similar findings were reported. Among second graders, 90 percent of the American children and 70 percent of the Japanese children chose favorable replies; among eighth graders the proportions dropped to 50 percent of the American and 5 percent of the Japanese.[25]

One obvious possibility is that Japanese youngsters' lack of affection for the prime minister reflects a generally cooler view of him among Japanese adults than the view American adults have of the president. Okamura found that few of the children in his study believed that the prime minister was popular with many people. Table 2-4, which presents some supporting evidence, compares the average percentage of popular support reported in the major public opinion polls received by each American president up to Richard Nixon, and the five major postwar prime ministers up to Eisaku Sato, as well as the highest and lowest levels of support received by each.

While again item wording differences must be taken into account in making any comparison, there seems little room for doubt that adult popular support for the Japanese prime minister is a significant notch lower than that for the American president. Prior to Tanaka Kakuei,[b] only one prime minister, Yoshida Shigeru who held office during much of the Occupation, had ever received more than 50 percent popular support. In contrast, all of the American presidents have enjoyed nearly 70 percent or more approval at some point, and except for Harry Truman and for Richard Nixon after the Watergate revelations, the average support for the American presidents far outdistances that for the Japanese leaders.[c] In short, it is clear that the cues Japanese youngsters receive

[b]Tanaka who held office from June 1972 to November 1974 and Miki Takeo who succeeded him are excluded from consideration because they took office after the study being reported here was conducted. Tanaka, who entered office on a crest of popularity, received the highest support ever attained by a prime minister in the *Asahi* poll (62 percent in July 1972). His early support in the *Mainichi* poll was also very high (53 percent in September 1972, the second highest on record after that received by Yoshida). But he suffered a precipitous decline in support—plummeting to 18 percent in the Mainichi poll of October 1972 just prior to his resignation due to the furor over his suspected illegal use of office for private gain. This was the lowest popular support for a prime minister recorded in the *Mainichi* poll up to that time. To complete the comparison with the figures in the table, Tanaka's average support was 32 percent. See *Mainichi Shinbun,* October 19, 1974, and *Asahi Shinbun*, December 16, 1973.

[c]An interesting comparison with the Japanese case is provided by that of Britain. Over the period 1945 to 1969, popular approval of the prime minister in the British Gallup Poll averaged 52 percent and ranged from a low of 26 percent for Harold Wilson in 1969 to a high of 68 percent for Harold MacMillan in 1960. See Fred I. Greenstein, Valentine Herman, Robert N. Stradling, and Elia T. Zureik, "The Child's Conception of the Queen and the Prime Minister," *British Journal of Political Science* 4:3 (July 1974), 261. In contrast, the French premiers of the Fourth Republic seem to have been equally unpopular as, and in some cases even more unpopular, than their Japanese counterparts. In the early years of the Fifth Republic, however, President de Gaulle enjoyed about as high a level of support as the American presidents. See the comparative data presented in Nishihira Shigeki, *Nihonjin no Iken (The Opinions of the Japanese)*, (Tokyo: Seishin Shobo, 1963) Figure II, p. 81.

Table 2-4
Adult Popular Support for Japanese and American Chief Executives

Prime Minister	Japanese Prime Minister (% supporting Cabinet)			President	American President (% approving handling of job)		
	High	Low	Avg.		High	Low	Avg.
Yoshida	54	31	41	Truman	87	23	46
Hatoyama	50	34	40	Eisenhower	79	49	66
Kishi	46	28	37	Kennedy	83	57	70
Ikeda	40	31	35	Johnson	80	35	54
Sato	46	19	32	Nixon	68	24	48
	Overall Average: 37%				Overall Average: 57%		

Source: Japanese data were computed from *Mainichi Shinbun*, October 18, 1971. Reprinted with permission. American data are from *Gallup Opinion Index*, March 1972, p. 2, and *The Gallup Poll Release*, August 15, 1974, p. 1. Reprinted with permission.

from adults about the prime minister are much less likely to be positive than those American children receive.

Yet, while Japanese children do not like or trust the prime minister, they apparently think he is doing a good job. As we saw in Table 2-2, the belief that he is carrying out his responsibilities as prime minister remains predominant throughout the grade school years. This mixture of respect and "dislike" is exemplified by the following comments of a tenth-grade Tokyo boy, which indicate that some children may begin with a naive, positive image of the prime minister that is soon overcome by the negative tone of adult discourse:

I: Well, what about Prime Minister Sato—is he doing a good job?
R: *He stands for the whole country. . . . I think he does his best, and is right for the job.*
I: Saying he's right for the job means he's fulfilling his responsibilities, doesn't it?
R: *Yes, I think he's doing the best he can.*
I: Do you like him or dislike him?
R: *Like or dislike? Well, I've no real reason to dislike him, but somehow since everyone says they dislike him, I feel as if I do too.*
I: Does everyone say that? Who's everyone?
R: *Everyone's—well, often on television they say things like "Sato's bad." And the price of rice keeps going up.*
I: They don't often say "Sato's good?"
R: *I've never heard anyone say "Sato's good."*

Over and above the obvious implications that the press may have a good deal to do with the prime minister's popularity—a point we shall return to—this admixture of respect and dislike may come out of an image of the prime minister's job that emphasizes importance rather than benevolence and is one of the few distinct pictures that Japanese children seem to have of the prime minister. In this image, the kinds of qualities that would stimulate affective identification are noticeably lacking.

The Prime Minister's Image: Some
Insights from a Comparison with
the Local Leader

What accounts for the remarkably low overall level of affect that Japanese children show toward the prime minister? Interviews with some 40 teenagers made it apparent that underlying much of their feeling was the sense that the prime minister is a distant and remote figure. The prime minister, one fourteen-year-old Tokyo boy said, leads a "separate existence" from the ordinary people.[d] In that separate existence, other interviews make clear, the prime minister is concerned about "big" things, not ordinary matters; about policies, not people.

I: Does the prime minister try to help the people?
R: *I think he tries to look after the big things rather than the little ones. Not so that people become individually better off, but so that Japan as a whole does . . . that's his responsibility.* (Rural eighth-grade girl)
I: What sort of person do you think the prime minister is?
R: *Sort of not too kind to the common people. I feel as if he does things that are far apart from us. I feel I'd like him to be closer to us.* (Tokyo tenth-grade girl)

This feeling of distance and separation from the prime minister apparently stems, at least in part, from two sources. First, the prime minister acts on the national level, from which Japanese youngsters feel far removed. Second, he is an impersonal figure whose image for most Japanese youngsters does not include the personal qualities, so prominent in American children's images of the president, that create an image of the president that has much the same kind of intimacy and familiarity as their images of their fathers. These points are best illustrated by showing the stark contrast in the images Japanese children have of the prime minister with those they have of another significant authority figure, the local leader.

In the interviews, there were frequent spontaneous and enthusiastic references from the Tokyo children to Minobe Ryokichi, the Governor of Tokyo. The following quote is illustrative of his appeal to the young:

[d]This echoes a comment made by a journalist in the *Asahi Shinbun*, July 9, 1971, that the prime minister always "sounds as if he is speaking in a different dimension from that of the people."

I: Is there a politician whom you like?
R: *Mr. Minobe.*
I: What's good about Mr. Minobe?
R: *Like I said, his seeming like one of the people is good. So everyone feels friendly, and he thinks about everyone's problems—perhaps it's that. He's on television a lot. He listens to everyone's opinions and says "If it can be done, I'll do it." I've seen that. . . .* (Tokyo tenth-grade girl)

Minobe has been unusually popular with adults as well; opinion polls have shown that more than two-thirds of Tokyo adults support him. His popularity also crosses party lines to an extent that is rare in Japan: not only do an overwhelming majority of Communists, Socialists, and Democratic Socialists support him, so too do a majority of Liberal Democrats.[26] Few politicians in postwar Japan have enjoyed that kind of suprapartisan support, so his relative popularity with children is no surprise. What is a surprise, however, is that children in other areas accord a similar level of support to *their* local leaders (mayors or village heads). This is the unexpected finding about local figures that emerges from Okamura's questions that were identical to those asked about the prime minister. Figure 2-1 summarizes the comparative support for prime minister and local leader among children in grades three through eight. The numbers shown, which are the mean scores among children of each grade for each authority figure on each of the items, were computed by scoring one point for the most negative response category up to five for the most positive.

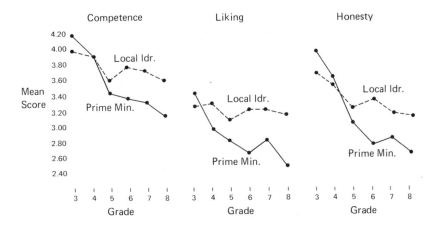

Note: Scores range from 1 (most negative) to 5 (most positive). Note also that *N*'s are as in Table 2-1 and that the items are as given in Table 2-2 and are identical for both prime minister and local leader.

Source: Okamura, 1968 Survey.

Figure 2-1. Mean Scores, by Grade, for Images of the Prime Minister and Local Leader.

As with the prime minister, the local leader is not highly salient to most children. But among those to whom the two figures are salient, we observe several notable differences. First, the prime minister enjoys a clear lead in support over the local leader only among the very youngest children, the third graders. By fifth grade, and to some extent even by fourth grade, the local leader enjoys more support. Second, whereas support for the prime minister declines grade by grade, support for the local leader remains fairly constant across all grade levels. Only evaluations of the local leaders' honesty show any really marked decline, and that appears to cease after fifth grade. In other words, for all practical purposes, the local leader appears to be much less susceptible to the corrosive effects of age on support that plagues the prime minister's image. Why? Though firm evidence is lacking, it seems, from a variety of sources, especially the interviews with young teenagers, that the factors they identify as negative and repulsive in the political world—remoteness, corruption, and the placing of narrow partisan interests ahead of the public interest—are widely perceived to be operative at the national level but not at the local level. And that distinction begins with the very notion of "politics," which is itself perceived as a national-level phenomenon. As one Tokyo tenth-grader said: "When you talk about local autonomy, that's something which is very close to home. Politics seems to be on a bigger scale." If politics seem remote, the notion of politician seems somehow "sort of wicked" and "unclean" in the words of one rural high school senior.[e] For many youngsters, however, local leaders such as Governor Minobe, or the city mayor or village head, don't really seem like "politicians."

I: So things that are right around you don't seem like politics? If that's the case, whom do you think of when I ask about politicians.
R: *The prime minister.*
I: What about Governor Minobe?
R: *He and some others have been on television a lot recently, making a fuss. . . . In a way, he's a politician too.*
I: But he's different from the prime minister?
R: *Yes, more like the working people.*
I: What do you mean by that? He feels closer to you?
R: *The things he does are basic . . . [sort of between doing] things for the country and for one's home.*
I: Things like garbage collection don't seem like politics?
R: *No.*

Our teenager is hesitant about classifying the governor as a politician. He is a politician only "in a way," but the sorts of things he does are different from those that the prime minister does. The interviewer in this case, herself a

---

[e]His words reflect the feelings of many youths. One sample of college students chose to describe politicians with the adjectives dark, dirty, cold, elderly, unintellectual, empty, closed and conservative. See Nishihira Naoki, *Gendai Seinen no Ishiki to Kodo 1 (The Attitudes and Behavior of Contemporary Youth)*, (Tokyo: Dai Nihon Tosho, 1970), p. 103.

Japanese college girl, provides us with the clue to the image of the local leader's job: not politics but "things like garbage collection." "Local autonomy" is not politics at the local level, but local officials looking after the practical, earthy needs of the common citizens. This uncynical view of local affairs and local leaders fits in with evidence suggesting that adults also feel less alienated when it comes to the local scene. In all areas of Japan, in the otherwise alienated city as well as in the country, consistently more people vote in local elections than in national ones. This may be because adults, like children, feel closer to the local leaders; Bradley Richardson, in a 1964 survey, found that both urban and rural adults were more likely to attribute concern about the people's needs to local officials and politicians than to national ones.[27]

Behind the apparently common tendency of youngsters and adults to view local leaders as more benign than national ones lies the fact that such leaders are expected to, and commonly do, run and serve as nonpartisans.[f] As a result, in contrast to national politics, in which party conflict and party interests occupy the limelight, at the local level the party label is widely deemphasized. Minobe, for instance, is supported by a Socialist-Communist-Komeito coalition organization, popularly known as the Tokyo Citizen's Party (*Tomin no To*). The nonpartisanship of local leaders has two important consequences for their support. First, it reflects and enhances community solidarity and harmony and thus accords well with some long-time cultural emphases that are still potent, especially in rural Japan. Second, their nonpartisanship insures that local leaders are less apt to incur critical treatment by the media, which operate, as Okamura has pointed out, on a principle of neutrality that permits the expression of positive support for nonpartisan figures only, while reserving for partisan figures negative comments.[28] Suprapartisan figures like Minobe receive generally positive treatment and of course nonpartisan local leaders often receive very little press attention at all. Meanwhile, the prime minister, as the most salient national partisan politician, is constantly criticized.

The local leader's job gets him out hobnobbing with the common people; he worries about the kinds of things they worry about, like garbage collection. How about the prime minister? What is the image youngsters have of him at his work? The chief executives of the United States, France, and Britain are all apparently

---

[f]Thus, among incumbents in office in January 1973, nonpartisans (*mushozoku*) accounted for only three of the 743 members of the two houses of the national Diet, but were overwhelmingly predominant among both urban and rural mayors, and constituted the largest group of prefectural governors as well. Nonpartisans comprised 94 percent of the 2,634 town and village mayors, and 82 percent of the 620 city mayors, including those of eight of the nine largest cities, excluding Tokyo, which, as a metropolitan prefecture, has a governor rather than a mayor. Tokyo's Minobe was among seven nonpartisan governors in office in the eight most populous prefectures. Of the total of 47 governors, nonpartisans outnumbered partisans 23 to 22, and the remaining two posts were occupied by men who had run as candidates of local groups (*shoha*) as distinct from the five major parties. Ministry of Local Autonomy figures cited in *Asahi Nenkan 1974 (The Asahi Yearbook, 1974)*, (Tokyo: Asahi Shinbunsha, 1974), pp. 229 and 415-60.

perceived by the children in those lands as doing rather awe-inspiring things: "ruling" or "commanding," engaging in foreign affairs and other statesmanlike enterprises.[29] No such aura of stately power and dominance characterizes Japanese teenagers' imagery of the prime minister's job. Rather, the common picture is that of one who "coordinates" (*matomeru*) the government and the opinions of the people, as an eighth grader put it. The picture is neither an inspiring—nor intimidating—one like those of the Western leaders; nor is it a familiar and ingratiating one like that of the local leader. At best, it might be seen as a rather idealistic picture of a representative leader seeking to harmonize government and people. A more negative interpretation might emphasize the power broker or bureaucratic manager, which is one component that may seem latent in the image. The latter interpretation would fit the personal style of Prime Minister Sato, who has been called a "model of the bureaucratic leader."[30] His personal appeal and identification with the common man were probably weaker than those of any of his predecessors, save only Kishi Nobusuke, his brother.[g] In his relatively infrequent television appearances, for example, Sato invariably seemed stiff and ill at ease. Minobe, who has made frequent television appearances, is always relaxed, full of smiles, and "folksy." The contrast is most vivid.

But the absence of personal imagery among Japanese youngsters' reactions to the prime minister reflects not merely the former incumbent's distant personality, but also the fact that the personal image-building that American presidents undergo, with the great attention focused by the press on their personal predilections, activities, and family life, has not occurred in Japan. One reason the press spotlight has been diverted from the personal life of the prime minister and his family is that to some extent the imperial family has stimulated more public curiosity and therefore more press coverage of their private lives. But perhaps more important is the aforementioned principle of neutrality under which the media operate, so that in seeking to avoid favorable treatment of partisan figures they downplay the personal life of the prime minister.

This lack of personal imagery in Japanese youth's views of the prime minister, which appears to be true also of French children's views of their president and premier,[31] while reflective of the psychic distance existing between children and the leader, is not necessarily detrimental to his overall role. What it may imply, indeed, is that his image is less important than his performance as a means to generating support even among the young. If that is so, then the kind of support he receives may be a conditional kind that helps keep leaders responsible and responsive, rather than an uncritical support that fosters irresponsibility. The fact that many children see him as carrying out his responsibilities even while they do not like or trust him supports such an interpretation. And the probability that for many children "dislike" is no more than that—and not

---

[g]Kishi was adopted from the Sato family into the Kishi family, a common practice among traditional Japanese families who lack a male heir to carry on their lineage.

hostility or hatred—may help keep such a critical stance toward the prime minister from becoming bitterly cynical.

An additional basis for the distant and impersonal image of the prime minister is the way he is chosen. The absence of direct popular election in the parliamentary system almost certainly diminishes the potential support and affection that the prime minister can generate. Popular identification is less easily created with a leader selected by a vote of the legislature than with one whose election is the culmination of a series of popular campaigns and personal appeals. The parliamentary system, that is to say, depersonalizes the leadership selection process; it lacks the drama of personal combat for popular esteem by two or more personalities who actively seek to create nationwide personal followerships. In the Japanese case, the process of depopularization of the leadership selection process is accentuated by the fact of one-party dominance. The head of the largest faction of the ascendant Liberal Democratic Party assumes the prime ministership almost as an automatic consequence of his selection as party president—a process in which there is no direct popular involvement and which creates little popular excitement.

The contrast with the election of the local leader is again noteworthy here as an instance of how a structural factor may contribute to both the distance of the prime minister and his impersonal quality. The local electoral process is one in which, as we have said, nonpartisanship is the rule. Deemphasizing the party label of course results in emphasizing the personalities of the contestants.[h] Moreover, the election is in fact head-to-head combat of two candidates who must use their personal appeal to gain followers.

The young Japanese child, in summary, sees the prime minister basically as a distant and impersonal figure who inspires neither awe nor affection but rather mild dislike and mistrust. Comparison of this image with that of the local leader makes it clear that a number of factors join to contribute to the erosion with age of the relatively positive evaluations of the prime minister that are held by the youngest children. But the local leader's advantages with respect to most of these factors appear to shore up his image against this erosion. Thus, in an interesting twist, the local leader may serve to fulfill some of the expressive functions of leadership for Japanese children that the American president and British and Dutch queens perform for children in those lands. It is clear, however, that the local leader is hardly a complete substitute for the missing national level benevolent leader. And it becomes necessary, therefore, to inquire as to whether any national level institution is able to generate broad-gauge support capable of contributing to the legitimacy of the regime. Or, on the other hand, do the negative feelings toward the prime minister spill over onto the rest of the political structure?

---

[h]Research in American electoral politics has shown that candidate appeal becomes more important in nonpartisan systems. See Fred I. Greenstein, *The American Party System and the American People* (Englewood Cliffs, N.J.: Prentice-Hall, 1970), p. 67.

The Spillover of Affect: Support
for Institutions among Teenagers
and Parents

Political cynicism, we are told, is a characteristic of adults, not of children. Fred Greenstein reported that the most striking finding of his study of New Haven children was that

... the prevailing adult skepticism and distrust of politics and politicians did not seem to be present. . . . [There] was no evidence even of a frame of reference which would make it possible to use questionnaire items tapping the dimension of political cynicism.[32]

But of course we have seen that even young Japanese children do exhibit such skepticism and mistrust of the prime minister. Does that cynicism develop into a systematic aversion to all political institutions at the national level, as we might expect if the spillover thesis is valid? Do older Japanese youngsters, then, develop anything approximating adult political cynicism? These are the questions that flow from what we have seen so far and to which we now turn our attention.

An essential element in the notion of the benevolent leader, and in the wider concept of political trust, is that political authorities care about the people. Table 2-5 summarizes how Japanese teenagers and their parents feel about the prime minister and three other national political institutions with respect to their concern for ordinary peoples' problems.

Table 2-5

Comparison of Political Institutions' Concern for Ordinary People

(Percent positive, neutral, and negative responses for students by grade, and for parents as a whole)

Students	Prime Minister			Government			Diet			Pol. Parties			
Grade	Pos	Neut	Neg	Pos	Neut	Neg	Pos	Neut	Neg	Pos	Neut	Neg	N
8	36	27	37	44	33	23	39	27	34	28	47	25	282
10	27	27	46	40	31	29	34	33	33	33	33	34	334
12	22	19	59	36	24	40	29	26	45	31	27	42	326
Parents	40	30	30	52	28	20	44	34	22	41	35	24	1637

Survey Item:
"How much does each of the following care about the problems in the daily lives of ordinary Japanese and try to help them?"

Note: Positive = Very much: Somewhat.
     Neutral = Can't say; Don't know.
     Negative = Not much; Hardly at all.

The table makes clear the lack of any intense belief in the concern of the institutions among the teenagers. It is especially noteworthy that fewer respondents believe the prime minister cares than believe that any of the other three institutions do. But no institution fares really well among the teenagers, and only the government gains consistent approval from a substantial proportion—but not a majority—of all age groups. The relationship between increasing age and increasing cynicism that we observed among children holds true for teenagers as well. What is more, by as early as eighth grade, they are more cynical about the concern of political institutions than are their parents. Indeed, more parents responded favorably than unfavorably regarding the concern of all four institutions, while twice as many parents were favorable about each institution than were the twelfth-grade children.

Another component of the concept of political trust is belief that political authority is responsive. The will of the people plays a large role in the democratic ideology, and the widespread belief of Japanese youngsters in popular sovereignty underlies the importance of their being able to feel that the people are listened to. Table 2-6 shows teenagers' and parents' evaluations of the responsiveness of the four institutions compared in the preceding table, plus elections. It confirms a number of the same points seen in Table 2-5. Once again, we observe that the students are more cynical than their parents and that insofar as the prime minister, government and Diet are concerned cynicism prevails over trust among the students. But only the Diet fails to get more positive than negative parental responses. A new note has been added, however, in that both parents and students exhibit markedly greater support for the responsiveness of the political parties and elections than for the prime minister, Diet and government. Moreover, there is a most significant reversal of the trend among teenagers toward increasing cynicism with age, in that their belief in the responsiveness of these two institutions—that is, the institutions' ability to make the government pay attention—actually increases with age. This finding is the first evidence of what is believed in this study to be an important source of support for the regime among Japanese teenagers: the belief that the input institutions of politics—those like parties and elections that mediate the political participation of the citizenry and convey their demands—are worthier of support than the output institutions—those like the prime minister, government, and Diet that represent authority. Parties and elections seem to be perceived in the role of the peoples' allies against authority. If this is so, then the apparent alienation from the output institutions and particularly from the primary political authority figure, the prime minister, may represent not an undifferentiated cynicism toward the institutional structure of the regime but rather a skepticism toward authority among a generation of Japanese brought up and socialized in a society that has repudiated but not forgotten authoritarianism.

A dimension of political trust that is particularly relevant to a society like Japan, where partisanship, cleavage, and factions often overshadow the idea of

Table 2-6
Comparison of Political Institutions' Responsiveness
(Percent positive, neutral, and negative responses for students by grade, and for parents as a whole)

Students Grade	Prime Minister			Government			Diet			Political Parties			Elections		
	Pos	Neut	Neg	Pos	Neut	Neg	Pos	Neut	Neg	Pos	Neut	Neg	Pos	Neut	Neg
8	23	42	35	22	50	28	21	52	27	38	53	9	36	53	11
10	21	37	42	23	42	35	19	43	38	47	38	15	46	38	16
12	41	11	48	22	34	44	14	37	49	53	32	15	50	37	13
Parents	38	37	25	38	39	23	23	37	40	60	30	10	61	32	7

Institution:	Survey Items:	Responses Scored Positive:
Prime Minister	"When the Prime Minister decides on a policy, he gives a great deal of consideration to what the people wish."	Agree; Agree strongly
Government	"Over the long run, the government gives a good deal of consideration to what the people want, when it decides on policy."	Agree; Agree strongly
Diet	"When it comes to deciding what to do in the Diet, most Diet members pay very little attention to the wishes of the voters who elected them."	Disagree; Disagree strongly
Parties	"The political parties play an important role in making the government pay attention to what the people think."	Agree; Agree strongly
Elections	"Elections make the government pay attention to what the people want."	Agree; Agree strongly

Note: *N*'s are as in Table 2-5.

the commonweal and the common interest, is that of the inclusiveness of political institutions—that is, whether they represent all the people or are beholden to narrow interest groups. Table 2-7 compares the institutions on this dimension, but the items, it should be noted, all differ substantially from one another and share only the common theme of inclusion versus exclusion of the people.

The trends in the table are clearly like those in Tables 2-5 and 2-6. Again, parties and elections, especially the former, receive more favorable evaluations from the teenagers, on the whole, than do the other institutions. The Diet suffers most, as indeed might be expected from the kinds of remarks made by the teenagers interviewed. A particularly common complaint against the Diet was that its members got there by unfair means, such as having a lot of money or being the son of a Diet member. There were also a number of references to corruption in the Diet and the government.

The corruption issue, which has been a recurring thorn in the side of Japanese politics, especially since the "black mist" scandals of the mid-1960s,[i] has made its mark on Japanese youngsters as well as their parents, as Table 2-8 indicates.

The interviews revealed no clearcut pattern about where teenagers believed corruption was greatest, although some had a feeling that, as one twelfth-grade Tokyo boy expressed it, "People in the government are more in the shadows, and so I think they are more dishonest." A rural high school senior, on the other hand, bemoaned the fact that Diet members, "no matter how often they do something wrong [i.e., break Japan's strict election laws], . . . win time and again in the elections."

What is intriguing is that though a number of youngsters made similar comments on the corrupt behavior of candidates for elective office, the comments showed virtually no evidence of disillusionment with the electoral process itself. And only a very few youngsters brought the political parties into their remarks on corruption. It was suggested earlier that elections and parties elicit more support because of their character as input institutions and that they thus might serve as important legitimizing agents for the structure of the democratic regime. Table 2-9 presents some additional evidence relevant to this hypothesis.

The items in the table share the common theme of tension between

---

[i]The "black mist" was the label attached by the press to a highly publicized series of scandals involving Liberal Democratic Party Diet members in 1966. The scandals included the indictment of a Diet committee chairman on eight charges of extortion, fraud, and tax evasion; alleged kickbacks by a sugar refining company to 11 LDP Diet members who had pressured government banking agencies to lend the firm huge sums; the forced resignation of the Speaker of the House of Representatives for alleged collusion with a stock brokerage official under indictment for fraud; the resignation under fire of the Minister of Transport, who had revised National Railway schedules so as to have express trains stop in his electoral district; and related cases involving the Ministers of Education and Agriculture and Fisheries, as well as the head of the Defense Agency. For full details, see *Asahi Nenkan 1967 (The Asahi Yearbook, 1967)*, (Tokyo: Asahi Shinbunsha, 1967), pp. 251-57, and 572.

Table 2-7

Comparison of Political Institutions' Inclusiveness

(Percent positive, neutral, and negative responses for students by grade, and for parents as a whole)

Students Grade	Prime Minister			Government			Diet			Political Parties			Elections		
	Pos	Neut	Neg	Pos	Neut	Neg	Pos	Neut	Neg	Pos	Neut	Neg	Pos	Neut	Neg
8	29	35	36	38	30	32	22	33	45	39	37	24	27	41	32
10	14	39	47	30	38	32	17	29	54	40	40	20	37	26	37
12	24	32	44	21	34	45	18	18	64	34	37	29	33	29	38
Parents	35	35	30	32	29	39	18	25	57	33	34	33	34	24	42

Institution:	Survey Items:	Responses Scored Positive:[a]
Prime Minister	"The Prime Minister truly works hard for the sake of all the people not just for himself or his party."	Agree; Agree strongly
Government	"The government's policies are increasing the gap between rich and poor, and work only for the benefit of the rich."	Disagree; Disagree strongly
Diet	"In the Diet, the majority ignores the rights of the minority, and the minority impedes majority decisions, so I don't think it is carrying out its responsibility to the people."	Disagree; Disagree strongly
Parties	"The political parties are all nothing more than groups of factions and influential men who think only of their own interests."	Disagree; Disagree strongly
Elections	"Since the same one party always wins, general election results don't really represent the will of the people."	Disagree; Disagree strongly

[a]Responses scored positive were those that supported the belief that the institution works for all the people.

Note: N's are as in Table 2-5.

Table 2-8

Corruption in the Government and Diet

(Percent positive, neutral, and negative responses for students by grade, and for parents as a whole)

Students Grade	Government			Diet		
	Pos	Neut	Neg	Pos	Neut	Neg
8	17	35	48	28	32	40
10	14	25	61	9	33	58
12	9	13	78	7	21	72
Parents	19	26	55	22	37	41

Institution:	Survey Items:	Responses Scored Positive:
Government	"A good many people in the government are dishonest and involved in corruption."	Disagree; Disagree strongly
Diet	"Most Diet members are trustworthy, honest men, who do not get involved in things like graft."	Agree; Agree strongly

Note: N's are as in Table 2-5.

diversified popular involvement in the political process and centralized authority. We note immediately that in contrast to the preceding tables, this one indicates that the parents are more negative about the institutions. Few teenagers, far fewer than parents, are willing to leave the people out of politics and leave politics to the leaders. Few would abandon elections and the multiple party system in favor of more harmonious and authoritarian modes of politics.

The other evidence available on this point is on the whole supportive. Okamura's data, for instance, included an item asking what would be the best thing for people to do to get their views reflected in politics. Among the high school students in the sample, voting in elections led the way, followed by writing to the newspaper and supporting the party of one's choice. Appealing to the Diet or the prime minister were chosen by few of the teenagers.[33]

It would of course be blindness to deny that Japanese youth are on the whole quite cynical about politics. The opinion polls show time and again that in Japan the young are more skeptical and distrusting of politics and politicians than are older people. Nevertheless, it seems evident that much of that cynicism is grounded in idealism—that is, in widespread belief among the young in the validity and legitimacy of the essential structural principle of democratic politics: rule by the people. But that idealism is accompanied by a skepticism about reality, a belief that government in a once antidemocratic system remains uncommitted to democracy.

Table 2-9

Willingness to Abandon Popular Input into Politics

(Percent agree, neutral, and disagree for students by grade, and for parents as a whole)

Students Grade	Leave Everything To Leaders			Abandon Elections			Single Party Would Be Better		
	Agree	Neut	Disagree	Agree	Neut	Disagree	Agree	Neut	Disagree
8	16	19	66	24	28	48	53	24	23
10	9	15	76	20	25	55	32	19	49
12	8	11	81	24	28	48	28	16	56
Parents	36	18	46	31	27	42	34	22	44

Survey Items:

"If we get good leaders, the best way to improve the country is for the people to leave everything to them rather than for the people to discuss things among themselves."

"It would be better if instead of all the present political parties there were only one political party which represented all the people and really did its best for the country."

"Since there are always so many election law violations, it would be better if our representatives were chosen by some other means such as competitive examinations, instead of elections."

Note: *N*'s are as in Table 2-5.

The authoritative institutions of government in this regard may suffer particularly from being linked with the past. In the new regime not only are the names of the institutions the same—which is not true for the parties and is irrelevant for elections and newspapers—but so are many of the faces. Prime Minister Kishi was not only a high-ranking civil servant in Manchuria under the old regime but was imprisoned as a war criminal. Prime Minister Sato was also a bureaucrat in imperial Japan. (Governor Minobe, on the other hand, has a link with the past too, but a most decidedly "democratic" link. His father was the author of the famous "Organ Theory," which characterized the emperor as simply one of the organs of the state, for which he was found guilty of *lèse-majesté*. The governor thus is a personal symbol repudiating the past.)

Nevertheless, the fundamental impediment to the prime minister's serving as a legitimating benevolent leader lies not in such personal links to the past, but rather in the role history has played in defining the very nature and basis of national leadership in postwar Japan.

**The Missing Leader and the
Missing Hero: Some Speculations
on the Role of History**

As in every nation the political regime of contemporary Japan is rooted, symbolically as well as institutionally, in a particular set of historical events. The events that define the contemporary Japanese polity are the defeat in World War II and the subsequent American Occupation of the country from 1945 to 1952. This historical definition of the contemporary political regime is in large part responsible for the absence of a benevolent leader in Japan.

Among the most common and effective ways in which political regimes seek to create allegiance is by sanctification of their historical roots. In the days when monarchs ruled as well as reigned, the history of the monarchy played this role and the monarch was the benevolent leader as a matter of course. But another pattern has come to predominate in the contemporary world—the emergence of a revolutionary tradition. The broad outlines of this pattern are common to the many otherwise disparate societies in which it is found: A new regime and a new social order are created and portrayed as the result of a great popular and national victory. It may be a nationalist revolution—victory over colonial occupation—as in the case of the many new nations that have emerged from among the former European colonies in Africa, India, Southeast Asia, and Latin America, as well, of course, as the United States, or it may be a popular defeat of the *ancien regime*, as in the cases of China, Russia, and France, among others. Whichever the case may be, the pattern is for the new regime to be the product of a revolution in the broadest and commonest sense of the term.

The profound changes effected by the Occupation in the social, cultural, political, and institutional life of Japan certainly qualify as one kind of revolution. But it was a *revolution without a victory*, not the culmination of a heroic struggle of patriots against the old order but the result of a defeat at the hands of a foreign conqueror. As a result the new political regime has lacked many of the means available to other regimes to create psychological bonds of allegiance among their members. The events of the origin of the democratic regime are not a source of national pride; there is little in them to serve as the catalyst for political emotions; no storming of the Bastille, no Long March, no Valley Forge to stimulate the patriotic urge and tie the new regime to the national identity. Thus, although Japan is a land of festivals, there is no real celebration of the democracy's founding. Constitution Memorial Day, May 3rd, is an almost entirely formal occasion with little or none of the power to kindle popular pride in the historical event and the regime it created that characterizes such days in other countries. Similarly, the flag and the national anthem are unrelated to, and therefore not directly supportive of, the new regime; they remain as holdovers from the *ancien regime*, as does that regime's foremost symbol, the emperor.

In creating a new political regime, the Occupation was inevitably limited in the means it could muster to legitimize that regime. It was able to create support for the new regime among some Japanese by reason of their belief in either its ideological or its structural legitimacy (to use David Easton's terms[34])—that is, their conviction that the moral and political principles of the new regime were right and proper for Japan or that the new institutions and norms were inherently worthy of acceptance.

But for most people, it is not principles or institutions that catalyze political affection and create legitimacy for a new order. Rather, it is a leader. Thus we come to the second and perhaps most important characteristic of the founding of Japan's new regime: it was a *revolution without a hero*. It was perforce a profound change of political regimes; but it was accomplished without a leader to embody the new values and to personify the new institutions.[j] The mission and purpose of the Occupation was of course not to create a regime based on such personal legitimacy; it was to destroy one—the emperor system of imperial Japan. As a result, not only did no new Japanese leader arise to serve as the personification of the new order; indeed, the popular identification of any prominent Japanese figure as the hero of the revolution and the creator of the new order was rendered impossible by the American authorship of the regime.[k] There was no Washington, Lenin, Mao, or Nehru to create for his successors the mantle and aura of personal legitimacy that characterizes the institutionalized leadership roles of many contemporary political systems. Today's Japan is, in short, a nation without a pantheon of political heroes.

A comparison of pre- and postwar children's heroes will serve to underscore this important point. In 1905 and 1915, children asked to name the "greatest man in Japan" overwhelmingly chose the emperor, who was followed by a small number of national military leaders and famous warriors—Admiral Togo, General Nogi, Saigo Takamori, and the fourteenth century warrior, Kusunoki Masashige.[35] Postwar grade school children, in 1958 and 1960, were asked a similar question—to name those whom they thought were great men. No single figure predominated in the responses, but Noguchi Hideo, the famous bacteriologist, was chosen most often by both samples. Very few children (about 6 percent of one sample and 4 percent of the second) chose the emperor and even fewer (5 percent and 0 percent, respectively) chose then Prime Minister Kishi.[36] No military figures were cited, while from history, a number of children chose the agriculturalist Ninomiya Sontoku instead of the warrior Kusunoki. But an even more telling difference was the appearance among the postwar children of foreign heroes. In the 1960 sample, it was Abraham Lincoln who was second only to Noguchi. In 1968, another sample, this time of Tokyo middle school pupils, overwhelmingly picked John F. Kennedy as the political leader whom they most respected.[37] In the same year, students at four universities—Tokyo, Nihon, Doshisha, and Kyushu—were asked the same question. Between 35 percent and 60 percent (the latter figure being of the students at Tokyo

---

[j]In his discussion of means for creating legitimacy, David Easton points out that abstract ideologies and ideas per se are usually ineffective in eliciting mass support. Rather, he says, "Typically, this has been achieved in part by the emergence of vigorous and trusted leaders who . . . embody the ideals and stand for the promise of their fulfillment. They are the personal bridges acting as ties to the new norms and structures of authority." See his *A Systems Analysis of Political Life* (New York: Wiley, 1965), pp. 304-05.

[k]That authorship was symbolized in a most concrete fashion by the dominating presence of General Douglas MacArthur, head of the Occupation.

University, the alma mater of nearly every Japanese prime minister) replied that there was *no* political figure whom they respected; moreover, those who did name a figure most frequently picked foreign leaders, of whom the four most often named were Kennedy, Lincoln, Lenin, and Churchill.[38] Only two Japanese prime ministers were mentioned—Yoshida Shigeru, who piloted Japan through the Occupation, was tied for fifth place with Charles deGaulle, and Ito Hirobumi, one of the founders of the Meiji regime, was tied for twentieth place.[1] In short, for the great majority of Japanese youngsters, political heroes either do not exist or are foreign leaders.[39]

Conclusion

Is Japan's democracy jeopardized by having no revolutionary hero, no benevolent leader? The answer depends greatly upon the success of other means for creating legitimacy. Japan has now been a democracy for nearly a generation. As we have seen here, during that time the political socialization process has inculcated among many young people a profound skepticism of government. But we have also seen that it has inculcated in many of them a commitment to popular sovereignty—that is, to the principle of popular participation in government and hence to support for an important element of the democratic ideal. An important part of the evidence and argument of this chapter has been that Japanese teenagers share a broad commitment to those elements of the structure of the regime—elections, parties, and the press—that mediate popular participation in politics. Moreover, the evidence suggests that local-level support may serve as a surrogate for national-level alienation; the local leader in Japan may be an important and safe personal agent of regime legitimation.

The very success of the Japanese democracy thus far must prompt us to ask the comparative question: How do most new regimes perform? Of course, there are too many unusual characteristics in the Japanese case—the Occupation itself, the high level of socioeconomic development of imperial Japan, her extensive bureaucracy, and even some domestic tendencies toward democracy, among others—to permit facile comparison with the experiences of new regimes in other nations. Still, it is obvious that all too often new regimes fail not in spite of the revolutionary hero and the benevolent leader, but in part because of him. The history of the postwar world is filled with the skeletons of young democracies and the ghosts of revolutionary heroes. Pakistan, Indonesia, Ghana, and others tell us of the sad but common tale of the revolution that is either betrayed by its own hero or unable to endure his passing.

---

[1]Tanaka Kakuei, who had not yet become prime minister, was also mentioned, but shared twentieth place with Ito and two foreign leaders. The only living Japanese politician to be among the ten names most frequently cited by the students was Nakasone Yasuhiro, who shared fifth place with Yoshida and de Gaulle. Nakasone is the leader of a major faction in the Liberal Democratic Party and a strong contender for the party presidency, and quite possibly the premiership in the future.

We might also ask whether, from the perspective of democratic theory, Japan is indeed not better off because of the missing leader. If the consent of the governed is to be an effective means of democratic control, then the presence of a benevolent leader who elicits a profound emotional response from those to whom he is responsible might prove someday too high a price to pay for stability. Japan already knows how high the price of the benevolent leader can be.

Notes

1. See Fred I. Greenstein, "The Benevolent Leader: Children's Images of Political Authority," *American Political Science Review* 54:2 (December 1960), 934-43, and *Children and Politics* (New Haven, Conn.: Yale University Press, 1965).

2. See Robert D. Hess and David Easton, "The Child's Changing Image of the President," *Public Opinion Quarterly* 114 (Winter 1960), 632-44; David Easton and Jack Dennis, *Children in the Political System* (New York: McGraw-Hill, 1969); and Robert D. Hess and Judith V. Torney, *The Development of Political Attitudes in Children* (Garden City, N.Y.: Anchor Books, 1967).

3. Dean Jaros, Herbert Hirsch, and Frederic J. Fleron, Jr., "The Malevolent Leader: Political Socialization in an American Subculture," *American Political Science Review* 52:2 (June 1968), 564-75.

4. Edward S. Greenburg, "Black Children and the Political System: A Study of Socialization to Support," paper delivered at the 1969 Annual Meeting of the American Political Science Association.

5. Fred I. Greenstein et al., "Queen and Prime Minister—The Child's Eye View," *New Society* 23 (October 1969), n.p., and "French, British, and American Children's Images of Government and Politics," paper delivered at the meeting of the Northeastern Political Science Association, 1970; Fred I. Greenstein and Sidney Tarrow, "Political Orientations of Children: The Use of a Semi-Projective Technique in Three Nations," *Sage Professional Papers in Comparative Politics*, Series 01-009, 1 (1970), pp. 479-588; Jack Dennis, Leon Lindberg, and Donald McCrone, "Support for Nation and Government among English Children," *British Journal of Political Science* 1, 25-48; and Paul R. Abrahamson and Ronald Inglehart, "The Development of Systemic Support in Four Western Democracies," *Comparative Political Studies* 2 (1970), 419-42.

6. Sidney Verba, "The Kennedy Assassination and the Nature of Political Commitment," in Bradley S. Greenberg and Edwin B. Parker, eds., *The Kennedy Assassination and the American Public* (Stanford: Stanford University Press, 1965), pp. 348-60. For a summary of many of the findings on which the argument rests as well as provocative criticism of the possible normative consequences of benevolent leadership, see Lewis Lipsitz, "If, as Verba says, the

State Functions as a Religion, What Are We to do then to Save Our Souls?" *American Political Science Review* 52:2 (June 1968), 527-35.

7. See footnote e in Chapter 1; hereafter his study is referred to as Okamura, 1968 Survey.

8. Alexander Leighton and Morris Opler, "Psychological Warfare and the Japanese Emperor," in Robert C. Hunt, ed., *Personalities and Cultures* (Garden City: The Natural History Press, 1972), pp. 255-56.

9. Greenstein et al., "Queen and Prime Minister—The Child's Eye View."

10. Ibid.

11. Greenstein, "French, British, and American Children's Images of Government and Politics," Table 3, p. 40.

12. Ibid., pp. 19 and 40.

13. Kazuo Kawai, *Japan's American Interlude* (Chicago: University of Chicago Press, 1960), p. 57.

14. Ardath Burks, *The Government of Japan* (New York: Crowell, 1961), p. 30.

15. Okamura, 1968 Survey.

16. Abrahamson and Inglehart, "The Development of Systemic Support in Four Western Democracies," p. 242.

17. See, for example, Ishida Takeshi, "Popular Attitudes toward the Japanese Emperor," *Asian Survey* 2 (April 1962), and David Titus, "Emperor and Public Consciousness in Postwar Japan," *Japan Interpreter* (Summer 1970).

18. Harada Shigeru, "Atarashii Aikokushin to wa Nani ka" (What is the New Patriotism?), *Seinen Shinri* 7:2 (February 1956), p. 32.

19. See David A. Titus, "Emperor and Public Consciousness in Postwar Japan," *Japan Interpreter* (Summer 1970), pp. 189-90; also, Yoshida Yoshiaki, David Titus, and Agata Yukio, "Shocho Tennosei no Ishiki Kozo" (The Mentality of the Symbolic Emperor System), *Meiji Daigaku Hosei Kenkyujo Kiyo*, n.d.

20. See Titus, "Emperor and Public Consciousness in Postwar Japan," p. 193.

21. Okamura, 1968 Survey.

22. Hess and Torney, *The Development of Political Attitudes in Children*, p. 43.

23. Easton and Dennis, *Children in the Political System*, Table 8-4, p. 179. These and all following figures on American children's affect toward the president are of pre-Watergate vintage. As this is being written there is still very little evidence regarding the overall intensity and permanence of the impact of the Watergate affair and Nixon's resignation in disgrace on American children's images of the president. In a study done during the period of the televised Senate hearings on Watergate in June 1973, Greenstein found only a slight diminution in children's tendency to idealize the president in comparison with pre-Watergate samples of children. "Children's Images of Political Leaders in Three Democracies," paper delivered at the 1973 Annual Meeting of the

American Political Science Association, New Orleans, Louisiana. See also Howard Tolley, Jr., *Children and War: Socialization to International Conflict* (New York: Teachers College Press, 1973) for evidence that the Vietnam War may have caused a decline in American children's perceptions of the president as an unerringly wise and infallible leader.

24. Robert D. Hess et al., *Authority, Rules, and Aggression: A Cross-National Study of the Socialization of Children into Compliance Systems*, Part I (Chicago: University of Chicago, March 1969, for Bureau of Research, Office of Education, U.S. Department of Health, Education and Welfare); see "PART B, Chapter 5: Japanese Data" by Akira Hoshino, and "PART C: Cross-National Comparisons and Conclusions" by Maria Tenezakis et al.

25. See Robert D. Hess, "The Socialization of Attitudes toward Political Authority: Some Cross-National Comparisons," *International Social Science Journal* 15 (1963) 542-59, and Okamura Tadao, "Political Socialization of Upheavals: A Case in Japan," unpublished paper (Chicago: University of Chicago, Department of Political Science, 1962).

26. *Asahi Shinbun*, July 9, 1969.

27. Bradley M. Richardson, "Urbanization and Political Participation: The Case of Japan," *American Political Science Review* 67 (June 1973), Table 7, p. 443.

28. Okamura Tadao, "The Child's Changing Image of the Prime Minister," *The Developing Economies* 6:4 (December 1968), 581.

29. Greenstein, "French, British, and American Children's Images of Government and Politics," Table 3, p. 40.

30. Shinohara Hajime, quoted in *Yomiuri Shinbun*, October 13, 1970.

31. Greenstein, "French, British, and American Children's Images of Government and Politics," p. 20.

32. Greenstein, "The Benevolent Leader," p. 935.

33. Okamura, 1968 Survey.

34. David Easton, *A Systems Analysis of Political Life* (New York: Wiley, 1965), pp. 286 ff.

35. Karasawa Tomitaro, *Asu No Nihonjin* (*Tomorrow's Japanese*), (Tokyo, 1964), pp. 52-53.

36. Ibid., p. 64.

37. Owaki Kenzo, "Chugakusei no Seiji Ishiki" (The Political Consciousness of Middle-School Students), *Ide* 77 (February 1968), p. 38.

38. *Asahi Shinbun*, November 24, 1968.

39. See Fred I. Greenstein, *Children and Politics*, p. 137 ff., for an interesting discussion of evidence indicating that the tendency of American children to choose political figures as heroes has shown a marked decline between the early 1900s and the present.

3

Symbols of Consensus: Democracy and Peace

Introduction

We have seen that the origin of the democratic regime in an alien military occupation effectively rendered impossible legitimation of that regime through the person of a national hero. Hence it was vital, if the new regime were to survive, that it become the vehicle of its own legitimation by instilling in the Japanese not merely acquiescence but conviction in and enthusiasm for its principles and values. Thus, Occupation authorities attempted to make democracy the legitimizing ideology of a new order in both political and social life. What was accomplished by that attempt is reflected in the role democracy plays in the political orientations of today's Japanese—both the youngsters born and raised in the atmosphere of the new regime and their parents resocialized under it.

To properly assay that role of democracy, we must ask two broad questions. What does democracy *mean* in today's Japan? And is it *valued*? We may respond to the first question, at the outset, by concentrating on the cognitive aspects of democracy to see what Japanese teenagers understand it to mean and how their conceptions differ from those of their parents.

The main question, however, concerns how democracy is valued. Is democracy valued positively? This leads us to consider elements in Japanese culture that might resist acceptance of democracy. "Traditional culture" has often been claimed to be the principal source of resistance; hence a fruitful source of pertinent information may be provided by a comparison of reactions to democracy among the older generation and rural residents (those members of Japanese society in whom traditional culture allegedly persists most strongly) and among the young and the urbanites (the group among which it is presumed to be least influential).

The analysis of affective feelings about democracy considers reaction to two aspects of democracy. The first is the term or symbol itself. The second is the democratic system of making decisions. Japanese culture traditionally placed a high premium on consensus and harmony and as a result sought unanimity in decisions and their acceptance by all concerned. The democratic rules of the game prescribe that decisions are to be based on the principles of majority rule and respect for minority rights. The question thus becomes to what extent the majoritarianism and tolerance of conflict or dissent of democracy have run afoul of the preference for consensus and unanimity.

51

The latter part of this chapter deals with the value of democracy to today's young Japanese and their parents from a rather different perspective. The focus shifts to an examination of the relative role of democracy in the hierarchy of values and ideals that form the framework within which the Japanese define national ideals and national goals. Here, as we shall see, another value propagated by the Occupation must be considered: pacifism. The discussion ends with a consideration of the place of these two symbols and values in the emerging political culture and some speculation on their role in national consensus and national identity.

The materials on which this chapter is based include, in addition to the survey questionnaires administered to the teenagers and their parents and the interviews with 40 of the teenagers, a set of compositions on the theme "Democracy, Capitalism, and Socialism" written by an eighth-grade class in a middle-class Tokyo middle school. The compositions were done at home without any supervision from either this author or the teacher other than the instruction regarding the topic. As a result, the contents quite often manifest not the spontaneous ideas, images, and attitudes of the youngsters themselves, but rather their reading of materials readily available at home—books, magazines, and frequently encyclopedias—on the three belief systems. They are thus useful less as indicators of the youngsters' own stable cognitive and affective states of mind regarding democracy or capitalism and socialism than as reflections of the substantive content of some important ambient socializing influences at play in adolescence in today's Japan.

The Meaning of Democracy

The democratic politics imposed on the Japanese by the Occupation were, as Japanese and American skeptics of the progress and the prospects of democracy in Japan have often noted, alien to the Japanese experience. Without the legacy of symbolism and imagery that infuses the concept of democracy in some of the Western nations, the United States and France in particular, the question thus arises as to how Japanese perceive and conceive of democracy. One particularly salient dimension of the question concerns the generational differences, if any, in Japanese views of the meaning of democracy. Older Japanese were raised under a political system that not only rejected democracy as inimical to traditional Japanese customs and values but portrayed it in negative terms and symbols such as "individualism." Younger Japanese have, on the other hand, been explicitly indoctrinated into the democratic belief system in their schooling.

We saw in Chapter 2 that popular sovereignty, especially the normative belief that the people should rule, was a major theme in Japanese youngsters' conceptions of the prominent actors in the political process. It is thus no surprise to discover that popular sovereignty is also a major, indeed the predominant, image in Japanese youngsters' conceptions of democracy. In interview after interview, almost identical words were repeated to define democracy as where "the opinions of the people are reflected in politics." Compare, for example, the following:

... when all sorts of peoples' opinions, the opinions of everybody in Japan, are brought together and the will of the people is emphasized. (Rural eighth-grade boy)

... a form of society where the government of a state listens to what the people say and reflects this in politics. (Suburban Tokyo twelfth-grade boy)

... where the people are made the basis. ... where what the people think is respected. (Rural tenth-grade girl)

In a pretest of the questionnaire conducted among more than 90 Tokyo eighth graders, 54 percent chose "the people have sovereign power" as the response that best expressed the meaning of democracy over seven other responses, none of which was selected by more than 9 percent. Comparative data here is scant, but Hess and Torney's data show that among their nationwide sample of American children, equality and voting were the most commonly perceived components of democracy while "the people rule" trailed in third place.[1]

The stress on popular sovereignty in Japanese youths' conceptions of democracy is not surprising. The new democratic regime, after all, was created to supplant a regime based on imperial sovereignty and, as a result, the constitution itself lays great stress on the role of the people. This emphasis is reflected in the stress laid upon popular rule in the inculcation of the young into the democratic belief system. Okamura Tadao and his associates found in a study of primary, middle, and high school social studies texts that by far the principal emphasis in the definitions of democracy given in those texts was popular sovereignty.[2] Moreover, of course, it must not be overlooked that the very word for democracy in Japanese, *minshushugi*, literally means "the principle of popular rule" and unlike the Greek-derived English word, it needs no linguistic explanation but is directly understandable.

In the interviews, few of the youngsters were spontaneously concrete as regards how the people rule or get their views reflected in politics. But those who did clearly understood the idea of representative democracy. Witness the following definitions of democracy:

... politics of the people. But in fact each one of the people can't directly participate in politics, so in Japan it's the Diet. (Suburban Tokyo twelfth-grade girl)

... when everyone's opinions are considered. But in Japan there are so many people that each person can't give his, and so there are representatives and politics is left up to them. (Urban Tokyo tenth-grade boy)

While popular sovereignty is obviously a prime component of every classic and contemporary definition of democracy, it is far from being the whole of the concept. To get at the other elements of the democratic conception in the minds of young Japanese (and those of their parents) the questionnaire included an item asking the respondent to select the two statements from a group of eight that best express the meaning of democracy.

The responses available included four broad categories of definitional emphasis: (1) libertarian, including safety to criticize the government and respect for human rights; (2) egalitarian, including the absence of poverty and discrimination; (3) participatory, including the right of all adults to vote, the rule of majority opinion in politics, and freedom of parties to compete in elections; and (4) pacifist, including the right to live in peace.[a] In the absence of popular sovereignty from the list of available choices, no single conception of democracy predominated among either students' or parents' first choices. The students' choices tended to be rather evenly split among majority rule (21 percent), respect of rights (22 percent), and egalitarianism or no poverty (16 percent). The parents, however, tended much more strongly than the students (23 percent to 7 percent) to emphasize the importance to democracy of voting—an important difference that shall be discussed shortly. One striking trend emerged in the second choices, with the right to live in peace leading all responses among both students (25 percent) and parents (21 percent). As we shall see later in this chapter, this theme of peace as a right and an ideal will occur over and over again in the images that young Japanese, and to a lesser extent even their parents, have of their ideal society.

Taken together, then, the cognitive orientations of Japanese youngsters with regard to democracy tend to be dominated by the notion of popular rule; once that is taken as a given component of their conceptions of democracy, the other constituent democratic values tend to draw roughly equal support both from parents and from students in all grades. It should also be noted, however, that as the age of students increases, they become less likely to choose egalitarian and pacifist ideas of democracy's essence and more likely to choose participatory and libertarian ones.

Democracy, then, is a familiar concept to Japanese, young and old alike, and the range of cognitive content that it takes on among them appears to be quite close to that found among Americans, even if the emphases differ. But the more important question is whether democracy has come to be valued in Japan. There are reasons of history and of culture why democracy should be alien to Japanese life and values, and it is to the success of democracy at establishing itself in the hierarchy of values in Japan in the face of such obstacles that we now turn.

---

[a]Popular sovereignty was intentionally excluded from the available options on the basis of the pretest results. The responses in the first three categories are components of most descriptions of democratic ideals and were derived from articles in the Japanese constitution. The fourth, peace, was included because it has a place of prominence in the new regime and its constitution, and because early interviewing revealed that it was closely linked in the minds of some youngsters to democracy.

The Value of Democracy

The values and virtues that have been emphasized in traditional Japanese culture, as has already been noted, are essentially undemocratic and in some respects even antidemocratic. The discreditation of the old ways caused by the defeat in World War II led many Japanese to seek a new basis for social conduct as well as for politics. But old values and symbols do not vanish overnight and the negative image of democracy continued to persist in the new Japan. An American sociologist found that even as recently as the late 1950s urban white-collar families in Tokyo tended, in their search for a new value system, to see democracy and individualism as "only a justification for selfishness and therefore not a solid basis for morality."[3]

Nevertheless, democracy is the formal ideal and value of the political system, and as such it is widely and uniformly propagated in the educational system and in the media. The result has been a constant recession of antagonism toward it and an increase in public acceptance of it over the postwar period, as the Japanese political scientist Shinohara Hajime has documented. In 1946, over 93 percent of a nationwide sample of adults felt that democracy had gone too far; in 1955, 64 percent of another sample believed that there were aspects of democracy unsuited to Japan that needed to be corrected.[4] Nevertheless, it was clear, as Shinohara points out, that by the 1960s democracy had become a positive symbol. The Research Committee of the Study of National Character of the Institute for Statistical Mathematics conducts a national survey asking many of the same questions every five years. In both 1963 and 1968, 38 percent of those surveyed thought that democracy was good, while roughly half felt that it depended on circumstances.[5] This acceptance of democracy thus appears to be a qualified one for many adults. For comparative purposes, the same organization asked the same question of Japanese-Americans in Hawaii. Seventy-four percent of them thought democracy was good, while only 21 percent believed it depends on the circumstances.[6] To gauge the comparative extent of attachment to democracy as a concept or symbol among Japanese of both the prewar and postwar generations, respondents in the study survey were asked whether they had a favorable reaction when they heard the word democracy.

The responses among both generations were overwhelmingly positive, with 76 percent of the students and 83 percent of the parents replying either "favorable" or "very favorable." But two things are noteworthy about the pattern of responses for both young and old. First, almost no one of any age rejects democracy outright; it has become in a sense sacrosanct. Second, and conversely, the support is surprisingly restrained in view of the duration and intensity of pro-democratic socialization in postwar Japan. Those responding "very favorable" were substantially fewer in number than those choosing simply "favorable" among both students (32 percent versus 44 percent, respectively) and parents (31 percent versus 52 percent). The more positive response, however, increased with the age of the student, from 24 percent among the eighth graders to 39 percent among the twelfth graders, which perhaps reflects the intensified exposure of the older youngsters to social studies texts, newspapers, books, and other sources that frequently sing democracy's praises.

Resistance to democracy is invariably asserted to stem from the traditional elements of Japanese culture. We have seen, however, that generation makes no significant difference. But if generation is one supposed cultural watershed, another such watershed variable, and one of probably longer-run significance, is place of residence. The "real" Japan of traditional custom and culture is rural Japan. It is here in the fishing or farming village where traditional Japanese culture evolved and where it is alleged to retain its greatest hold. The village is the archetype of Japanese society, and its human relations are the classic model of the norms and values governing Japanese social conduct. We would expect therefore that rural residents would be less receptive to democracy as a symbol and value. But we would expect, also, that the universal propagation of the democratic faith through Japan's uniform national educational system would lessen the difference in reaction to democracy on the part of young urban and young rural Japanese by comparison with that between their respective parents.

In fact, however, an examination of the responses revealed that urban and rural adults responded in identical fashion to the question; indeed, the very same percentages of both groups chose each of the available response options. The rural youngsters, on the other hand, actually exhibited a slightly but statistically significantly more positive reaction than did their urban fellows (83 percent to 78 percent, chi-square value of $p < .05$). This is of course directly contradictory to the hypothesis that those who live in the countryside are less likely to value democracy than their city cousins. Two points must be made in this connection. To begin with, as we shall see in later chapters, rural youngsters tend to be generally more supportive of the institutions of politics and government. Their more positive stance toward democracy may reflect this. Secondly, expressed attitude and actual behavior may not agree. The rural Japanese may in fact be less attracted to democracy than appears to be the case—a point we shall return to shortly in the discussion of consensus that follows.

Insofar, at least, as the general abstract term itself is concerned, there seems to be widespread agreement, across generations and across the main social line of cleavage in today's Japan, on its positive value. But democracy carries with it an important set of associated concepts and ideals with quite specific implications for the behavior of individuals and groups. Let us turn now to one of these, which is a central element of democracy, majoritarianism.

Consensus versus Majority Rule

The emphasis on majority rule that we have observed to be prominent in Japanese youngsters' first choice of ideas expressing the meaning of democracy is a significant problem for the analysis of the present and future role of democracy in Japanese political culture because it runs head on into a widely noted cultural norm of a preference for deciding by consensus and avoiding decisions in which one part of group, even a majority, wins and another loses. Robert Ward's description of this preferred decision pattern is thorough and lucid:

The traditional Japanese system of decision making is different [from the adversary system of the West]. It operates by consensus, that is, by unanimous agreements. A problem is posed and is then discussed by the group concerned with a minimum of open commitment to positions by participants. Eventually a sense of generally acceptable compromise emerges from the discussion; this is formulated by a senior member of the group and is then adopted by unanimous consent. In such a system no one is openly defeated or humiliated, "face" is preserved, at least the semblance of unanimity is achieved, and group harmony is thus maximized. Also the explicit recognition of minorities is avoided. Reciprocally, if the system is to operate along traditionally approved lines, it becomes an obligation of the majority faction not to ignore or ride roughshod over the opinions of the minority elements which do in fact exist. If they do so, the minority can then raise the cry of tyranny of the majority and solicit and obtain public sympathy on this ground.[7]

In order to ascertain the extent to which the preference for consensus exists among Japanese of both pre- and postwar generations and has for each group the implications it appears to have, a number of items included in the questionnaire dealt with group decision-making, and these were followed up in the individual interviews. Table 3-1 presents the results of an item designed to evoke preferences toward three varieties of group decision-making—authoritarian, consensual, and majoritarian.

The results appear unquestionably to accord with the antimajoritarian thesis. The teenagers overwhelmingly prefer the consensual path to decision. So too do their parents, but in a surprising reversal of what we would expect and predict on the basis of *presumed* change in the content of political socialization in childhood and adolescence, especially in school practices, the parents were *more* apt than the teenagers to choose the majoritarian mode.

That consensual methods are preferred by the great majority of young Japanese, and majority versus minority contention avoided, in day-to-day life is clearly evident also from the results of the individual interviews conducted. When asked how they themselves made decisions in their school clubs, and so forth, the great majority of the students interviewed replied that they all talked it over until they came to an agreement. Interestingly enough, several of the students noted that their clubs had strong leaders and so decisions tended to follow the leader's preferences. Deciding by majority rule—by choosing sides and taking a vote or a show of hands—was felt, with only one or two exceptions among all those interviewed, to be a disagreeable solution to be used only as a

Table 3-1

Preferred Method of Group Decision Making

(Percentages of students by grade, and parents as a whole, choosing each response)

Students Grade	Authoritarian	Consensual	Majoritarian	Don't Know; No Response	Total
8	12	67	16	5	100%
10	16	72	10	2	100%
12	10	71	16	3	100%
Parents	12	58	26	4	100%

Survey Items:

"Let's suppose you belong to a certain group (such as a club, etc.). Suppose that group had decided to go on a trip. But there were some people who wanted to go to the mountains and others who wanted to go to the seashore. Circle which one of the three ways of deciding where to go that you think would be best.

A. One person says that since the group's affairs have been put in the charge of its leaders, you should rely on them and have them decide [*Authoritarian*].

B. Another person says that everyone should give his opinion, and discussion should be continued until all agree on one opinion [*Consenual*].

C. Someone else says that it should be decided by majority rule, even if there is a large minority [*Majoritarian*]."

last resort. Nevertheless, it was apparent that in the students' own group experiences instances did arise in which consensus was impossible and majority vote decisions were taken.

In response to a related item in the questionnaire, 88 percent of the students and 78 percent of the parents felt that in such instances, when a vote did have to be taken, two-thirds or more of the group members should agree for the decision to be fair to all. And as many as 16 percent of the students and 11 percent of the parents replied that nearly all of the group—nine-tenths or more—should agree. Once again, slightly more parents than students (15 percent to 9 percent) were prone to the majoritarian position that a bare majority should agree. However, the overwhelming preference among both generations for at least a two-thirds majority is clear secondary corroboration for the antimajoritarian thesis.[b]

The emphasis on unanimous consensus in Japanese culture appears to have two major implications for democracy in the Japanese setting. These have been aptly summarized by Robert Scalapino who in noting that "Japanese society

[b]It must be noted that this finding is not unique to Japan. Social psychologists researching small group decision processes in the United States have reported that American subjects in experiments tend to seek decisions agreed to by two-thirds or more of the group members. See William W. Lambert and Wallace E. Lambert, *Social Psychology* (Englewood Cliff, N.J.: Prentice-Hall, Inc., 1964), p. 42.

denies the moral validity of majoritarianism" asserted that "the right of the majority to govern is not accepted by all, nor is the right of the minority to oppose."[8] Two fundamental democratic principles, the majority's right to make its position law and the liberty of the individual and the minority to dissent and oppose, are thus alleged to be jeopardized by the consensus norm. Let us examine each of these in turn.

The first problem for democratic politics has to do with the right of the majority to impose its will on the minority. It does seem clear that the Japanese preference for unanimity both hampers the operation of this principle in Japan and that the principle itself is not wholly accepted among influential elements of the public. In particular, it has been the case in national politics for most of the postwar period that the governing party has held a majority that while clear has been a good deal less than the two-thirds most Japanese apparently recognize as fair. Hence when controversial issues, such as the renewal of the United States-Japan Security Treaty, have arisen, the opposition parties in the Diet have either forcibly resisted the taking of votes or have refused to take part, claiming that the imposition of the government position as national policy in such controversial matters is "tyranny of the majority." Some of the popular feeling on this point is suggested by the following remark of one of the interviewees, a twelfth-grade Tokyo boy:

I feel this way a bit about the force of the majority. Our teacher has said that at times when a decision is made in the Diet, you can tell even from the beginning what the outcome's going to be. I think I read in a book that in England the people who hold the majority opinion don't ignore the minority; it said that they intensify talks until they're unified. I think that's ideal, but in Japan it feels as if it's like war, somehow, and sometimes there're fights, and the majority always crushes the minority, and there's the feeling that the minority can never make itself heard.

As the quote suggests, not only does the imposition of the majority rule principle seem illegitimate, but it casts something of a blight on the perceived moral character of the Diet and the actors in the political process and induces a feeling of political impotence. These are serious consequences for the prospects of democracy in Japan. Just how common among young Japanese and their parents is this rejection of the legitimacy of majority rule in the face of a large minority? Table 3-2 presents the results of an item in the questionnaire designed to get at this question.

The table leaves little room for doubt that among both youngsters and adults there is little taste for majority rule in a close contest. Scalapino's assertion that "the right of the majority to govern is not accepted by all" would appear to have some validity among both generations of Japanese. We might explain the rejection of majority rule here on the part of the adults by reference to traditional cultural norms and practices. But how can we explain its also holding for the students in the survey who have been raised under the new democratic

Table 3-2
Attitudes toward Majority Rule: The Large Minority
(Percentages of students by grade, and parents as a whole, choosing each response)

Students Grade	Strongly Agree; Agree	Don't Know; No Response	Strongly Disagree; Disagree	Total
8	45	31	24	100%
10	57	22	21	100%
12	66	20	14	100%
Parents	61	23	16	100%

Survey Item:
"When you're trying to decide something, if there is a relatively large number of people in the minority, those in the majority shouldn't insist on their own opinion."

regime and presumably schooled in the values and beliefs of democracy? One important explanatory factor may be traceable directly to the school experiences of Japanese youngsters. In the questionnaire, the students were asked whether they had ever in the past three years been candidates for club or school office and if they had ever served as officers. While only 27 percent had ever run for office, fully 65 percent had actually served, as officers. In other words, it would appear that elections for office do not occur in most cases. Frank Langdon's assertion that "Japanese social experience does not provide sufficient socialization in the ritualized hostility that lies behind the operation of party politics in Western countries"[9] would appear to be correct insofar as schooling in the process of electoral competition is concerned.

To put another perspective on the resistance to majoritarianism, however, it might be useful to consider the role that consensus is supposed to play in democracy by contemporary political theorists. Robert Dahl lists consensus as one of eight standards of achievement by which the democraticness of a political process should be judged:

Consensus in political discussion and decision making [is necessary] in the sense that solutions are sought that will minimize the size, resentment and coercion of defeated minorities, and will maximize the numbers of citizens who conclude that their goals have been adequately met by the solution adopted.[10]

It may be that in a political system, such as that in Japan, in which government and opposition are deeply divided over fundamental policy issues and where their respective forces are fairly evenly split with but a slight edge to the former, bare majority rule without any attempt at consideration of the opposition's views would be likely to produce conflict too severe for the system to resolve peacefully. The fact is, of course, that the parties have worked out a system of majority-minority consultation and accommodation of minority principles on most issues, so that the frequency of majority-minority confrontation on fundamentals has been sharply reduced.

The second implication for democracy in Japan of this cultural preference for unanimous consensus is that it restricts the freedom of the individual or of the minority to oppose and dissent. It allegedly attacks, that is to say, not only the majoritarian but also the libertarian basis of democracy. As Ezra Vogel has put it with respect to the urban middle class:

... there is no fully legitimate basis for standing against the group. Once group consensus is reached, one should abide by the decision. Although some deviants attempt to justify their failure to follow group consensus in terms of democracy or freedom, these values have not been internalized sufficiently to justify the deviant's behavior to himself, let alone to other members of the group.[11]

This subordination of the individual to the group is a classic theme in treatments of Japanese culture. But there is evidence from several sources to indicate that in some important realms the principle of the freedom to dissent and to oppose is in fact now widely recognized and practiced in Japan. In the first place, comparative studies of support for civil liberties have shown that high school and college students in Japan are much more likely than their American fellows to express support for civil liberties, especially the rights of minorities and of individuals to espouse and express unpopular views.[12] In a less abstract and formalistic context, Whitehill and Takezawa found that Japanese workers were more likely to resist what they considered illegitimate group pressures toward conformity than were American workers.[13] Certainly there is clearly no suppression of dissent in the political realm. The Japanese government is probably criticized more often and more bitterly by both the press and the opposition than that of almost any other nation. How do Japanese youngsters view the rights of the minority to persist in their views in the face of group pressure to conform? Table 3-3 presents the results of an item used in the questionnaire expressly designed to get at this.

It is immediately apparent that here, in contrast to the case of the large minority, there is a decided generational split in attitudes. Slightly more parents agree than disagree that the persistent small minority should be condemned as selfish. The teenagers, on the other hand, overwhelmingly reject this position and their rejection increases with age, which suggests that a new libertarian norm may have taken the place of the old conformist one. We have already seen in Chapter 2 that there is strong evidence that young Japanese reject the symbols of authority. Here is evidence that they also reject the coercive, authoritarian aspects of consensus. When we consider this in comparison with the other available evidence on Japanese youngsters' reactions to authority—the Kato and McGinnies studies of attitudes toward civil liberties and the Whitehill and Takezawa study of workers' attitudes toward their bosses—it would appear that

Table 3-3

Attitudes toward Majority Rule: The Small Minority

(Percentages of students by grade, and parents as a whole, choosing each response)

Students Grade	Strongly Agree; Agree	Don't Know; No Response	Strongly Disagree; Disagree	Total
8	20	31	49	100%
10	16	27	57	100%
12	14	24	62	100%
Parents	36	32	32	100%

Survey Item:

"When you're trying to decide something, and only a very few people disagree, for those people to continue insisting on their opposing opinion should be condemned because it is selfish."

there may be taking place a major shift in Japanese culture—away from the authoritarianism of the past to a new emphasis on the liberty of the individual. Robert Frager, a social psychologist, found in replications of the Asch conformity tests among Japanese college students that a substantial proportion had to be classified as either "autonomous" (i.e., those who made correct judgments in the face of an incorrect majority) or as "anti-conformist" (those who disagreed with the majority when the majority opinion was correct).[14] We shall explore the psychological aspects of this question as they bear on the political personality of young Japanese in a later chapter. Suffice it to say here that the old stereotype of the Japanese as ridden with conformity and hence incapable of governing themselves freely appears to be inaccurate and inapplicable as regards the young people of today.

What still might be the case, however, is that the decline of coercive conformity and the other antidemocratic aspects of the consensus norm might be confined to young people in the most "modern" sectors of the society, particularly the urban areas. Urban society is neither so tightly knit nor so communally interactive as rural society; the urban resident, working in one place and living in another, belongs to several disparate worlds, and the roles of friends, co-workers, and neighbors are not mutually overlapping as they tend to be in the rural village. The sanctions impelling the urban adult to subordination to group consensus in any of his spheres of life are thus less imposing than those faced by the rural adult.

How does this commonly expressed view of the differences in the pressures toward consensus and conformity of city and country life fit the data presented so far? Are rural adults and children more prone to choose antimajoritarian decision modes and to emphasize conformity with the will of the group? The evidence is on the whole negative. Cross-tabulation of urban-rural residence with the four items just discussed—preferred decision mode, size of a fair majority, imposition of the bare majority's will, and condemning small minority opposition—revealed no statistically significant (chi-square) differences between urban and rural students. Among the parents, rural parents were indeed significantly more likely than urban parents to choose the consensual decision mode and to opt for a very large size for a fair majority. In each case, however, the difference between the urban and rural adults is a matter of degree, a question of the size of the proportions supporting the old ways rather than a matter of direction. A substantial majority of both urban and rural adults chose the consensual responses to the two questions. Moreover, there is no significant difference between the urban and rural adults on the other two questions.

It would appear then that insofar as patterns of decision-making and the rights of the majority and those of the minority are concerned, urban-rural residence has no significant impact on the attitudes of young Japanese; while older Japanese attitudes are significantly distinguished by this urban-rural split only with regard to what we might refer to as the "harmonizing" aspects of consensus, but not its coercive aspect. On balance, then, the stereotype of the traditional consensus norm as finding its most intense and antidemocratic form in rural Japan no longer appears valid. Whether expressed attitudes and actual behavior are congruent is another question. It may be that village Japan is still ridden with conformity and suppression of the individual, but the norms of today's culture no longer permit the verbal expression of antidemocratic attitudes. That fact in and of itself is noteworthy, because it indicates that at a minimum the attitudinal supports for traditional modes of suppression of dissent and subordination of the individual are giving way, and without such supports the behavior itself is unlikely to continue unchanged.

The analysis of the value of democracy and of support for democracy among Japanese teenagers and their parents is based in part on interview discussions of their reactions to democracy as a general, nonspecific symbol, their reactions to democratic procedures and "rules of the game," and how each has been affected by elements of Japanese culture that are often asserted to be inherent impediments to democracy in Japan. The analysis shows that the impact of these allegedly inhibiting factors is neither particularly great nor consistent. Positive feelings about democracy in general appear to prevail even among those—the older generation and the rural folk—to whom they are alleged to be most alien and repugnant. And the old values of consensus and conformity appear to have bent to accommodate the new; the pattern of responses suggests a blending of a desire for harmony with an acceptance and tolerance of nonconformity and dissent.

If democracy has become an integral part of the value structure of contemporary Japanese political culture, how centrally located is it in that structure? One answer to that may be gained by comparing it with other positive values. If there is a national set of ideals and values in today's Japan, and particularly among today's youth, how does democracy rank in comparison with the other values? Indeed, what other values are to be found there?

Democracy, Peace, and National Identity

There is little question that democracy as a political creed—a set of ideals and principles of political conduct and a blueprint for government—is widely accepted among the young. Nearly every interview and composition revealed a picture of an ideal Japan governed by democratic procedures and institutions. Chapter 5 discusses the perceived relationships of democracy to other belief systems, in particular socialism and capitalism; here it suffices to note that it is unquestionably accurate to describe democracy as the accepted creed—that is, it is not only the system of principles and institutions within which the overwhelming majority of Japanese youngsters desire and expect that politics will take place, but also the criterion against which they feel political conduct should be judged.

Democracy as a creed is thus a legitimating ideology in the sense that David Easton uses the term. For American youngsters, democracy's role as the preeminent political creed and legitimating ideology is supported by its role as the central political symbol. The very word evokes in the American a host of great events, rhetorical phrases, and heroic figures: the Constitutional Convention, Washington at Valley Forge, and Lincoln at Gettysburg: "Give me liberty or give me death"; "We hold these truths to be self-evident . . . "; "A new nation conceived in liberty and dedicated to the proposition that all men are created equal." The single word democracy thus encapsulates the political heritage and the national identity of the American who hears or utters it.

Democracy in this sense is more a symbol than a creed. Indeed, it must be said to be the central symbol of American political life. It is what has been called by Harold Lasswell a "key sign," a symbol that "provide[s] a unifying experience fostering sentiments that may transcend limitation of culture, class, organization, and personality."[15] Murray Edelman in *The Symbolic Uses of Politics* has referred to such symbols as "condensation symbols":

Condensation symbols . . . condense into one symbolic event, sign, or act patriotic pride, anxieties, remembrances of past glories or humiliations, promises of future greatness: several of them or all of them.[16]

Democracy, given its history in Japan, could hardly play such a role there as it does in America. In a sense, democracy has the flavor, for the Japanese, of an important lesson to be learned and mastered, almost like a catechism lesson, rather than the evocative magic of a source of national identity and pride. But there is a Japanese political condensation symbol that brings forth something of the same kind of emotional response among Japanese youngsters, and indeed among many adults, that democracy evokes from Americans. That symbol is peace.

Something of the importance of the role played by peace in the political lives of young Japanese is suggested by the contents of the compositions written by some 43 Tokyo eighth graders. They were asked to discuss their "ideal Japan" and the role therein of democracy, capitalism, and socialism. Nearly all of the children did, as expected, describe democracy as a requisite of their ideal Japan. In addition, however, and despite the complete lack of any mention of peace when they were given the assignment to write the essay, 23 of the 43 included peace as an essential attribute of their ideal Japan, and most treated it as the *sine qua non*, prior to all other attributes. The following excerpts from the compositions are illustrative:

... *I think that provided Japan always has peace, freedom and prosperity, that any kind of "ism" is alright.*

... *I think that no matter what, peace is the most ideal.*

... *My ideal is a country like this: first, a country which is peaceful and where there is no war. That is because, when there is war, even children who have committed no crimes end up being entangled in it.*

... *I think that an ideal Japan would have: (1) lots more playgrounds... (2) no traffic violations... (3) not going to war. My favorite country is Switzerland. If you ask what I like about it, the first thing that comes to mind is that it absolutely does not go to war.*

Table 3-4 presents the reactions of students and parents to the term pacifism as compared with their reactions to democracy by way of further evidence of the importance in contemporary Japan of peace as a symbol and value. While the

Table 3-4
Reactions to Pacifism and Democracy Compared

	Very Favorable	Favorable	Don't Know; Can't Say[a]	Unfavorable	Very Unfavorable	Total
Students:						
Pacifism	54	35	9	2	0	100%
Democracy	32	47	19	1	1	100%
Parents:						
Pacifism	37	42	18	2	1	100%
Democracy	31	52	15	2	0	100%

[a]Includes a small number of nonresponses.

great majority of both students and parents respond positively to both terms, it is clear that pacifism evokes a more enthusiastic reaction, especially among the young, than does democracy. While very few students (or parents) responded negatively toward either of the two terms, twice as many students were uncertain about democracy as were about pacifism. The central difference, however, is that many more students felt "*very* favorable" about pacifism than did so about democracy, or for that matter about any other of a group of "isms" that also included liberalism, capitalism, socialism, and communism. Pacifism was the only symbol with respect to which "very favorable" was the modal response. (The reactions to the other "isms" are discussed in Chapter 5.) It should be noted that the parental response to pacifism was also more positive than that for democracy, though among the parents the gap between the two symbols was much less than among the students.

These responses to the terms themselves should not, of course, lead us to overlook the size of the majority of both students and parents alike who felt positive about democracy. The point to be made here is only that democracy, while highly prized, is second to peace as a symbol and value, especially among the young Japanese of today. The historic experience of Hiroshima and Nagasaki and the renunciation of war in the constitution continue to evoke in Japanese, young and old, a sense of a special mission and role for Japan in today's troubled world. Indeed, the constitution of 1946 is often referred to as the "Peace Constitution," an identification which has been most significant for many youngsters, as the words of one eighth grader's composition suggest:

Ideal Japan, for me, would be peaceful. Since this is even now decided by the Constitution, if we really obey the Constitution, it will be alright as things stand.

To test the relative values Japanese youngsters and their parents place on peace and on democracy in a more direct fashion, the questionnaire included an item asking them to choose between the two in a hypothetical dilemma. Table 3-5 shows the results, which are interesting in a number of respects. To begin with, for no group in the table is there any question that peace is by far the preferred value. But the generational difference is noteworthy; it is somewhat of an anomaly that the parents, nearly all of whom experienced World War II, should be less inclined to prefer peace over democracy than their children, who are, as the Japanese themselves frequently remark, without any direct knowledge of war. But inspection of the age trends in the students' responses reveals that as age increases there is a distinct shift toward the parental pattern of responses. Hence it may very well be that the difference is attributable to age rather than generation and that the preference for peace over democracy may diminish with age.

One important component of the explanation of the preeminence of peace in the hierarchy of Japanese youngsters' values, and more particularly of its

Table 3-5

Peace versus Freedom

(Percentages of students by grade, and parents as a whole, choosing each response)

Grade	Peace	Democracy	No Response	Total
8	76	23	1	100%
10	70	27	3	100%
12	63	34	3	100%
Parents	56	36	8	100%

Survey Item:

"Everyone would like to live in a peaceful and free country. But unhappily, not all countries are always peaceful and free at the same time. Suppose you had to live in one of the two countries given here. Which would you choose?

A. In this country, there is peace and its people don't have to worry at all about war. But this country's government severely restricts the liberty of the people. Hence the people of this country can live in peace but not in freedom [*Peace*].

B. In this country, there is freedom; fundamental human rights are guaranteed, so its people don't have to worry at all about tyranny. But this country is at war with another country. Hence the people of this country can live in freedom, but not in peace [*Democracy*]."

predominance over democracy in this respect, may be found in the social studies course in the Japanese school. Okamura and his associates found in a study of the most commonly used social studies textbooks an overwhelming emphasis on the Western origins and development of democracy and a linking of democracy with foreign figures such as Lincoln and Rousseau. But in the case of peace, however, they found "dramatically fewer" references to Western men and history and a pronounced tendency for the discussions of peace to be rooted in the Japanese Constitution and the experiences of World War II.[17] From their analysis and from direct examination of the texts themselves, it seems clear that peace is portrayed as being uniquely and integrally rooted in the history and value system of contemporary Japan. The implication often appears to be an almost exclusive relationship between Japan and peace that stresses Japan's singular role among the world's powers as a "peace" power and the intimate and personal significance of peace as a value to each and every Japanese.

The treatment of democracy in the texts is a study in contrast. Okamura et al. point out first that there are frequent references to abstractions such as "spirit of democracy" or "the courage to protect human rights," but few concrete links to consciousness of the citizen's role in the conduct of politics. As a result, they assert, Japanese youngsters tend to think of democracy as something of an "intellectual game" that is not directly linked to their own lives. Moreover, being invariably described with Western referents, it comes across in the texts as an "import." The survey data also suggest that Japanese, young and old, do continue to perceive democracy as an import. Thirty-two percent of the eighth and tenth graders and over 40 percent of the twelfth graders and the parents agreed that "Japan's democracy is not a real democracy because it was forcibly imposed by foreigners," in contrast to less than 25 percent (or 30 percent in the case of the tenth graders) of both generations who disagreed. Doubts as to the democraticness of a foreign-imposed democracy have been widespread and persistent throughout the postwar period, but, it can be argued, they do not augur ill for Japan's democracy. On the contrary, such doubt helps keep the Japanese more concerned and sensitive to inadequacies and failings in the concrete process and institutions rather than causing criticism of democracy per se. For many Japanese, especially the young, democracy is an ideal that will require effort and commitment to attain. It is the commitment of Japan's leaders to attain that ideal; not the desirability of the ideal itself that they question. Forty percent of both students and parents alike agreed with an item in the questionnaire stating that "most Japanese politicians don't really believe in democracy; they only pretend to."

Conclusion

The question to which this chapter ultimately has been addressing itself is whether democracy will be able to establish itself firmly as the legitimate principle of government and of political life in the emerging political culture of Japan. The question is all the more important because of the absence in Japan of an historical heritage and contemporary leadership that would provide the kind of personal legitimation that has been so instrumental in cementing the allegiance of citizens in other lands, and especially in the United States, to their democratic regimes.

As we have seen, there is substantial and consistent evidence to indicate that democracy has become established in the attitude structure of young Japanese, and indeed of their elders as well, as the preferred system of government. The symbol itself draws an overwhelmingly favorable response among members of both generations. Moreover, although it was hypothesized that rural residence would tend to diminish acceptance of democracy as a value given the presumably greater persistence of old antidemocratic norms and values in the village than in the city, no difference whatever in its acceptance among urban and rural adults was observed. Among the students the difference that was observed was in the opposite direction from that expected, with rural children being more positive than urban children.

At the more specific level of the actual application of democratic rules for decisionmaking, however, the data showed that both generations retained the traditional preference for consensus over majoritarianism. The preference for consensus, however, held across the urban-rural gap as well, and, although the rural adults were more inclined toward consensus than the urban adults, it was only a difference in degree rather than in direction. The one surprising finding was that although the bulk of both generations favored consensus options in the various questionnaire items, more parents than children chose majoritarian responses. This finding of course runs counter to expectations. The explanation may lie in the fact that many parents have experienced decision-making situations, including voting, in which a desired outcome has come about as the result of simple majority rule. The children, on the other hand, clearly lack experience with decisions involving contest and conflict. Even school experiences do not appear to socialize Japanese youngsters into majoritarianism, for, as pointed out, the data on school office-holding indicate that many offices are filled by means other than contested elections. The greater preference for consensual decision-making on the part of the children may thus reflect more strongly the influence of general cultural values, in comparison with the influence of experience with voting and decision-making in the work place and so forth on the part of parents. The fact that far more parents than children chose voting as one of the two principal meanings of democracy tends to reinforce this interpretation and suggests that socialization into democracy also takes place as the result of adult experiences in the political system and not simply as the result of pre-adult, pre-political learning.

The general pattern of responses to the consensus versus majority rule items suggests, however, that while consensus has retained its significance in Japanese political culture, it has become modified so as to be compatible with the main elements of democracy. In turn, democracy, as assimilated into the value structure of the two generations of Japanese, has also become adapted to incorporate elements of consensus. In this new synthesis of democracy and consensus, only the ameliorative and harmony-inducing aspect of consensus has been retained; the oppressive anti-libertarian intolerance of individual or minority group dissent that was characteristic of pre-1945 consensualism is no longer apparent. Indeed, what is remarkable about this new blend of consensus and democracy is that it seeks to remove even the slightest vestige of authoritarianism from democracy. "If," the position of most young Japanese seems to be, "the majority cannot persuade the minority of the rightness of the majority view, or if the two cannot agree on some compromise, then it is preferable that nothing be done rather than that the majority impose its will." Conversely, under no circumstances should the minority be silenced or coerced or ignored. In other words, there is in this area of beliefs about the rules of the game, a widespread and prevailing belief in the legitimacy of minority dissent and resistance to authority coupled with a belief in the illegitimacy of the use of majority rule to coerce dissenters. This is fully consistent with the attitude found in Chapter 2—that is, the prevailing pattern in which many youngsters support the input institutions of politics that may be viewed as "on the peoples' side" but are suspicious of the authoritative institutions of government.

This ideal of a consensual democracy is, of course, understandable—but it is also problematic. Government often must take decisions that offend substantial minorities. If aversion to majority rule is untempered by the realization that consensus is often unattainable, then it is possible that "tyranny of the majority" would be thwarted by an even more objectionable "tyranny of the minority." But nearly all of the youngsters interviewed, with few exceptions, were willing to concede, however reluctantly and grudgingly, that sometimes, no matter what, unanimity is impossible and then the majority view should and must prevail. In the end, the legitimacy of the majority's right to prevail is not denied; rather, the majority is denied the right to ignore or casually override the minority view. Only when the majority has tried consultation and discussion and found agreement or compromise to be beyond achievement, can it legitimately impose its will. Such a notion of consensual democracy, based on consultation and accommodation between conflicting sides in a dispute, is most appropriate to Japan. It is appropriate first of all because it is in keeping with her cultural norms. But even more importantly, it is appropriate because it provides a political cultural rationale for democratic politics in a system that is so polarized ideologically that dissensus rather than consensus is the rule. The more frequently that majority and minority can accommodate one another's interests in the face of their ideological differences, the smaller and less dangerous the tides of dissensus become.

Finally, it has become fashionable of late to speak of Japan as a nation in search of an identity on the one hand and, on the other, as undergoing a rebirth of militarism. Insofar as the beliefs and images and visions of Japan that the youngsters harbor are concerned, neither of these generalizations is anywhere near the mark.

It is clear that Japanese youngsters overwhelmingly share a belief in and desire for a Japan in which democracy is the operative principle of politics and of social conduct and whose major goal is peace. The importance of peace in the values and ideals of young Japanese, its centrality in their conceptions of the requisites of an ideal society, and their belief that Japan is specially and uniquely entrusted with the mission of peace make it clear that for the great majority of young Japanese, Japan's national goals and national identity are bound up with peace. In the emerging Japanese political culture, peace and democracy serve as the two central elements of national consensus.

Notes

1. Robert D. Hess and Judith V. Torney, *The Development of Political Attitudes in Children* (Garden City, N.Y.: Anchor Books, 1968), Table 13, p. 75.
2. Okamura Tadao et al., "Seijiteki Shakaika ni Okeru 'Minshushugi' to

'Heiwa' " ("Democracy" and "Peace" in Political Socialization), *Shakai Kagaku Janaru* (1969), see especially pp. 4 ff.

3. Ezra Vogel, *Japan's New Middle Class* (Berkeley and Los Angeles: University of California Press, 1963), p. 142.

4. Shinohara Hajime, *Nihon No Seiji Fudo* (*Japanese Political Culture*), (Tokyo: Iwanami Shinsho, 1968), p. 74.

5. Tokei Suri Kenkyujo, Kokuminsei Chosa Inkai, *Dai-ni Nihonjin no Kokuminsei (Japanese National Character: Second Study)*, (Tokyo: Shiseido, 1970), p. 443.

6. *Mainichi Shinbun*, June 10, 1972.

7. Robert E. Ward, "Japan: The Continuity of Modernization," in Lucian W. Pye and Sidney Verba, eds., *Political Culture and Political Development* (Princeton, N.J.: Princeton University Press, 1965), p. 62.

8. Robert A. Scalapino and Junnosuke Masumi, *Parties and Politics in Contemporary Japan* (Berkeley and Los Angeles: University of California Press, 1962), p. 152.

9. Frank Langdon, *Politics in Japan* (Boston: Little, Brown, 1967), p. 73.

10. Robert A. Dahl, *Political Opposition in Western Democracies* (New Haven, Conn.: Yale University Press, 1966), p. 387.

11. Vogel, *Japan's New Middle Class*, p. 148.

12. See Elliott McGinnies, "Attitudes Toward Civil Liberties Among Japanese and American University Students," *Journal of Psychology* 58 (1964), 177-86; and Kato Takakatsu, "Political Attitudes of Japanese Adolescents in Comparison with American," *Psychologia* (Kyoto) IV (December 1961), 198-200.

13. Arthur Whitehall and Shin'ichi Takezawa, *The Other Worker* (Honolulu: East-West Center Press, 1965).

14. Robert Frager, "Experimental Social Psychology in Japan: Studies in Social Conformity," *Rice University Studies* 56:4 (Fall 1970), 250.

15. Harold D. Lasswell, "Key Signs, Symbols, and Icons," in L. Bryson et al., eds., *Symbols and Values: An Initial Study* (New York and London: Cooper Square Publishers, 1954), p. 201.

16. Murray Edelman, *The Symbolic Uses of Politics* (Urbana: University of Illinois Press, 1964), p. 6.

17. Okamura, "Seijiteki Shakaika ni Okeru 'Minshushugi' to 'Heiwa' " ("Democracy" and "Peace" in Political Socialization), p. 5.

4 Symbols of Dissensus: The Growth of Partisanship

Introduction

In the preceding chapter we saw that there are symbols and values, notably peace and democracy, that are widely inclusive in their appeal to today's Japanese youth and to the majority of their elders as well. These symbols may be said to constitute the nuclear elements of consensus in contemporary Japanese political culture. This chapter, in contrast, is concerned with those symbols that divide rather than integrate and are the source of the conflict that fuels much of the political process; specifically, the focus here is on the development of party identification.

In Japan, as in many polities, the scope of national consensus often appears to be exceeded by that of cleavage and dissensus. Partisan conflict extends over a broad range of issues, and is often—perhaps even usually—accompanied by hostility and harsh rhetoric. An important difference from American partisan politics is that in Japan the most significant partisan division is based on explicit and profound ideological cleavage. The ruling conservative party and the capitalist economic system it supports are confronted by the challenge of a "progressive" camp led by the Japan Socialist Party whose philosophy of society and economics has been greatly influenced by Marxism. Much of party politics then and, by extension, party identification as well takes on a decidedly ideological character, and our analysis of the origins of partisanship must of necessity give careful attention to the development of ideology in adolescence as well. For analytic purposes, however, it is useful to treat the development of these two orientations sequentially since, as studies of American youth have shown and as the evidence of Japanese youth will corroborate, party identification occurs substantially earlier in the life cycle than even the embryonic stages of ideology. This chapter therefore deals with the development of party identification, while discussion of the emergence of ideology is reserved for the chapter that follows.

After setting the stage with an abbreviated introduction to the Japanese party system and to the ideological themes and overtones of Japanese political life, four substantive questions about the acquisition of party identification are raised. First, how many young Japanese develop party identifications and from how early in childhood? Second, what role does the family play in transmitting partisanship? Third, to what extent do Japanese youngsters' partisan loyalties reflect the impact of sources alternative to, or supplementary to, the family—in

73

particular, to what extent are they grounded in the major social bases of adult political cleavage, urban-rural differences and socioeconomic status differences. And finally, what does having a party identification mean in terms of affective feelings as well as of cognitive awareness of policy and ideology differences?

The questions of how many Japanese youngsters from how early an age acquire party identification are important because each bears on the potential stability of the party system. The age at which partisanship develops is significant because it has been shown that the strength of an individual's attachment to his party depends on how long he has had it. In particular, if the attachment was formed early in childhood, it is, like the attachment to the leader discussed in Chapter 2, especially apt to endure and to color the political learning and experiences that come later. It becomes a deeply rooted part of the individual's political self-identification.

The widespread existence among the electorate of personal attachments to political parties that date from childhood has been linked to the stability of the American[1] and British[2] party systems and its absence to the turmoil of partisan politics in Third and Fourth Republic France.[3] New parties have found it extremely difficult to gain a foothold in the American and British systems, whereas in pre-de Gaulle France the great reservoir of unattached loyalties made possible the sudden emergence and equally sudden demise of small parties often concerned with only a single issue. This instability of the parties, conversely, kept most French adults from forming party loyalties, which meant, in turn, that parents in most French families did not transmit such loyalties to their children.[4]

In some important aspects, the Japanese party system bears a certain resemblance to that of France. Most of the parties have had only a short history, and during the relatively brief period of the postwar, new parties have emerged while others have disappeared. Moreover, the surviving parties have nearly all changed their names or split apart and merged and, in some cases, split once more. Since about 1960 or so, however, when the Democratic Socialist Party and the Komeito made their appearances, no significant changes have occurred. Still, for many Japanese adults, the depth or even the existence of party loyalties is problematic. Thus, a major concern of this chapter is whether the members of the present Japanese electorate are transmitting loyalties to the existing parties to the upcoming electorate or whether, deprived of this cross-generational source of stability, the party system is likely to continue in a state of flux and volatility. Hence, particular attention is paid to the correspondences between parents' party identifications and those of their children.

The significance of the third question lies in the recognition that there are important alternative sources of partisanship that are often supplementary to, or compensatory for, family socialization. Specialists on Japan have long noted the profound impact on political attitudes and behavior of whether one lives in the city or the country. The link between the level of urbanization of a community and the level of political conservatism suggests the possibility that the social milieu may reinforce the family's transmission of party identification when it occurs and compensate for it when it does not occur. An examination across generations of this relationship between urban-rural residence and partisanship is important, too, because on the strength of the association rests the continued validity of one of the major themes of Japanese mass politics, namely, that the status or class-based politics of systems like England and other Western European countries do not prevail in Japan where partisanship is rooted not in class but in culture, the competing cultures of city and countryside.[5] Hence, the discussion of the social bases of partisanship compares the effects of both of these social characteristics on the patterns of party loyalties of both generations of Japanese.

Finally, the discussion in this chapter turns to the cognitive and affective meaning of party support to young Japanese as a prelude to the discussion of ideology that follows in the next chapter. Much of the impact of party support on politics in the United States derives from the strength of the affective attachment to and identification with the party—its "feeling tone" so to speak. Conversely, the cognitive bases of partisanship, awareness of policy differences, and especially of ideological differences, appear to play a lesser role. In Japan, where the parties have shorter histories and shallower roots and are also more divided ideologically, the question of the relative weight of affective and cognitive components of party support takes on a special interest and significance.

Parties and Ideologies: The Nature of Political Confrontation

The present party system in Japan is the product of a series of evolutionary changes that have taken place over the postwar period.[6] The most important of these occurred in 1955 when the Liberal Party and the Democratic Party, the two leading conservative parties, merged to form the Liberal Democratic Party (LDP), which has held national power ever since. The Liberal Democrats are usually portrayed as the champions of capitalism, of big business, and of farm interests. It would be difficult, however, to pin any ideological label on them, other than the generic term of conservative, with a small "c." Under their rule and that of their postwar predecessors as mentioned above, the Japanese government has actively pursued a national policy placing priority on economic growth. It is important to note that these conservatives do *not* share the American right's ideals of "rugged individualism" and laissez-faire. Government control and *care* of big business is overt and manifest in LDP policy. Further, the Liberal Democrats are not averse to having the government run certain industries and services. Under conservative rule, there has been a government monopoly on tobacco; the largest railway is nationally owned and operated, as is the major radio and television network; and the government has placed great stress on economic planning. In short, the Japanese conservatives are a pragmatic political party—a "catch-all" party—interested above all in continuing to win at the general elections. Ideology plays no role whatever in their rhetoric and very little if any in the substance of their politics.

There could be no greater contrast to these pragmatic conservatives than the major opposition party, the Japan Socialist Party (JSP). Although there remain a few right-wing socialists in its midst, the mainstream of the party is firmly committed to Marxist principles of socialism. The party identifies itself with the proletariat and proclaims itself as a "class-based" rather than "mass-based" movement. Its campaign themes are heavily interlaced with ideological opposition to the socioeconomic status quo. They frequently focus on the allegedly inegalitarian, antidemocratic, and repressive nature of Japan's big business-dominated capitalist system and on the links of that system to militarism and, through the United States-Japan Mutual Security Treaty, to imperialism.

The preeminence of ideological considerations within the party has caused it to suffer several major schisms. By 1960, the tension between the right and left wings eventuated in the secession of most of the right wing, which in that year formed the Democratic Socialist Party. The DSP is an evolutionary, rather than revolutionary, socialist party that seeks to achieve reforms within the capitalist system rather than to replace it entirely. The party's lack of a systemic opposition to the established socioeconomic order, coupled with its willingness to cooperate with the LDP both in the Diet on some government legislative proposals and in some local electoral contests, have led the DSP to be labelled the "second conservative party." Many Japanese analysts believe the party's lack of a clear image that is distinct from that of the LDP has been the cause of its inability to gain popular support at the polls.

Sharing the middle of the spectrum with the DSP is a party that does not fit neatly into the classic left-right classification. The Komeito (literally, clean government party) appeared on the scene only in the early 1960s. Since then, it has made strong inroads into the support among the urban working class for the socialists and, probably to a lesser extent, for the communists. The party is not readily classifiable because, although it often advocates positions similar to those of the socialists and communists, it is religiously based and has until recently been the official political arm of a popular new Buddhist sect, the Soka gakkai (value creation society). This sect has caused a furor over its nationalistic principles, the pressure tactics it employs in proselytization, and the authoritarian complexion of its organization. Much of the electoral support for the Komeito comes from the bloc vote of Soka gakkai adherents. But the success of the party, until 1972 the third largest in the Diet, has also been due in large part to the fact that its candidates have stressed bread-and-butter issues and taken stands on the practical kinds of problems—such as hygiene in the wholesale food markets—that have broad appeal to ordinary citizens.

The third of the smaller parties is the Japan Communist Party (JCP), which is an orthodox Marxist-Leninist party that is found farthest to the left on the spectrum of party politics. Of the five parties that now constitute the Japanese party system, only the JCP has maintained the same name and the same organizational continuity from the beginning of the postwar period and before. The party, of course, makes extensive use of ideological rhetoric. But its real impact on politics lies not in its membership or in its electoral strength, which is growing but still slight, but rather in its influence among intellectuals, scholars, and teachers. Of particular note for our purposes here is that the party's influence extends to important elements in the Japan Teacher's Union, the nationwide organization of school teachers. This fact and the fact that the party maintains a large youth organization, popularly known as the Minsei or "Democratic Youth," magnify its potential importance in the political socialization process far beyond its numbers in the Diet or supporters in the electorate.

The Japanese party system, then, is one with a diversity of parties and with a history of changing party labels and changing party structures and organizations. Its present five-party line-up dates back only a dozen years or so, but the basic cleavage between two camps—"conservatives" versus "progressives"—has been a continuing characteristic of partisan politics throughout the postwar period.

The Extent of Party Identification

Partisan conflict is of course endemic in democratic nations. In varying degrees, depending on the party system of the nation in question, the involvement of individual citizens in the political process is deeply bound up in their attachment to and self-identification with a political party. In the United States and Great Britain, where the major parties are long-established organizations with deep historical roots, such party affiliation is extremely widespread among adults (about 70-75 percent and 90 percent, respectively[7]). Such widespread identification with existing political parties has two important consequences. First, it strengthens the stability of the party system and hence of the political process generally by making abrupt changes in the loyalties of the electorate unlikely, and thus impeding the easy formation of new parties. Second, at the individual level, political participation becomes primarily, even perhaps exclusively, mediated through partisanship; it is the single most influential determinant of political and especially electoral behavior. Thus, for the political life of both the system in general and of the individual citizen, party identification assumes major importance.

In Japan, however, the postwar party system has been anything but stable, in either the names of the parties or their numbers. Frank Langdon argues that the frequent changes in the composition and labels of the parties

. . . lessen the chance of strong or long-continued party attachment. In the more frequent party reorganizations before 1955, many politicians could carry their voters with them despite a switch in their party affiliation. Some informants even admit to identification with a party faction. This suggests an underlying stability of partisanship yet to be transferred to the party.[8]

If Langdon is correct, Japanese adults are unlikely to bequeath enduring party identifications to their children. But the data on the whole do not bear out Langdon's assertion that partisanship has not been transferred to the parties. Examination of the national opinion polls on the question of party liking or support establishes that between 65 and 70 percent of the national samples polled consistently proclaim their support for one or another of the five parties.[9] And a nationwide survey of adults conducted for a University of Michigan project on the Japanese voter, which made use of a literal Japanese adaptation of the standard party identification item also used in the Michigan studies of the American voter, likewise found that 61 percent of the Japanese sample identified with one of the parties in 1967. This compared with 69 percent of the Americans who did so in the 1968 Michigan survey of American voters.[a] These figures appear, then, to indicate that adult partisan affiliation is nearly as widespread in Japan as in the United States. They implicitly contradict Langdon's assertion. So, in more direct fashion, does the fact that over the two decades between 1955 and 1975 support for the Liberal Democratic Party has remained remarkably constant in the polls. Indeed, up to 1968 (the year in which the present study was conducted) the percentage of respondents in the *Asahi* poll who were classified as LDP supporters or "indirect supporters"—that is, who said that "liking aside" they would vote for the LDP in an election—never went below 45 percent or above 51 percent. Support for the JSP showed a similar constancy, if the entrance onto the scene of the Democratic Socialists is taken into consideration. What the figures do show, in fact, is that the proportion of those who claim to support no party or who will not answer—those, that is, who are neither party identifiers or indirect supporters—dropped in half, from an average of 20 percent during the period between 1955 and 1960 to 10 to 11 percent during the late 1960s and early 1970s.[10] In other words, while the two new parties have caused some defections among supporters of the JSP, their major impact appears to have been to decrease the proportion of nonidentifiers in the electorate. Though the time frame is too short to permit firm prediction, the direction of the evidence runs counter to the thesis of unstable partisanship, and in support of the emergence of a five-party system with healthy roots in the political culture.

To what degree has the institutionalized basis of conflict become stabilized in

[a]The biggest difference between the American and Japanese samples came in the proportions of those who, having not chosen any party on the initial party identification question, reported that they felt "close" to a particular party in response to a follow-up probe question. Nineteen percent of the Americans fell into this category as opposed to only 5 percent of the Japanese. See Bradley M. Richardson, "Party Loyalties and Party Saliency in Japan," *Comparative Political Studies* 8:1 (April, 1975), Table 1, p. 36.

Japanese politics? The foregoing evidence on the extent of partisanship among Japanese adults has provided some evidence on this point. Perhaps more important from the perspective of this study is the evidence on the acquisition of party identification by Japanese children. One of the major findings of Greenstein's work was that American children typically acquire a party identification at a very early age. In his New Haven sample he found that by as early as fourth grade, 60 percent of the children chose to call themselves Democrats or Republicans despite their inability to describe how the two parties differed.[11] This nearly equalled the percentage of adults professing a party identification in the polls. Greenstein concluded that since partisanship, like the image of the president, was acquired so early it was likely to have an enduring impact on the political self-definition, attitudes, and behavior of the individual and ultimately therefore to form an enduring basis for party stability.

Do we find a similar pattern of early acquisition of party affiliation in Japan? Okamura asked the children in his 1968 survey: "If you could vote, which party would you vote for?" As in the United States, from the earliest grades onward a majority of the Japanese children were willing to name a party preference: 56 percent of the third graders and 58 percent of the fourth through sixth graders did so, while the percentages declined somewhat to 50 and 51 percent of the seventh and eighth graders, respectively.[b] These are close to the proportions of identifiers among the Greenstein sample of American primary school children. Moreover, as was also true in the American case, the proportion of identifiers among the children closely approximates the proportion among the youngest adult voters: for example, 59 percent of those between twenty and twenty-four in the 1967 survey conducted for the University of Michigan project on the Japanese voter identified with one of the parties.[12]

A somewhat broader cross-national comparison is presented in Table 4-1, by using data from this study's survey as well as Okamura's in an adaptation of a table on comparative proportions of party identifiers among American and European children at various age levels. At the youngest level, the proportion of identifiers among the Japanese children is exceeded only by that among the British. And, even though the Japanese trail the Americans and the Germans as well in the two older groups, the gap is not great.[c] Only the English youngsters

[b]The response options to the partisanship item in Okamura's 1968 survey included one ("would vote without relation to party") that has normative connotations—"vote the best man regardless of party"—not found so explicitly in the more typical residual categories of "independent" or "support no party." This may have resulted in depressing somewhat the proportions of youngsters naming one of the parties, and it seems probable that the figures represent minimum proportions of party identifiers among Japanese children.

[c]The specific items used in the countries other than Japan can be found by consulting the citations in Jack Dennis and Donald McCrone, "Preadult Development of Political Party Identification in Western Democracies," *Comparative Political Studies* (July 1970), 257. Okamura's item is given in the text. The item used here was one of a series in which the child was asked to choose which party he thought each of the following person supports: himself, if he could vote, his father, his mother, his teachers, his friends. In addition to the

Table 4-1

Cross-National Comparison of Party Identification among Japanese, American, and European Youth

(Percent of youths at each age level, by nation, who profess a party affiliation)

Nation	Age Level[a]		
	Youngest	Middle	Older
Japan: 1968	58	49	46
1969	–	53	59
United States	49	56	64
Britain	80	79	79
West Germany	50	62	68
Italy	45	51	55

[a]The age groups are: *Youngest:* 9-10 years for the United States, West Germany, and Japan; 8-10 years for Britain, and 10 years for Italy; *Middle:* 12-13 for the United States and Japan, 11-13 for Britain and West Germany, and 13 for Italy; *Older:* 17-18 for the United States and Japan, 14-16 for West Germany, 14-17 for Britain, and 16 for Italy.

Source: For Japan, the 1968 data are from Okamura, 1968 Survey, and for 1969, from Massey, 1969 Survey. The remainder of the table is an abbreviated version of a table in "Preadult Development of Political Party Identification in Western Democracies," by Jack Dennis and Donald McCrone, *Comparative Political Studies* Vol. 3, No. 2 (July 1970), p. 252 by permission of the Publisher, Sage Publications, Inc.

show a markedly higher degree of party identification, and that is reflective of the significantly higher levels of partisanship found among English adults than among adults in any other nation yet studied.

The Inheritance of Partisanship: The Family as Source

Insofar as children's own identifications are concerned, then, Japan appears to have nearly as extensive pre-adult partisanship as most of her Western counter-

five parties, the other responses included were "other," "support no party," and "don't know."

There are some obvious dangers in using the data in Table 4-1 for comparative purposes. First of all the ages of the children included in each age level differ from country to country; only the Japanese and American groups are identical in age across all three age levels. Secondly, the items used to elicit party identification also differ from country to country and even within countries by age group. There is no way of estimating how these differences affect the validity of the findings, and thus the figures must be used only with caution. But at present this is the only comparative data available. It is presented in lieu of better data, mainly to suggest that there is probably no reason to believe Japanese youngsters to be especially unusual in the extent to which they identify with political parties or fail to do so.

part democracies. But how stable are these likely to be over the long run? One obvious approach to an answer to this question is to compare the distribution of party affiliations across generations to see whether the socialization process is recreating the adult pattern of identifications among the young. The Japanese polls have long broken down party affiliation by age, and the finding that has been most prominently emphasized has been that the youngest members of the electorate, those in their twenties, have shown a markedly lesser propensity to identify with the Liberal Democrats than older adults.[13] What does the data from the present survey tell us on this point? Table 4-2[d] presents the distribution of responses to the party support items in both the student and parent samples.

We observe that as in the polls mentioned, young supporters of the Liberal Democrats and, to a lesser degree, the Democratic Socialists are proportionally fewer than their parents. But the disparity between the two generations appears to be based not on defections among the young to the left, but rather in the abstention of many youngsters from support for any party. The polls do show that young adults tend more than their elders to support the parties of the left. But since they have been showing that very same phenomenon over the past twenty-five years without any significant change in the overall distribution of partisanship having taken place, the inevitable conclusion is that even when such defections to the left do occur they are impermanent. That young adults give up their support for the left as they grow into middle age is a phenomenon apparently unique to Japan (from among the major party systems on which empirical research has been done) and is one for which Donald Stokes has coined the phrase "political senescence."[14]

Nevertheless, while in gross terms teenagers may not yet be rejecting the LDP partisanship of their parents but rather abstaining from partisan commitment, and despite the identical rank orderings of partisan preferences in the two generations, it is clear that the socialization process is not simply reproducing parents' party affiliations in the younger generation. It behooves us, therefore, to give careful attention to the correspondence between the partisan affiliates of parents and children at the individual level.

The degree to which an individual's party identification is rooted in a family tradition bears ultimately on the stability and durability not only of his own identification but through it, in mass terms, on the stability and durability of the party system and the legislative process. In their study of French and American

[d]By comparison with an *Asahi Shinbun* poll for the period just prior to the date of this survey, the pattern of partisanship in the study's adult sample appears slightly more conservative, LDP and DSP supporters being somewhat overrepresented (by 6 percent and 3 percent, respectively) and JSP supporters somewhat underrepresented (by about 8 percent). This slight bias of course makes no difference to the point being discussed here, since the concern is with the degree to which the distribution of partisanship among parents is being reproduced among children. The *Asahi* figures for all adults are as follows: LDP, 47 percent; DSP, 7 percent; Komei, 6 percent; JSP, 26 percent; JCP, 3 percent; other and no reply, 11 percent. *Asahi Shinbun*, November 17, 1968.

Table 4-2

Distribution of Party Support, by Age and Generation: Parents and Students Compared

(Percentages of students by grade, and parents as a whole)

Grade	LDP	DSP	Komei	JSP	JCP	Other; None	Don't Know; No Response	Total	N
8	26	6	5	13	3	17	30	100%	282
10	30	5	3	15	2	19	26	100%	334
12	34	5	3	14	4	24	17	100%	326
Total	30	5	4	14	3	20	25	100%	942
Parents	53	10	5	18	2	7	5	100%	1637

adults' political interest and participation, Converse and Dupeux found that far fewer Frenchmen than Americans acquired their partisan affiliations from their parents. This was due in no small measure to the fact that few Frenchmen could even recall knowing what party their fathers supported. Converse and Dupeux blamed this gap in the family political communication process for the French party system's instability.[15]

There is strong reason to believe that much the same failure of the family to transmit partisan affiliation took place in the childhood of today's adult Japanese. To begin with, as Bradley Richardson has pointed out, prewar restrictions on the suffrage—property qualifications for voting disenfranchised most men until 1925, and women did not get the vote until 1946—made the learning of parental partisanship irrelevant for many of those adults.[16] Moreover, during the decade before 1945, the parties had been gradually abolished, until, during the years of World War II, there remained only one "party," the Imperial Rule Assistance Association, which was in fact nothing more than an arm of the government and a device for suppressing opposition. Thus, the childhood of today's adults would have come during the wartime period when the parties had been dissolved, or else earlier, in the twenties and thirties, when the party system was made up of now-defunct parties.

We have seen, however, that despite the absence or the irrelevance of family socialization to partisanship in the childhood of today's Japanese adults, most of them have developed identifications with the contemporary parties. Are they, in turn, communicating those identifications to their children? Has there developed a pattern of intra-family generation-to-generation transfer of party loyalties that is likely to provide an ongoing basis for the stability of the present party system? The data from the present survey permit us to ask two related questions here. First, to what extent do today's Japanese youngsters *know* their parents' partisanship? And second, to what extent do they *share* it?

On the first point, only 32 percent of the teenagers in the sample were unsure of their fathers' party preferences; 68 percent placed their fathers in one of the preference categories (including "supports no party"), while 67 percent did so for their mothers. But a comparison of the teenagers' perceptions of the parents' party preferences with the parents' own reports reveals a substantial degree of inaccuracy. When all father-child and mother-child pairs—including those cases where the student replied that he did not know—were used as the bases for the calculations, only 43 percent of the students accurately named their fathers' partisanship and only 44 percent, their mothers'. Very much the same pattern of inaccurate perception was observed by Zureik among a sample of young Englishmen and their parents: only 42 percent of the English youths, aged 9 to 18, correctly assigned their parents to one of the parties.[17] And the evidence from the United States is also similar when age differences in the student samples from the United States and Japan are taken into account. The Tau-B correlation between American high school seniors' reports of their parents' party preferences and the parents' own reports was .59;[18] for the high school seniors in the present Japanese sample, the Tau-B correlation was .51 in the case of the father's party preference and .55 in the case of the mother's.

The consistency across cultures of a pattern of inaccuracy in children's perceptions of parental partisanship provides ample reason for skepticism about the value of relying on recall data, such as adults' recollections of their parents' partisanship during the adults' childhood. More important for present purposes, these data on Japanese teenagers' perceptions of their parents' partisanship are at the same time preliminary evidence weighing against a determinist role of the family in the creation of party identification and evidence that at least in respect to their apparent *knowledge* of parental partisanship, Japanese youngsters resemble their British and American peers.

In answer to the question of the extent to which Japanese children share the party identifications of their parents, Table 4-3 provides the basic data on the extent of partisan inheritance in Japan through cross-tabulations of students' and parents' party preferences. As the table makes clear, the degree of correspondence in partisanship between parents and children is moderately high. Expectations—like those implied in the Langdon quote cited earlier—that the changing nature of the party system would result in a breakdown in the transmission of partisanship from parent to child are shown to be unfounded; neither, however, is there the complete identity of the two generations' affiliations that a naive application of the alleged "Mendelian law" of political inheritance would predict. With the parties arranged from conservative to progressive in the order shown in the table,[e] the rank-order correlations between parents and children that result are the highest of the parent-child correlations on political attitudes that occur in the data used in this study. Jennings and Niemi found this to be the case in American families as well.[19] Hence, it seems clear that in Japan, as in the United States, the family's role in the direct transmission of political orientations to the young is at its highest in the passing on of partisanship, even though the transmission is far from perfect.

Still keeping to the comparative perspective for the moment before turning to an analysis of the differences in the Japanese parties' rates of inter-generational continuity in support, the main question is how the Japanese family compares with families in other countries in transmitting partisanship. Table 4-4 presents a summary of the available evidence, in terms of one or both of two measures: correlations between parents' and children's identifications, and percentages of children and parents with the same identification. It should be

---

[e]That this constitutes the basic left-right ordering of the contemporary parties is abundantly clear, not only from the parties' own policy and ideological positions, but from the way in which the electorate perceives the place of each of the parties in terms of the "conservative"-"progressive" spectrum as well. See, for example, the proportions of a national sample of adults who identified each of the parties as either "conservative" or "progressive" reported in the *Mainichi Shinbun*, March 23, 1975.

Table 4-3
Students' Party Identification, by Parents' Party Identification

Students by Fathers:

Fathers' Party Identification	Students' Party Identification						
	LDP	DSP	Komei	JSP	JCP	Total	N
LDP	69	8	2	16	5	100%	261
DSP	48	23	2	21	6	100%	52
Komei	28	4	52	16	0	100%	25
JSP	32	8	4	52	4	100%	77
JCP	27	0	0	46	27	100%	11
Total	56	9	5	24	5	100%	426

Goodman and Kruskal's Gamma = .45
Kendall's Tau-B = .30

Students by Mothers:

Mothers' Party Identification	Students' Party Identification						
	LDP	DSP	Komei	JSP	JCP	Total	N
LDP	67	8	3	17	5	100%	263
DSP	61	18	0	18	3	100%	38
Komei	22	7	59	7	4	99%	27
JSP	33	11	1	52	3	100%	94
JCP	33	0	0	0	67	100%	3[a]
Total	56	9	6	24	5	100%	425

Goodman and Kruskal's Gamma = .42
Kendall's Tau-B = .27

[a]Marginal frequency in this case is too small, strictly speaking, to permit percentaging. Percentages are given for the sake of convenience only.

noted that there are some problems of comparability in the figures. The first is that the children's ages differ from country to country. Second, the Japanese correlations and percentages of agreement are based necessarily[f] only on those students and parents who identify with one of the five parties; nonidentifiers were excluded from the tables from which the figures were calculated. In the

[f]Necessarily, because while independents may fit neatly between two parties, as in the United States, there is no way of knowing where they or other nonidentifiers should be placed along a multi-party spectrum as in Japan. Hence, with their inclusion no ordinal correlation could be calculated. On a related point, it should be noted that Tau-B is used only when comparisons with American or British data are necessary. The author's preference is for Goodman and Kruskal's Gamma, another ordinal measure, which has an intuitively more meaningful interpretation similar to that of the commonly used measures of correlation of interval-level data.

Table 4-4
Cross-National Comparison of Parent-Children Agreement in Party Identification

Country	Correlation[a]	Percentage Agreement
Japan: with fathers	.30 (.41)[b]	58% (63%)
with mothers	.27 (.38)	59% (63%)
United States	.47	59%
Britain	.45	41%
West Germany	–	57%
France	–	29%

[a]Kendall's Tau-B

[b]Figures in parentheses are for high school seniors (ages 17-18) only. The other age groupings are for Japan, 13-18; United States, 17-18; Germany, 14-16; and France, 15-16. Source: For the United States, M. Kent Jennings and Richard G. Niemi, "The Transmission of Political Values from Parent to Child," *American Political Science Review* 62:1 (March 1968), Table 1, p. 173; for Britain, Elia Zureik, "Party Images and Partisanship among Young Englishmen," *British Journal of Sociology* 25:2 (June 1974), 196-97; and for West Germany and France, Dennis and McCrone, "Preadult Development of Political Party Identification in Western Democracies," *Comparative Political Studies* 3:2 (July 1970), Table 2, p. 257.

American data, however, independents were included in the calculations, and this fact suppresses both the percentage agreement and the correlation. Whether independents are included in the figures for the other nations in the table is not clear, but if they are, the figures must also be considered as probably understating the degree of agreement between parents and children. Nevertheless, so long as these caveats are taken into consideration, comparison is possible, if it is understood as being suggestive rather than precise and definitive. In this rough and suggestive sense, then, the data appear to indicate that Japanese parents pass on their partisanship to their children at rates similar to parents in America, England, and West Germany and higher than that of French parents.

A somewhat stricter comparison is possible with the American data by limiting the Japanese figures to those for the high school seniors (and their parents) and excluding nonidentifiers. When this is done, it is clear that there is a higher degree of partisan agreement among the Americans (87 percent[20]) than among the Japanese (63 percent in the case of both father-child and mother-child pairs). And, even when the Japanese parties are lumped into two camps—conservatives (LDP and DSP) and progressives (Komeito, JSP, and JCP)—the rate of children's defections to the "enemy camp" is markedly higher than that found among the Americans: 27 percent from the father's camp and 29 percent from the mother's, as compared to the 13 percent of the American youngsters who defect to the opposite party from that of their parents.

Nonetheless, the nearly two-thirds of the party identifiers among the oldest

Japanese youths who share their parents' partisanship is a surprisingly high proportion in view of the strong reasons to expect a low rate of parent-child agreement on partisanship. The implication that the early postwar instability of the Japanese party system would result in an absence of family socialization to partisanship similar to the French pattern is clearly disconfirmed. Indeed, it seems safe to say that parent-child partisan correspondence in Japan is close to the modal level found in the Western democracies and substantially higher than that found in France.

An additional and significant finding on the Japanese family's role in transmitting partisanship to the child is that parent-child agreement increases with the age of the child, from Tau-B's of .21 and .14 between the eighth graders and their fathers and mothers, respectively, to Tau-B's of .41 and .38 between the twelfth graders and their fathers and mothers. In other words, despite the growing teenager's increasing exposure to such socializing agencies other than the family as the peer group and the mass media, the family actually strengthens its influence on partisanship. This again contrasts sharply with France, where Dennis and McCrone found that the rate of agreement with parental partisanship *declined* among older children as compared to younger ones, which suggests, in their view, "low familial reinforcement for whatever partisan cues are transmitted."[21]

On the whole, then, the Japanese family compares favorably with families in other countries in the extent to which parents succeed in transmitting their partisanship to their children. But not all families are equally effective in this regard. In particular, a second look at Table 4-3 will reveal that the rate at which children retain or defect from their parents' party identifications varies by party. Clearly, Liberal Democratic parents outdistance all others in the degree to which their children share their partisanship. And their children were substantially more likely than those of any other party's supporters (except the Komeito's) to correctly identify their partisanship (55 percent accuracy for both fathers and mothers). Both of these facts probably reflect the reinforcement of the LDP family's impact made possible by the fact that LDP supporters are far more likely than others to have politically homogeneous marriages: 86 percent of the LDP husbands in the survey had LDP wives, and 85 percent of the LDP wives had LDP husbands.

The Democratic Socialist parents present a striking contrast. Their retention rate is so low as to suggest serious difficulties for the party even to maintain its already small following in the electorate. DSP parents tend more frequently than others to have spouses from the other parties, especially the LDP. The obvious effect of this fact is the great loss of their children to the ranks of the LDP that DSP parents incur. What is equally intriguing is that this tendency to be married to supporters of the LDP apparently works to blur the party identification that DSP parents project to their children; indeed, more DSP parents were reported by their children *as LDP supporters* than as DSP supporters (39 percent to 16 percent in the case of the fathers and 35 to 21 percent in the case of the mothers).

Among the other parties' supporters, the Komeito parents come closest to rivalling the LDP parents' transmission rate. And their party identification was even more likely to be correctly perceived by their children (67 percent for the fathers and 65 percent for the mothers) than was true of the LDP parents. Since Komeito support is usually linked to adherence to the Soka gakkai sect of Buddhism, a religion in which fervent belief is accompanied by extensive group activities and proselytization, such support is almost certain to play a more prominent role in the self-identification and daily life of the Komeito supporter than purely secular partisanship would. This no doubt has much to do with the relative success of Komeito parents at transmitting their partisanship to their children.

The supporters of the Japan Socialist Party just barely manage to bring half of their children into the Socialist fold. Like their right-wing fellows in the DSP, JSP parents appear to have some difficulty in communicating a clear image of their partisanship to their children: only 36 percent of JSP fathers and 34 percent of JSP mothers were correctly assigned by their children to the JSP. Similarly, the Socialists' neighbors to the left, the supporters of the Japan Communist Party, also do not appear to be effective at inducing their children to follow in their partisan footsteps, although the small size of the sample must make any inference here quite tentative. Nevertheless, the likelihood that this impression is accurate is enhanced by the fact that so many children of the JCP supporters in the sample misperceived their parents' party identification: only 29 percent of the fathers and 38 percent of the mothers were correctly identified.[g]

There is an intriguing similarity here between the cases of the JCP and DSP parents. As in the case of the DSP's large losses of its supporters' children to the LDP, the communists lose their offspring mainly to their larger ideological neighbors, the JSP. Moreover, most JCP supporters are married to JSP supporters. These parallels suggest that there is a principle of "political gravity"

---

[g]Akira Kubota and Robert E. Ward, "Family Influences and Political Socialization in Japan," *Comparative Political Studies* 3:2 (July 1970), 150, reported that the JCP parents in their survey were the *most* effective of all the party supporters in transmitting their partisanship to their children. But their sample of JCP supporters was even smaller than the sample in the present study. Obviously, the resolution of this question awaits a study with a large sample of JCP supporters and their children. But in the meantime, indirect evidence in support of the conclusion that JCP parents are *not* particularly effective in transmitting partisanship exists in the results of a panel study of Tokyo voters carried out in March and November, 1967. While 83 percent of all party identifiers in the March survey maintained the same identification in November, only 44 percent of the March JCP identifiers also identified with the JCP in November. If JCP identification is less stable than that for other parties over time, it follows that JCP identifiers should be less consistent, and less effective, in transmitting such identifications than those with more stable identifications. In a 1961-62 panel study, however, JCP identifiers were no less stable over time than other identifiers. Both studies are reported in Miyake Ichiro, "Seito Shiji no Ryudosei to Anteisei" (Stability and Instability of Party Support), *Nenpo Seijigaku*, 1970, Tables 1.4 and 1.5, p. 93.

involved in the family transmission of partisanship in multi-party systems like Japan's, in which the parent who identifies with one of the larger parties exerts a greater "pull" on his child's partisan inclination than the parent who identifies with one of the smaller, numerically less dominant parties. Moreover, at least in the Japanese case, the principle even seems to extend beyond the boundaries of ideological camps and to affect the relative pull of the two largest parties: while JCP families lose their children mainly to the JSP, the Socialists themselves lose a substantial number—roughly a third—to their arch-rivals in the opposing camp, the Liberal Democrats. JSP to LDP defections are twice as high as those in the reverse direction, which would seem a bad omen for a party that has laid great stress on its appeal to youth. Indeed, a striking finding in the table is the significantly greater success of the Liberal Democratic Party in retaining the offspring of its own supporters and at acquiring the offspring of all the other parties. Still, in absolute numbers, the LDP suffers a net loss from one generation to the next; in the case of fathers and children, for example, the LDP lost the children of 81 of its supporters to one or another of the other parties and gained 60 of the children of the other parties' supporters for a net loss of 21. The figures in the case of the mothers were roughly the same: 87 lost to 61 gained, for a net loss of 26. This loss to the ruling LDP of 8 to 10 percent of its supporters from one family generation to the next represents a potential source of major change in the distribution of party identifications in Japan with all the consequences that would entail for Japanese politics. But, as was noted earlier, many young adults appear to adopt an LDP identification as they enter their thirties and forties. It may be that the continuing gradual decline in the electoral strength of the LDP reflects a small but constant net loss in LDP identifiers as the result of the two transition processes in partisanship, one of which is generational in nature and the other, age-related, as outlined here.

The foregoing discussion has emphasized the effect of the accuracy of the child's perception of his parents' partisanship on his adoption of that partisanship. It bears mentioning that one of the characteristic trends in the data was a notably greater degree of correspondence in the teenagers' own identifications with their *perceptions* of their parents' identifications than with the parents' *actual* identifications. This tendency is most evident among the youngest teenagers who, like American and British youngsters,[22] tend to exaggerate their partisan solidarity with the family, perhaps as Niemi has suggested, as a result of a psychological need to make it "appear to themselves that they are not really so different from their parents."[23] That this solidarity is misplaced is indicated by the low correlation of their perceptions of their parents' partisanship with the parents' actual partisanship: Tau-B = .22 for both parents in the case of the eighth graders. The older teenagers, who are more interested in politics and more consciously aware of their parents as political role models, tend to be much more accurate about their parents' partisanship: as noted earlier, in the case of the twelfth graders, the Tau-B between perceived and actual partisanship of the fathers was .51 and that of the mothers was .55. Hence, by twelfth grade there is little or no appreciable difference between the Japanese youths' degree of agreement with their parents' actual partisanship (Tau-B = .41 and .38 with fathers and mothers, respectively) and with the parents' perceived partisanship (Tau-B = .39 and .40).

The discussion so far has focussed on the direct role of the family in the genesis of partisanship with emphasis on the transmission from parent to child of an identification with a party. But the influence of the family on a youngster's partisanship may come about not only through the internal parent-to-child communications net of the family, but through the family's external links with the wider society. Being born into a family means also being born into a social class and into a community—into the village or the teeming city. It means being placed into a particular social environment—into relationships with other people, most of whom are likely to share the same values and beliefs and identifications as the family. Almost inevitably, then, the influence on the political attitudes and beliefs of the growing child of the family and the influence of such basic social characteristics as social status or urban-rural residence overlap. What, then, is the impact of these social characteristics on the partisanship of young Japanese?

Social Determinants of Partisanship:
Urban-Rural Residence and Socioeconomic
Status

In adult politics in most polities, social factors—notably, whether one lives in urban centers or rural areas as well as one's social status—have an impact on two aspects of partisanship. The first is whether one identifies with a party or remains uncommitted or alienated; the second, the direction partisanship takes among those who do identify with parties. Among the adults in this study, typically for Japan and contrary to the United States, urban dwellers and upper-status individuals were found significantly more likely than rural and lower-status individuals to avoid affiliation with a party. Excluding those who did not respond to the questionnaire item, 10 percent of the urban residents supported no party as compared to only 4 percent of the rural residents, while 10 percent of the upper SES group expressed no party support as opposed to only 5 percent of the lower SES group.

The same pattern held true for the teenage sample as well. While roughly equal proportions (25 and 23 percent) of urban and rural students replied "don't know" to the item asking which party they would support if they could vote, substantially more urban than rural youngsters (24 to 14 percent) chose the "don't support any party" response. The relationship between the socioeconomic status of the respondents' families and nonidentification had a somewhat different pattern. Here, significantly more low-status than high-status youngsters (33 to 22 percent) replied "don't know." But, conversely, more upper-status teenagers than lower-status teenagers (25 to 19 percent) chose the intentional nonidentification response. On the whole, then, the impact of urban-rural residence and socioeconomic status on the adult pattern of nonidentification appears to be reflected among the teenagers as well.

The association of intentional nonaffiliation (as opposed to the "don't know" variety) with the upper-status and urban teenagers has some interesting comparative implications. Greenstein's data, and those of Hess and Torney, show a clear trend for more upper-status American children to call themselves independents, while lower-status children in the Hess and Torney study appeared to have a less clearly based lack of commitment behind their nonaffiliation.[24] The American evidence thus appears to corroborate the tendency apparent here for upper-status children to be more apt than lower-status children to intentionally refrain from identifying with a party. In Japan, as we shall see in a later chapter, this is symptomatic of the greater alienation of upper-status and urban youth from some aspects of politics.

A second important question confronting us here is how these two social factors affect the *direction* of partisanship. Table 4-5 presents the distribution of partisanship among both teenagers and parents according to urban-rural residence and socioeconomic status.

As is immediately evident, urban-rural residence does have a moderate impact on party identification among both generations. Socioeconomic status, however, appears to be only weakly related to partisanship among the adults and not at all among the teenagers. This appears to corroborate Watanuki Joji's interpretation of Japanese politics as "cultural politics" or "value politics" rather than status politics—that is, cleavages in Japanese politics seem to be founded in differences in cultural outlooks and values, in particular those between the traditional values and norms of country folk and the modern challenges to the traditional beliefs and practices that have grown up in the city.[25]

Status differences, however, are not so totally irrelevant to partisanship as Table 4-5 would lead us to believe, for, in fact, there is a negative relationship between socioeconomic status and rural residence: rural families have lower incomes and typically lower levels of parental education. Hence, we must take account of this before simply dismissing any place for socioeconomic status in the molding of partisanship. Table 4-6 presents the relationship between SES and partisan affiliation among both generations with urban-rural residence controlled.

When the impact of area of residence is held constant, it is clear that there is a correlation between the family's socioeconomic status and the direction of partisanship among both children and adults. Higher-status families produce more adults and children who affiliate with the conservatives than do lower-status families, which produce more Socialists and Communists. But the striking

Table 4-5

Party Identification of Students and Parents, by Urban-Rural Residence and Socioeconomic Status

By Urban-Rural Residence:

Party Identification	Students		Parents	
	Urban	Rural	Urban	Rural
LDP	46	61	54	68
DSP	11	8	16	7
Komei	7	6	7	3
JSP	28	22	21	21
JCP	8	3	2	1
Total	100%	100%	100%	100%
(N)	(274)	(255)	(789)	(680)
	Gamma = −.26		Gamma = −.23	

By Socioeconomic Status:

Party Identification	Students			Parents		
	High	Med	Low	High	Med	Low
LDP	50	56	51	60	62	56
DSP	15	6	8	19	9	8
Komei	4	6	11	4	5	8
JSP	25	25	26	16	22	26
JCP	6	7	4	1	2	2
Total	(100%)	(100%)	(100%)	(100%)	(100%)	(100%)
(N)	(168)	(229)	(132)	(466)	(370)	(333)
	Gamma = −.02			Gamma = .08		

aspect of the distributions in the table is that while the drift from right to left as one proceeds down the status level is quite clear among rural adults and teenagers, in the urban sample we note an interesting generational difference. Support for the parties of the left (JSP and JCP) does not change markedly from high- to low-status groups among the teenagers; it is nearly the same in both high and low groups (32 percent and 35 percent, respectively) and slightly higher among the middle group. This contrasts with the parents among whom there is a clear upward progression of left support as status decreases.

It is noteworthy that when the student's age is added as a second level control, we discover that among the urban, though *not* the rural, teenagers, the correlation between SES and partisanship decreases with age, from .16 among the eighth graders to .07 among the twelfth graders. This is the result of

Table 4-6

Interaction of Urban-Rural Residence and Socioeconomic Status on Party Identifications of Students and Parents

Urban Residence:

Party Identification	Students' SES			Parents' SES		
	High	Med	Low	High	Med	Low
LDP	48	44	39	57	53	39
DSP	15	8	4	21	11	7
Komei	5	8	22	4	8	20
JSP	26	30	26	17	24	32
JCP	6	11	9	1	4	2
Total	100%	100%	100%	100%	100%	100%
(N)	(144)	(107)	(23)	(387)	(327)	(75)
		Gamma = .12			Gamma = .20	

Rural Residence:

Party Identification	Students' SES			Parents' SES		
	High	Med	Low	High	Med	Low
LDP	62	67	54	77	71	62
DSP	17	5	9	8	6	8
Komei	0	5	8	1	2	5
JSP	17	21	26	13	20	24
JCP	4	2	3	1	1	1
Total	100%	100%	100%	100%	100%	100%
(N)	(24)	(122)	(109)	(79)	(343)	(258)
	Gamma	= .16		Gamma	= .20	
	Partial Gamma	= .14		Partial Gamma	= .20	

concurrent increases with age of the proportions of upper-status urban youths identifying with the left parties and of lower-status urban youths identifying with the conservatives. Meanwhile, in further support of Watanuki's notion of the prevalence of "cultural politics" over status politics, the correlation between urban-rural residence and partisanship increases with age, from −.21 among the eighth graders to −.32 among the twelfth graders, which is a stronger association than that found among the adults (−.23).

It would appear, then, that the principal social correlate of partisanship among both adults and teenagers in Japan is whether they live in the relatively conservative countryside or the relatively progressive metropolis. But the social status of the family also makes a difference, though this is only apparent when the effect of urban-rural residence is held constant. For both parents and teenagers, higher social status is associated with increased support for the conservatives in both urban and rural areas. The correlation is fairly weak, however, especially among the urban teenagers. Nevertheless, while it is generally true that the lines of partisan cleavage among Japanese young and old are drawn principally along the classic dichotomy of culture and values in Japan of city versus country, there is also a basis for partisan differences in the lines dividing economic and social strata. "Cultural politics" continues to prevail as the social basis of partisanship, but "status politics" plays a role as well, even though it is one of less impact and less consistency.

The Cognitive and Affective
Content of Partisanship

However they are acquired, party affiliations among young Japanese seem to be rather less salient and ego-involved than they are for young Americans and Britons. Bradley Richardson, in a secondary analysis of the Kubota and Ward data, found substantially fewer strong identifiers than is true of adults in the United States and England as well as those in three other countries.[26] In this study, interviews with Japanese teenagers provided the impression that much the same was true for most of them. No student interviewed spontaneously identified himself verbally as a Liberal Democrat, or a Socialist, or whatever. Clearly this particular component of the galaxy of groups and symbols that might be used to make reference to one's identity is little used and not very salient foı most young Japanese. Nevertheless, although not at the forefront of their self-definitions, their partisanship is significant because, as we shall see, it has a systematic impact on their ideological perspectives and on their attitudes toward other political objects, including their support for the input and output institutions of the regime.

Before turning to a discussion of the place of ideology in the socialization of young Japanese and its relationship to partisanship, it is appropriate to ask whether party affiliation is founded on an awareness of what the parties stand for. Greenstein found that few of his New Haven children could or did distinguish between the Republicans and Democrats in terms of policies or ideologies.[27] Unfortunately, the kind of spontaneous data evoked by Greenstein's open-ended question is not available on Japanese children's perceptions of differences between the parties. But Okamura provides us with some useful data on Japanese youngsters' ability to recognize the positions of the two major parties. He asked children in grades seven through twelve to "pick two things that the Liberal Democratic Party maintains" from a fixed list of choices and then to pick two that the Japanese Socialist Party maintains. Table 4-7 summarizes the proportions of children who chose accurately and inaccurately for each party, by grade.

Table 4-7

Accuracy of Children's Perceptions of Policies of the Two Major Parties (LDP and JSP)

(Percentages of accurate and inaccurate choices, by grade)

	LDP Positions		JSP Positions	
Grade	% Correct	% Incorrect	% Correct	% Incorrect
7	98	53	87	64
8	117	49	99	65
9	124	49	116	56
10	157	23	149	28
11	162	20	159	20
12	183	17	168	19

Issues and Positions:	LDP Position	JSP Position
Existence of Self-Defense Forces	Supports	Opposes
Seating of Mainland China in the U.N.	Opposes	Supports
United States-Japan Mutual Security Treaty	Supports	Opposes

Note: Since two choices were permitted, percentages total to 200; nonrespondents are omitted.

Source: Okamura, 1968 Survey.

The three issues to which the questions refer have been among the most debated policies of the entire postwar period. The Self-Defense Forces and the Security Treaty with the United States, especially the latter, are the targets of sustained opposition attacks that have continued to receive wide coverage in the press. At election time, abolition of each is usually among the principal themes of the Socialist and Communist campaigns. It may be something of a tribute to the persistent attempts of the opposition parties to keep these issues at the forefront of public awareness that so many youngsters—indeed, a rough majority from eighth grade onward—are able to accurately perceive (or guess) the parties' positions on them. But underlying the division between the Japanese parties, and the conflict over these issues of national policy, is a cleavage between left and right that goes to basic questions about the nature of government and society. How far that cleavage has penetrated into the political learning of Japanese adolescents constitutes the subject matter of the next chapter.

Conclusion

Despite its newness and the changes that have occurred in it during the past several decades, the multi-party system in Japan has apparently laid down its roots in the political culture. The evidence indicates that partisanship among

Japanese adults is comparable in extent to that among Americans and Western Europeans. Levels of party allegiance among Japanese children, from early in childhood through adolescence, were found similar to those prevailing in the Western nations studied. But there appear, on impressionistic evidence, to be fewer strong identifiers among the Japanese youths. The influence of the family on partisanship also seems similar in Japan to the Western countries. Not only do Japanese youths show a level of knowledge of their parents' partisanship that equals that of British youths and rivals that of Americans, but they also share their parents' party affiliations to a degree that approaches their Western peers. And even though they tend to imagine their parents as being more similar to themselves in partisanship than in fact they are, their actual partisan agreement with their parents increases with age. In short, the family does appear to play a comparable if slightly weaker role in the genesis of partisanship in Japan to that which it plays in the United States and Britain.

Because of the importance of social factors to both the ideological aspects of partisan politics and the overall bases for the aggregate balance of party support, the analysis then considered to what extent socioeconomic status and urban-rural residence function as sources of partisanship among young Japanese. The evidence pointed to an important inter-generational continuity in the overall predominance of urban-rural "cultural" differences over status differences as influences on partisanship. Coupled with evidence of low net transition rates of defection from the conservative party to the parties of the left, the continued clear impact of urban-rural residence among the young as compared to the inconsistent and weaker, but still present, impact of status differences suggests that change in the distribution of party strength is likely to occur only gradually and incrementally as the younger generation replaces its elders in the electorate.

It would appear, in short, that partisanship, at both the level of the individual's party affiliation and the aggregate level of socially based distribution of party strength, is being reproduced from one generation to the next to a degree that exceeds what we might expect in a party system with such a short and checkered history. To explain this continuity, we may have to look beyond the relationship of the individual to a particular party and turn our attention to the basic continuity of the ideological camps, conservative and progressive, into which the parties fall.

Notes

1. The literature on party identification and its effects on politics in the United States is vast. The seminal source remains Angus Campbell, Philip E. Converse, Warren E. Miller, and Donald E. Stokes, *The American Voter* (New York: Wiley, 1960); see also by the same authors, *Elections and the Political Order* (New York: Wiley, 1966). Fred I. Greenstein, *The American Party System*

and the American People, 2nd ed. (Englewood Cliffs, N.J.: Prentice-Hall, 1970), provides a useful overview of the literature.

2. See David Butler and Donald E. Stokes, *Political Change in Britain* (New York: St. Martin's Press, 1971).

3. See Philip Converse and Georges Dupeux, "Participation of the Electorate in France and the United States," in Campbell et al., *Elections and the Political Order*, pp. 269-91.

4. Ibid., pp. 279-80. See also David G. Cameron, "Stability and Change in Patterns of French Partisanship," *Public Opinion Quarterly* 36 (1972-73), 19-30. Cameron's reanalysis of the 1958 Converse and Dupeux data showed that even among those in the sample who did identify with a party, over 60 percent did not know their father's partisanship, a finding which suggested that parental transmission is not a necessary condition for partisanship to develop. He also found, from data from a 1968 survey, that a substantial increase in the proportion of Frenchmen possessing a party identification had occurred since 1958—an increase in which various factors other than family socialization appeared to have played significant roles. Nevertheless, the 1968 data, like that of 1958, showed that knowledge of parental partisanship was the most powerful predictor of whether the respondent in the survey himself had a party identification, which thus reaffirms the importance of family socialization to partisanship.

5. See Watanuki Joji, "Patterns of Politics in Contemporary Japan," in S.M. Lipset and Stein Rokkan, eds., *Party Systems and Voter Alignments* (New York: The Free Press, 1967), pp. 447-66.

6. The literature in English on the Japanese party system is growing, but there has been no really adequate overview since Robert Scalapino and Junnosuke Masumi's *Parties and Politics in Contemporary Japan* (Berkeley and Los Angeles: University of California Press, 1962) appeared nearly a decade ago. This slim volume remains useful even today but is somewhat dated and of little value as regards the Komeito. A more recent but abbreviated treatment can be found in Theodore McNelly, *Politics and Government in Japan*, 2nd ed. (Boston: Houghton Mifflin, 1972). On the policies and ideologies of each of the parties consult: for the LDP—Haruhiro Fukui, *Party in Power* (Berkeley and Los Angeles: University of California Press, 1970), Nathaniel Thayer, *How the Conservatives Rule Japan* (Princeton, N.J.: Princeton University Press, 1969), and Chitoshi Yanaga, *Big Business in Japanese Politics* (New Haven, Conn.: Yale University Press, 1968); for the JSP and DSP—Allan B. Cole et al., *Socialist Parties in Postwar Japan* (New Haven, Conn.: Yale University Press, 1966); for Komeito and Sokagakkai—James White, *The Sokagakkai and Mass Society* (Stanford: Stanford University Press, 1970); and for the JCP—Robert Scalapino, *The Japanese Communist Movement, 1920-1966* (Berkeley and Los Angeles: University of California Press, 1967).

7. On Great Britain see Butler and Stokes, *Political Change in Britain*, p. 27.

There has been a gradual decline in partisanship in the United States over the past several decades; according to Gallup Poll figures, 80 percent of Americans in 1940 identified with either the Democrats or Republicans as compared with only 73 percent who did so in 1969 and 68 percent who did so in 1975. See the *Gallup Opinion Index*, June, 1975, p. 22.

8. Frank Langdon, *Politics in Japan* (Boston: Little, Brown, 1967), p. 213.

9. The *Asahi Shinbun* and *Mainichi Shinbun* polls, both of which are conducted several times yearly. See in particular *Asahi Shinbun*, December 27, 1968.

10. *Asahi Shinbun*, December 27, 1968, and September 18, 1972. A slight rise in the size of this group to an average of between 13 and 14 percent was noted in the polls taken in 1973 and 1974. See *Asahi Nenkan 1974 (Asahi Yearbook, 1974)*, p. 669, and *Asahi Nenkan 1975*, p. 690.

11. Fred I. Greenstein, *Children and Politics* (New Haven, Conn.: Yale University Press, 1965), pp. 71-72.

12. See Bradley M. Richardson, "Party Loyalties and Party Saliency in Japan," *Comparative Political Studies* 8:3 (April, 1975), Table 4, p. 41.

13. See, for instance, the polls reported in the *Asahi Shinbun*, June 26, 1971, and in Nishihira Shigeki, *Nihonjin No Iken (The Opinions of the Japanese)*, (Tokyo: Seishin Shobo, 1963), p. 146.

14. Donald E. Stokes, "The Study of Political Generations," Noel Buxton Lecture, University of Essex (London: Longmans, 1969), p. 9.

15. See the discussion on this point in note 4, above.

16. Richardson, "Party Loyalties and Party Saliency in Japan," p. 37.

17. Elia T. Zureik, "Party Images and Partisanship Among Young Englishmen," *British Journal of Sociology* 25:2 (June 1974), 196.

18. Richard G. Niemi, *How Family Members Perceive Each Other: Political and Social Attitudes in Two Generations* (New Haven, Conn.: Yale University Press, 1974), p. 53.

19. See M. Kent Jennings and Richard G. Niemi, "The Transmission of Political Values from Parent to Child," *American Political Science Review* 62:1 (March 1968), 179. The precedence of partisanship among political values transmitted in the Japanese family was also observed by Kubota and Ward in their pilot study of fifteen- to nineteen-year-old Japanese. See Akira Kubota and Robert E. Ward, "Family Influences and Political Socialization in Japan," *Comparative Political Studies* 3:2 (July 1970), 152.

20. My recalculation of the figures in Table 1 of Jennings and Niemi, "The Transmission of Political Values," p. 173.

21. Jack Dennis and Donald McCrone, "Preadult Development of Political Party Identification in Western Democracies," *Comparative Political Studies* 3:2 (July 1970), 257.

22. See Niemi, *How Family Members Perceive Each Other*, p. 63, and Zureik, "Party Images and Partisanship Among Young Englishmen," pp. 197-98.

23. Niemi, ibid., p. 62.

24. Greenstein, *Children and Politics*, Table 4.3, p. 73, and Robert D. Hess and Judith V. Torney, *The Development of Political Attitudes in Children* (Garden City, N.Y.: Anchor Books, 1968), p. 190.

25. Watanuki Joji, "Patterns of Politics in Contemporary Japan," pp. 456 ff.

26. Richardson, "Party Loyalties and Party Saliency in Japan," Table 1, p. 36.

27. Greenstein, *Children and Politics*, p. 68.

5 Symbols of Dissensus: The Emergence of Ideology

Introduction

The role of ideology in contemporary mass societies has been a source of continuing controversy and debate. A major element of that debate has grown out of studies of the American electorate, in which it has been argued that the sphere within which ideology is relevant and significant is a very limited one involving only a small segment of the population.[1] This chapter is meant to contribute to the debate, by examining the development of ideology among young people in a country in which ideological symbols are very widespread.

One need not look long or far to find the traces of ideology in Japan. They can be found in the latest acts of urban guerilla warfare committed by revolutionary students or in the gory ritual suicide of a famous novelist after the failure of his rightist putsch. They can be found, too, in less violent places: on the spines of countless popular books about the ills of present-day life in Japan and in the civil suit against government control of school texts brought by a famous historian.

Ideology, highly articulated and logically constrained, asserting universal social principles and prescribing specific courses of action for both society and the individual, is a vital force in the political life of today's Japan. Among its most characteristic features has been its attraction to the young, and it is this characteristic that demands the attention of any study of the political learning process.

This chapter, then, focuses on the development of ideological thought among Japanese adolescents. More specifically, it concentrates on their reactions to the ideological dimension that overshadows all others in contemporary Japan: the symbols and substance of the confrontation between capitalism and socialism. As in so many of the world's nations, political conflict in Japan is characteristically phrased and framed in support of or opposition to the Marxist view of man and society. The Socialist and Communist Parties, as well as the student movement, make extensive use of the Marxist framework and terminology in their rhetoric. But ideological rhetoric and a terminological framework within which to articulate a unified social and economic philosophy have never been an important part of postwar Japanese conservatism. So it is in a sense by default that the ideological stimulus to which Japanese young and old respond, positively or negatively, more than to any other is the leftist critique of the contemporary socioeconomic system.

101

This dominance of the Marxist-derived left-right ideological dimension in the rhetoric and substance of partisan conflict makes Japan of particular interest for the comparative study of political learning in adolescence. Studies of the development of ideological thought during the teenage years have so far been largely confined to the United States.[2] But despite the differences between the two major parties and the existence of groups and movements like the Students for a Democratic Society and the Black Panthers, it continues to be the case that the main currents of American politics are notably devoid of ideological content. In particular, the absence of a strong ideologically based socialist movement or party with a national following sets America apart from most other industrial nations. As a result, definitions of what is "ideological" in the context of American politics are apt to involve high levels of conceptualization and abstraction. In other political systems, such as Japan's, however, ideology manifests itself not only in the intellectual domain of ideas and abstractions but also in the popular domain in which concepts become political labels that, like party labels, serve as simplifying screens through which political complexity can be reduced to readily understandable categories by the common citizen.

This chapter, then, investigates the predominant ideological concepts and labels, specifically "socialism" and "capitalism," and their role in the political learning that takes place in adolescence in Japan. The first objective will be to examine the cognitive and perceptual aspects of these concepts and labels. What do "socialism" and "capitalism" mean to Japanese teenagers? How do they perceive these "isms" to relate to their country? How much of the content of these concepts is understood, and how does age affect the depth of understanding?

A second and related objective will be to assay the affective responses to these ideologically related concepts of both the teenagers and their parents. How do evaluations of these ideological symbols compare with each other and with those of other leading political symbols such as democracy and peace? How do they rank in the political value hierarchies of the two generations? What do youngsters believe to be the merits and faults of the two "isms"? To what extent do these responses to the labels parallel their responses to the unlabeled concepts?

There is another perspective on ideology that must also be considered and dealt with. In it, ideology is taken to refer to a *style* of thought—a *way* of putting ideas and attitudes together to form an overall, integrated view of social, economic, and political processes. The literature on ideology in this latter sense is extensive.[3] But running through nearly all the definitions of ideology in that literature are several elements usually considered fundamental prerequisites of ideological thought. Two that are of particular relevance to the study of teenagers' political attitudes are the *constraint* of the attitudes and the use of *causal reasoning* about society and politics based on general principles or beliefs.

"Constraint" is a term coined by Philip Converse to refer to the degree of consistency between attitudes:

.. the probability that a change in the perceived status (truth, desirability, and so forth) of one idea-element would psychologically require . . . some compensatory changes in the status of idea-elements elsewhere in the configuration.[4]

Thus, for example, in the most straightforward case in the present context, we would expect that among ideologues, attitudes toward both socialism and capitalism would be mutually constrained. To the extent that positive attitudes toward socialism are coupled with negative attitudes toward capitalism, the constraint or consistency of the component beliefs of an individual's political attitude structure or belief system would be high, and an important condition of ideology would be satisfied.

A second condition of ideology is that attitudes toward political issues and objects be founded on certain basic, general principles, or what Converse has called "crowning postures—like premises about the survival of the fittest in the spirit of Social Darwinism."[5] It will be evident that this latter condition is a rather stringent one, in that it requires both a fairly sophisticated grasp of abstract concepts and abstruse theories as well as the capacity to use those concepts and theories in evaluating the real world. Such knowledge and use of abstract concepts and principles in politics obviously is apt to be more characteristic of political elites than of common citizens, and more characteristic of adults than of children and adolescents.

The development among Japanese teenagers of these two conditions of ideological thought thus constitutes a third major focus of this chapter. Particular attention will be paid to the applicability of two alternative models of the growth of ideology in adolescence to the data. The first model derives from the work of developmental psychologists, notably Joseph Adelson and his associates.[6] It stresses the growth of cognitive capacities, and posits a series of stages as prerequisite to the emergence in mid-adolescence of the capacity for ideology.

The second model derives from an empirical study of the development of policy thinking among American teenagers by Richard Merelman.[7] Merelman found that cognitive capacity alone is inadequate to explain the process through which an adolescent forms a style of political thought that could be considered ideological. He tentatively concluded that the nature of politically related stimuli in the environment was of greater importance to the development of ideology than the adolescent's cognitive capacities. The contrast between the near total absence of vivid and salient ideological symbols in American political life and their widespread presence in Japanese politics (at the national level at least) makes this political stimulus model of particular relevance. It will be argued here that the overlapping and mutual reinforcing of party labels and ideological labels is a particularly important way in which stimuli in the political environment affect the ideological development of Japanese youngsters. Thus, the fourth focus of the chapter will involve the manner in which the party identification that young Japanese develop interacts with their beliefs and attitudes about and reactions to ideological symbols and values.

Cognitive and Perceptual
Aspects of Ideology

It is readily apparent that the lexicon of politics in both the popular and elite cultures in Japan differs from that in use in the United States. When Americans discuss politics, the terms heard most often are "democracy," "freedom," "liberty," and so on. These terms are used in political discourse in Japan too. But there are others that rarely appear in American political discussions that occur often in Japan. "Socialism," "capitalism," and associated terms are encountered not only in the slogans of the leftist parties and of the radical students but also in the titles of endless popular books and articles—and even in the social studies texts in the schools.

Capitalism is particularly prominent among the terms, since it refers to the present economic system, which is the target of the critical ire of the opposition in Japan. Something of the degree to which this term has become not just common but prominent in political discourse and hence ultimately in the political learning process is suggested by Table 5-1. As is apparent, capitalism far outdistances democracy as the primary defining characteristic of their society in the eyes of Japanese teenagers from as early as the tenth grade. Only among the eighth graders in the sample does democracy prevail. This suggests that there may be a learning sequence involved in which democracy precedes capitalism in the political consciousness of Japanese youngsters. It is significant, in this regard, that while one can find mention of democracy in the social studies texts and curricula from early in the primary grades, capitalism and socialism do not appear in any significant fashion until ninth grade, in the "politics and economics" course in social studies taken by all students.

It should be pointed out that it is the *precedence* of these two characteristics that is being stressed here. When, in the interviews, youngsters were asked to

Table 5-1

Capitalism versus Democracy as Defining Characteristics of Japan

(Percentages of students by grade, and of parents as a whole, choosing each response)

Students Grade	Socialist	Capitalist	Dictatorship	Democratic	Don't Know; No Response	Total
8	10	24	0	46	20	100%
10	4	60	2	25	9	100%
12	0	70	2	24	4	100%
Parents	3	41	0	45	11	100%

Survey Item:
"What kind of country is Japan? Pick the one that you think suits Japan best."

choose *two* characteristics, nearly all chose *both* capitalism and democracy. But there was no doubt that among the older students the majority believed capitalism to be more characteristic of Japan than democracy. As one fourteen-year-old Tokyo boy said, "I think capitalism is the more important, because before the war Japan wasn't democratic but it was capitalist. The war didn't change that."

The interviews also provided an insight into the teenagers' conceptions of the ideological terms. It was apparent that both capitalism and socialism were conceived in rather skeletal fashion, with little complexity or descriptive richness. Capitalism seemed to be an especially elusive concept for most of the students. Few were as off the mark as the rural eighth grader who thought it was "where they do foreign trade and such." But even the more accurate verbalizations were conceptually limited and sparse in content. One relatively frequent definition centered around the image of *rule by capitalists*:

... Well, capitalism is where people with money—big capitalists—run the economics of the country. (Eighth-grade Tokyo boy)

... With capitalism, you get capitalists, after all. ... I have an image of being controlled by capitalists when you say capitalism. (Tenth-grade Tokyo boy)

A number of youngsters, however, showed a somewhat more specific grasp of a principal element of the concept of capitalism, the relationship between work and reward:

... [It's where] you get the return you work for yourself. (Eighth-grade Tokyo boy)

... when a person by his own efforts ... well, only that person becomes better off ... and there is free competition. (Tenth-grade rural girl)

Socialism seemed to be more widely and easily understood:

... With socialism, there is a planned economy, and everyone works hard and things are divided equally among everyone. (Twelfth-grade Tokyo boy)

... when the state provides social security. The state does everything and there isn't free competition. (Eighth-grade Tokyo boy)

A planned economy, social security, and public ownership of enterprise—these seem fairly widely understood to be what socialism is all about and how it differs from capitalism with its somewhat less distinct image of private ownership and free competition. Table 5-2 provides some evidence from Okamura's survey on the extent to which these characteristics are correctly associated with each "ism."

It is clear at a glance that a major increase in the frequency of students understanding both capitalism and socialism takes place after ninth grade. This is

Table 5-2

Meaning of Capitalism and Socialism: Correct and Incorrect Associations

(Percentages of students by grade, associating the responses shown with capitalism and socialism)

Grade	Capitalism		Socialism	
	Correct[a]	Incorrect[b]	Correct[c]	Incorrect[d]
7	37	56	83	14
8	54	62	102	16
9	73	49	107	12
10	143	17	159	6
11	148	15	158	5
12	151	13	154	5

[a]"Private ownership; free competition."
[b]"Public ownership; planned economy; social insurance."
[c]"Public ownership; planned economy; social insurance."
[d]"Private ownership; free competition."
Note: Since two choices were permitted, percentages total to 200; other ambiguous responses were also possible.
Source: Okamura, 1968 Survey.

probably in large part a consequence of what is learned in the latter half of the "politics and economics" social studies course given in all middle schools in the ninth grade. It is also apparent that at all age levels more youngsters are aware of the basic elements of socialism than of those of capitalism, though the disparity decreases sharply by tenth grade. The closing of the awareness gap between the two is also due no doubt to the aforementioned social studies course. But why should so many more youngsters in the earlier middle school grades understand socialism than understand capitalism?

To begin with, of course, capitalism does seem to present greater intrinsic cognitive difficulties. Socialism is definable essentially by reference to a simple notion—that of public ownership. Capitalism, however, is less clearcut, especially since abstract notions of private ownership and free enterprise are confused by images the youngsters have of concrete capitalist countries. Almost without exception the youngsters interviewed chose Japan and the United States when asked to name capitalist countries in today's world. But in their own country, at least, they are likely to have heard that there is economic planning, social security, and other forms of social insurance, and they all are aware of the publicly owned railway (popularly called by its abbreviated name of *Kokutetsu*— the National Railway), airline, television network, national monopolies, and utilities. Second, again almost invariably, the most prominent characteristic that the students attributed to capitalism was—in a direct translation of a phrase used by nearly all—"the gap between rich and poor." Yet, their discussions of their own country in the interviews revealed little tendency on their part to see Japan as riven with such a gap, and their image of the United States as a land of affluence and prosperity clearly did not mesh with the abstract image of what a capitalist state is supposed to resemble.

When it came to naming socialist countries the responses were somewhat less quick and sure. Most of the youngsters listed the Soviet Union and the Eastern European nations. But few knew anything about non-Soviet socialism. None of the interviewees had any idea of what sort of economic system could be found in Sweden, for example. It was obvious that socialism is equated with Marxian socialism insofar at least as the best-known socialist states are concerned. This is not surprising in view of the emphasis on Soviet style socialism in the texts and the relative inattention to the Scandinavian states.

More surprising, however, was the clearcut pattern that emerged from the interviews with regard to communism. There was a striking lack of conceptual clarity and differentiation in the notions of communism. Many of those interviewed were unable to say anything whatever about what communism means. Those who did venture definitions usually said only that it was a stronger or harsher form of socialism. It was apparent that the teenagers' understanding of the relationship between socialism and communism was at best a fuzzy one. Interestingly enough, however, a number of the students interviewed—even including those who could say nothing about the meaning of communism—were willing to choose certain nations as communist nations as opposed to socialist ones. In nearly every case, the nation identified as communist was the People's Republic of China, along with North Korea and North Vietnam. Many of the youngsters may have carried over their awareness of a split between the Soviet and Chinese blocs into their perceptions of socialism and communism.

It is also highly likely that the common Japanese abbreviations for the Soviet Union (Soren) and the People's Republic (Chukyo) have something to do with this, especially the latter. The second character of Chukyo is the initial character of the word for communism (Kyosanshugi), and the term thus is roughly similar to the English phrase *Communist* China. No such reference to communism is associated with the term Soren for the Soviet Union; nor indeed is communism usually mentioned in discussions of that country, which is almost always referred to in the textbooks and in the newspapers as a "socialist state" and the leader of the "socialist bloc."

Capitalism, then, is the characteristic most widely felt by young Japanese to typify their society. By the mid-high school years, a substantial majority of youngsters can recognize the basic elements of both capitalism and socialism, although communism appears to be much less well understood. In view of the importance of capitalism in teenagers' views of their society, it is important then that we turn to an analysis of their attitudes toward it and toward the other concepts associated with it.

Affective Responses to Capitalism, Socialism, and Other Symbols

We saw in Chapter 3 that so many youngsters place a high positive value on peace and democracy that they may be considered consensual elements in the emerging political culture in Japan. But we have also seen here that more youngsters believe capitalism to be Japan's most important characteristic than believe that democracy is.

In order to know what this implies in regard to their evaluation of their society, we must first ascertain how they feel about capitalism in comparison with other relevant concepts and symbols. The students and parents to whom the questionnaire was administered were asked whether they reacted favorably or unfavorably when they heard a number of political terms. Table 5-3 presents a summary of the results for each of the terms and ranks them in decreasing order of favorable responses. The same overall preference ranking obtains for both generations of Japanese. Peace and democracy, as noted, receive an overwhelmingly positive response. But the three socioeconomic terms, which are what concern us at present, show much less overt support. Table 5-3 corroborates a finding from the interviews that communism is clearly a negative symbol for many. Indeed, significantly more teenagers (11 percent) responded that they felt "*very* unfavorable" to it than to any of the other terms.

More important here, however, is that capitalism is positively valued by only

Table 5-3
Affective Reactions to Various "isms" of Students and Parents
(Percentages of all students and parents choosing "react favorably" plus "react very favorably" or "react unfavorably" plus "react very unfavorably")

	Students		Parents	
	Favorable	Unfavorable	Favorable	Unfavorable
Pacifism	89%	2%	79%	3%
Democracy	79	2	76	3
Liberalism	58	10	50	13
Socialism	29	14	26	22
Capitalism	29	22	21	31
Communism	11	40	5	67

Note: The actual order of the terms as they appeared in the questionnaire was: pacifism, socialism, liberalism, capitalism, democracy, communism. The items were modeled on similar ones included in a major continuing study of Japanese attitudes being carried out by the Tokei Suri Kenkyujo Kokuminsei Chosa Iinkai (National Character Study Committee of the Institute for Statistical Mathematics). See *Nihonjin no Kokuminsei* (*Japanese National Character*), (Tokyo: Shiseido, 1961), pp. 503-04, and *Dai-ni Nihonjin no Kokuminsei* (*Japanese National Character: Second Study*), (Tokyo: Shiseido, 1970), pp. 443-44.

a minority of students and of parents. Almost as many students reported an unfavorable reaction to the term as reported a favorable one. Second only to communism, capitalism received a higher proportion of "*very* unfavorable" responses than any other term (6 percent). Overall, then, capitalism falls near the bottom of the list in popularity, negative feeling toward it being surpassed only by that for communism. But a large group of students and parents, indeed a majority of the former and a near majority of the latter, remained noncommittal.

Socialism appears to evoke a pattern of reaction similar to that brought out by capitalism. But there is less hostility toward socialism and an even greater degree of neutrality. Nevertheless, there is no evidence in the table of a wholesale rejection of capitalism by the young in favor of socialism. This is in keeping with other findings on the attitudes of the young toward these two competing ideological symbols.[8]

It is noteworthy that despite the relatively primitive cognitive content of the youngsters' images of capitalism and socialism, they not only hold opinions about each but many were willing to make comparisons of the relative merits of each with respect to a set of other values. Table 5-4 shows the percentages of all students who felt that each of several attributes was to be found more or much more in capitalist countries or more or much more in socialist countries. Parental responses are also given for the sake of generational comparison.

The table confirms what was found, as illustrated by the quotes below, in the interviews: liberty and democracy are widely identified as positive attributes of capitalism that are missing in socialist countries.

Table 5-4
Capitalism and Socialism Compared on Five Attributes

	Students		Parents	
	Pro-Capitalism[a]	Pro-Socialism	Pro-Capitalism	Pro-Socialism
Liberty	66%	9%	58%	13%
Democracy	46	17	43	18
Peace	19	32	32	22
Inequality[b]	11	67	13	54
Poverty[b]	8	73	13	60

[a]Pro-Capitalism responses were "found more in capitalist countries" and "found much more in capitalist countries"; pro-Socialism responses were "found more in socialist countries" and "found much more in socialist countries."

[b]Response categories were reversed to accord with the direction of favor,—that is, the respondents who picked "more in capitalist countries" for inequality and poverty were counted as pro-socialist and vice versa.

. . . [In socialist countries] there isn't any freedom of speech; you can't say the things you want to say. (Eighth-grade Tokyo boy)

. . . Socialism is strong. It's really tightly controlled. There's no freedom such as in Japan. (Tenth-grade Tokyo girl)

Conversely, capitalism was believed to promote discrimination, inequality, and poverty, as can be seen in these excerpts from two eighth-grade compositions:

. . . in order to have real, out-and-out democratic politics, it is wrong to have a social system like capitalism, in which the difference between rich and poor gets bigger.

. . . [In capitalist countries] people who are strong succeed; people who are weak are used. That is, there is discrimination. So, looking at it as a person who isn't strong, it isn't a very good country.

But, not surprisingly for a people who have been said to have a "work ethic," the youngsters' compositions also show a number of them were put off by socialist-style egalitarianism, as for example:

. . . With socialism, everyone is equal, but I think it's sad that people of ability can only get the same amount of money as people with no ability.

. . . If no matter how hard a person works, he gets the same wages as other people, wouldn't his will to work be blunted?

So far, the analysis has concentrated on the labeled concepts of socialism and capitalism. But what kinds of responses to socialism and capitalism occur when their basic ideas are presented *without* the identifying labels? In a related item in the questionnaire, respondents were asked which of three unlabelled societies came closest to their ideal for Japan. The majority of the students (56 percent) chose the society "where the government controls the economy, so one can't become very wealthy, but where a minimum standard of living is firmly guaranteed," a description meant to represent socialism. A smaller group (33 percent) chose the welfare capitalist option of a society "where able men can become wealthy, but where such people are highly taxed by the government to help look after the disadvantaged." Very few, only 5 percent, chose the laissez-faire capitalist society "where men of ability can readily become wealthy, but where there are people who have difficulty earning a living." Interestingly enough, however, support for the welfare capitalist society increased with the age of the student, reaching 43 percent among the twelfth graders where it rivalled the 48 percent support for the socialist one. But, although socialist support diminished with student age, even the twelfth graders were to the left of the parents on this item, 47 percent of whom chose the welfare capitalist society as opposed to 37 percent who chose the socialist one.

How do these preferences accord with the students' reactions to the labelled concepts of capitalism and socialism? Cross-tabulation of the preferred ideal societies with each of the concepts produced a moderately strong correlation (gamma = .29) with reactions to capitalism among the students as a whole, but a much weaker (gamma = −.09) one with reactions to socialism. However, when we control for age, the latter correlation rises to −.30 among the twelfth graders and rivals the former, which goes up slightly to +.33. In other words, we see in the one case but not the other an increase in the strength of the association between reactions to ideological labels and unlabeled ideals that suggests that ideologically relevant attitudes become increasingly crystallized and coherent as age increases. The difference in the two cases must prompt our investigation into the factors that compete with age to promote the development in adolescence of ideology as a style of thought.

Constraint and Causal Reasoning: Ideology as a Style of Thought

Intellectuals, academicians, journalists, and others who think a good deal about politics tend to appraise political issues and occurrences by applying a set of abstract, integrated principles to them. But in doing so, they are, at least in the United States, in a very small minority.

Among a sample of American adults, Philip Converse and his associates found only a handful, about 2.5 percent, who could be classified as ideologues who consistently evaluated political issues by reference to such general principles. Another 9 percent were classified as "near-ideologues" whose use of the liberal-conservative—or any other ideological spectrum—as a yardstick of evaluation appeared either inconsistent or based on a shaky understanding of the terms.[9] Unfortunately, directly comparable evidence, based on open-ended questions, is not available on the extent to which Japanese adults use general principles in a consistent way to evaluate political issues. In response to similar, structured questionnaire items, only a slightly higher proportion of Japanese adults (89 percent) identified themselves as either conservative or progressive in a 1975 survey than Americans (84 percent) in a 1969 survey who identified themselves as conservative or liberal.[10] But, on purely impressionistic grounds, it seems almost certain that a larger—probably a substantially larger—proportion of Japanese than Americans classify as ideologues or near-ideologues, in the above sense, given the much greater penetration of popular politics by ideological symbols and rhetoric. It is equally certain, however, that the absolute number of such ideologically conscious individuals is a small minority of all adults—probably no more than one in four or five at a maximum.

If only a minority of adults can meet this condition for ideology, how much more likely it is that even fewer pre-adults will be able to do so. There is, above all else, the problem of whether they have the cognitive capacity for such abstract and deductive reasoning. Studies of American children and adolescents suggest that there are stages in the growth of such cognitive capacities and that it may not be until mid-adolescence that the so-called stage of "formal operations" is attained and the ability to apply general principles to specific cases and to reason deductively is developed.[11]

This analysis of the antecedents of ideology in adolescence must therefore take into account two conditions for ideological thought: constraint and the use of general principles. The data permit us to do this, though in each case to an imperfect degree. Let us look first at the problem of the constraint on consistency between Japanese teenagers' attitudes regarding socialism and capitalism. As a standard against which to judge the relative level of constraint among the teenagers' attitudes, parents' attitudes will be analyzed concurrently.

Of necessity, the survey could not include items dealing with the whole range of specific issues on principles relevant to socialism and capitalism. So, as was discussed earlier, primary emphasis has been placed on the very terms themselves and on their relationship to other symbols and values. Needless to say, however, the correlations between reactions to the terms and the other values provide a readily interpretable measure of the degree to which the basic elements of the ideologically relevant attitudes cohere. The developmental psychology model of the growth of ideology would predict that the coherence of attitudes toward socialism, capitalism, and communism will increase with age. Table 5-5 presents the ordinal level gamma coefficients of correlation between reactions to these three "isms" among the students as a whole and by grade and for parents as a whole.

The level of congruence between reactions to socialism and capitalism among eighth graders is not only strikingly low but is in the *opposite direction from what we would expect*, being slightly positive. The same is true for the correlation between capitalism and communism. It is not until tenth grade that consistency begins to emerge in these basic attitudes. But by twelfth grade, the

Table 5-5
Correlations between Reactions to Capitalism, Socialism, and Communism
(Goodman and Kruskal's Gamma)

Students Grade	Capitalism and Socialism	Capitalism and Communism	Socialism and Communism
8	.07	.03	.32
10	−.08	−.12	.55
12	−.27	−.15	.59
Total	−.10	−.10	.50
Parents	−.16	−.15	.56

teenagers evince as much or more congruence as do their parents. It is also evident that there is a substantially greater degree of consistency between the reactions to socialism and communism, among both parents and students. As was pointed out earlier, a large proportion of all students were antipathetic to the term communism. Among those favorable to socialism, the proportions favorable and unfavorable to communism were about even (26 percent to 28 percent, respectively). However, those unfavorable to socialism were also overwhelmingly unfavorable to communism (5 percent favorable to 78 percent unfavorable). On the whole, as a second glance at Table 5-3 will remind us, the students were neutral toward capitalism and socialism. Few—only about one in seven—reported an unfavorable reaction to socialism. But that so many of them should reject communism as well hints at an unexpectedly strong stream of anti-left coherence among the students insofar as attitudes toward these conceptual labels are concerned.

Attitudes toward communism are not our central concern here. Rather, we are interested in attitudes toward socialism and capitalism, which are more widely employed and legitimate terms and ideas. Thus, it is important to reiterate that despite the modest value of the correlation between reactions to these terms in comparison with that between reactions to socialism and communism, the correlation does point to a pattern of consistency prerequisite to the development of ideology as being present among a significant minority of the oldest teenagers. Does a similar pattern of emerging consistency appear in the relations between other attitudes as well? Let us take the reactions to the terms capitalism and socialism once more, and this time compare them to evaluations of whether a number of values are to be found more in capitalist or in socialist countries. Table 5-6 presents these correlations for both parents and students, with the latter again broken down by grade.

The overall student correlations (zero-order gammas) on the whole show a moderate degree of association between the evaluations of the attributes and the two terms. But while the correlations with reactions to capitalism show an increase with the age of the student in four out of five cases, no such developmental pattern is evident in the correlations with reactions to socialism, where indeed there seems to be a small but uniform decrease in the strength of association with age. Part of this anomalous finding may be due first to the fact that there takes place an increase with age (grade) in the proportion of students who are noncommittal toward socialism, from 52 percent of the eighth graders to 61 percent of the twelfth graders. Fewer of the older than the younger students, on the other hand, are noncommittal about capitalism.

Second, many of the youngsters appear to be trying to be objective—that is, to judge the two systems on what they believe to be the systems' merits rather than giving their own preferences. What they know of the relative merits of the two systems is often a set of generalized images reinforced through the social studies courses, if the content of the texts is reflective of the tenor of the

Table 5-6

Correlation of Students' and Parents' Reactions to Capitalism and Socialism with Comparison of Values in Capitalist versus Socialist Countries

(Goodman and Kruskal's Gamma for students by grade and as a whole, and for parents as a whole)

	Reaction to Capitalism				
	Students:				Parents:
Value	8	10	12	Total	
Liberty	.19	.33	.36	.32	.40
Democracy	.23	.39	.33	.33	.36
Peace	.22	.37	.38	.32	.28
Inequality	.22	.12	.25	.13	.23
Poverty	.29	.28	.02	.13	.17

	Reaction to Socialism				
	Students:				Parents:
Value	8	10	12	Total	
Liberty	−.16	−.22	−.31	−.22	−.27
Democracy	−.42	−.33	−.32	−.36	−.28
Peace	−.42	−.19	−.38	−.33	−.36
Inequality	−.26	−.31	−.20	−.24	−.22
Poverty	−.29	−.26	−.16	−.21	−.28

courses, and through stereotypes they absorb from adult political discourse. Capitalism is often connected with war and socialism with tyranny or suppression in such stereotyped thinking. A good many youngsters seem to have absorbed *both* such anticapitalist and antisocialist images. One twelfth grade rural boy, for instance, told me that "socialism is better than capitalism and democracy [*sic*] so far as equality is concerned, but . . . the people don't have freedom." Third, if we examine the intercorrelation of the evaluations themselves, by age, we also note almost no increase with age in the average strength of the relationships.

One implication of these facts is that while development of the *capacity* for ideology may take place during adolescence, concurrent development of actual attitudes and stances toward ideological objects and of consistency between such attitudes does not necessarily occur. The evidence from the Japanese case is mixed; some pairs of attitudes show increased congruence with age, and others show decreased congruence. Clearly other influences supplementary to and in some instances unrelated to age and the development of cognitive capacities are at work in shaping the ideological tendencies in Japanese teenagers' thought.

The second requisite of ideological thought is that of arguing from general principles about causes and consequences in social and political life. An excellent example of such cause and effect analysis based on "crowning postures" is this passage from one eighth grader's composition:

> ... *In modern Japan, capitalists with lots and lots of money give out money to use laborers for their own profit. And then, because no one says anything to those capitalists, they compete with each other. So, because there is free competition, there is no planning in society as a whole, and there are the unemployed who have met with misfortune. So the gap between the rich capitalists and the poor laborers gradually becomes wider.*

Such an articulate, sophisticated grasp of causal reasoning about economics and politics is unlikely to have been achieved by a thirteen year old, and this statement no doubt reflects the influence, if not the hand, of an adult or elder brother or sister, or even perhaps a book. But one can find politically interested high school students with such ability to discuss society with full competence in causal reasoning and a reliance upon general principles, as, for example, the editor of one of the "organs" (journals) of the high school student movement who was interviewed. The son of working-class parents who had had little formal education, he himself was nevertheless impressively well versed in the basics of Marxism and claimed to have begun to read *Das Kapital* in ninth grade. In our discussion of the state of world politics and of Japanese politics and society, he brought to bear in his positions many of the central concepts and principles of Marxist and Leninist thought. His beliefs were manifestly ideological in the sense of both being constrained and in being derived from a set of general principles that he applied in analyzing contemporary problems.

But of course, neither the eighth grader's composition nor the wide-ranging, well-integrated beliefs of this high school activist are representative of the caliber of most Japanese teenager's causal analyses of political and economic reality. Much more typical are such statements about the merits and debits of capitalism and socialism as were noted earlier in which the causal link is often only implicit. But, as is apparent even in these statements, a number of teenagers link socialism or capitalism in a cause-effect relationship with democracy: "Capitalism promotes a gap between rich and poor, so it is opposed to democracy."

Since a major concern of this study is to examine the sources of support for democracy in the political attitudes of young Japanese, the decision was made, after several pretest interviews in which teenagers linked democracy and socialism or capitalism in a manner similar to the above, to incorporate a set of items on this theme in the questionnaire. First of all, on an abstract plane, the respondents were asked to agree strongly, agree, disagree, or disagree strongly that (1) "real democracy is impossible in a capitalist society" and (2) "real democracy is impossible in a socialist society." They were then asked in specific terms about Japanese democracy and whether they agreed or disagreed with the following items: (1) "Japan is not really a democracy because the capitalists hold power. For Japan to become a real democracy, the socialist forces must take power" and (2) "In a socialist country, individuals do not have freedom, so it is necessary to preserve capitalism in Japan." Table 5-7 presents a summary of the students' responses to these four items, as usual broken down by age and accompanied by the responses of the parents.

As anticipated, a substantial proportion of the students at all age levels responded "don't know" to each of the items. Even so, given the fact that, in Okamura's survey, only one eighth grader in four was able to choose the correct characteristics of capitalism, it seems likely that many of the youngest students are exemplifying that dictum that "affect precedes information." It is also interesting to note that markedly fewer students, especially among the eighth graders but also at nearly all grade levels, replied "don't know" to the items about democracy and capitalism or socialism in Japan than those about the interrelation of those principles in the abstract.

The use of general principles as a basis for political and social judgment would, of course, have to be consistent to qualify an individual's thought as ideological. Once again, the pattern of intercorrelations of items reveals a moderate degree of association, an average gamma of .29 for all students as

Table 5-7

Attitudes toward the Relationship between Democracy and Capitalism and Socialism

(Percentages of students by grade, and parents as a whole)

In the abstract: Democracy is impossible in . . .

Students Grade	Capitalist Countries			Socialist Countries		
	Agree	Neutral	Disagree	Agree	Neutral	Disagree
8	26	59	15	24	58	18
10	23	49	28	21	52	28
12	29	42	29	18	52	30
Parents	34	39	27	34	45	21

In Japan: To be democratic, Japan should have . . .

Students Grade	Capitalism			Socialism		
	Agree	Neutral	Disagree	Agree	Neutral	Disagree
8	27	47	26	26	49	25
10	32	45	23	14	36	50
12	25	45	30	15	40	45
Parents	35	41	24	21	39	40

Note: Responses coded agree = "agree strongly" plus "agree"; those coded disagree = "disagree strongly" plus "disagree."

compared with .31 for the parents. When cross-tabulated with reactions to capitalism and socialism we find these items showing stronger degrees of association than did the evaluations of socialism and capitalism with regard to the five values. In this sphere—the area of prescriptive attitudes as opposed to the more descriptive character of beliefs about relative distribution of attributes—it would appear that affective and emotive responses to the ideological stimuli play a more influential role in shaping teenagers' attitudes.

It is particularly noteworthy here that the strength of the relationships between these four items and reactions to the two economic systems increase sharply with age in six of the eight cases. By twelfth grade, students' attitudes toward the relationship between democracy and capitalism and socialism are as strongly related to whether they are favorable to capitalism or to socialism as are those of their parents. But in a reversal of the previous findings, it is the relationship between these attitudes and reaction to socialism that shows the strongest increase with age.

Even among teenagers, then, there are those whose attitudes toward socialism and capitalism are so organized that they satisfy the criterion of constraint. The evidence indicates that similarly, some teenagers—indeed, probably more than levels of information would suggest—respond to ideological arguments based on "crowning postures" or the deductive application of general principles in political and social affairs. However, it is likewise clear that the model proposed by developmental psychologists, in which political learning occurs in stages, does not serve as a wholly adequate guide to the Japanese data. We saw that consistency in attitudes and beliefs relevant to socialism and capitalism increased with age generally, but that there were a number of cases in which increased age did *not* yield larger proportions of teenagers with congruent attitudes. Moreover, there did not seem to be a greater increase between the fifteen year olds (tenth graders) and the thirteen year olds than between the fifteen and seventeen year olds. Indeed, it was more often the case, with specific reference to ideologically related beliefs and attitudes, that the real jump in attitude coherence came in the last year of high school. The growth of ideology in adolescence would appear to be influenced not merely by the individual's capacity to absorb ideological learning but by the nature of those factors in his environment that reinforce or dilute the ideological stimuli themselves. In Japan, where ideology is at the heart of partisan politics, party support takes on a special significance as a potential source of and reinforcement for ideology.

Ideology and Partisanship

Much of the path-breaking work on the political socialization of American youth was concerned with the experiences and learning undergone by young children. One important reason for this focus on political learning in early childhood was the belief that those attitudes and values acquired early in childhood become deeply rooted and endure as determinants of adult values and behavior; that they endure to a greater degree than those acquired later in life; and that they pervasively affect and color what is learned later in pre-adult life. It was quickly established that party identification was one of the orientations that developed early in the socialization process and that ideology was not. Even the oldest of Greenstein's sample of New Haven grade school children made so few "ideological" references to the differences between the parties that he concluded that there was probably a stage of childhood before which the acquisition of so abstract and complex a thing as ideology was impossible for most.[12] Similarly, Zureik reported finding that British youngsters exhibited little awareness of the class interests represented by their preferred parties.[13] Hess and Torney, noting the low level of ideological consciousness among their eight- to thirteen-year-old sample of American children, suggested that the tendency of young children to identify with the personalities of leaders might be compensatory for this inability to ideologize.[14]

Richard Merelman has pointed out that these findings imply ideological instability:

Because the earliest stages of human thought are not conducive to . . . ideological development, it seems fair to speculate, accepting the Freudian position on the psychological dominance of earliest modes of thought, that adult political ideologies always rest on an unstable base.[15]

But of course, such a consequence is most likely where party and ideology are only weakly related, if at all. Such is true in the United States where one can be either a conservative or a liberal Democrat or a conservative or a liberal Republican. In Japan, however, the lines of partisan cleavage overlap to a great extent with the lines of ideological cleavage. The unambiguous ideological position of most of the parties means that party support supplies both an intense and unequivocal stimulus to the development of ideology, as well as a stable basis and reinforcement for that ideology.

To begin the discussion of how party support and ideology interact in the political socialization of Japanese teenagers, let us look at Table 5-8, which summarizes the correlations between party support and a capitalism-versus-socialism scale made up of a number of the items just discussed.[a] (For convenience, the composite scale is referred to hereafter as the ideology scale.)

---

[a]The scale was formed as follows: a factor analysis was performed on the responses to the political attitude items of the eighth graders in the sample, and a varimax rotation performed on the principal components. Eight items loaded at a level of .30 or higher on one rotated factor. These were all related to attitudes toward capitalism and toward socialism and included most of those mentioned so far. All of these were five point Likert-scale items, and were recoded so that a strongly pro-socialist response was given a score of 1 and a strongly pro-capitalist response a score of 5. The scores on the eight items were then cumulated for each individual in a summary index. This index was then trichotomized into the three-point ideology scale.

Table 5-8
Students' Party Support and Ideology
(Percentages of students supporting each party who are pro-capitalist, neutral, or pro-socialist)

Party Support	Ideology Scale			
	Pro-Capitalist	Neutral	Pro-Socialist	Total
LDP	44	40	17	100%
DSP	16	50	34	100%
Komei	34	26	40	100%
JSP	17	30	53	100%
JCP	7	33	60	100%
		Goodman and Kruskal's Gamma = .50		

As the table makes clear, there is indeed a strong general association between the students' partisanship and their overall ideological tendency. Inspection of the breakdown by each party, however, reveals differential patterns of party-ideology correspondence. One particular hypothesis suggests itself in this regard. We would expect that supporters of the parties of the left, the JSP and JCP, would show the highest degree of party-ideology congruity. These are the parties that use ideological rhetoric in politics, and the very terms of that rhetoric derive from their philosophical and conceptual vocabulary. Moreover, these two parties carry primary ideological terms or labels as their *names*. As already suggested, ideological labels like "socialist" and "communist" play the same sort of simplifying role that party labels play: they reduce complex ideas and complex realities to images that are easily comprehensible and have strong affective color. A common pair of such images is the fat capitalist with his cigar, and the idealistic and dedicated socialist working for the good of all. When such ideological labels as these, which are the real "building block" elements of ideologies, are also the labels of political parties, they create a synthesis of party and ideology that forms a unified object of support and affection, or of rejection and hostility.

This hypothesis is supported by the figures in the table, as it is generally in the cross-tabulations of party support with nearly every individual item relevant to socialism and capitalism. Interestingly enough, when we examine the relationship between party support and reactions to the terms socialism, capitalism, and communism, we observe that while indeed more JSP and JCP supporters are favorable to socialism and communism than, for example, the proportion of Liberal Democratic supporters favorable to capitalism, we find that significantly fewer of them are *unfavorable* to capitalism than were favorable to socialism and communism. Apparently, the reinforcement of positive party and ideological labels that takes place is stronger than the generation of hostility toward the opposing label.

The importance of party support to ideology among Japanese teenagers is underscored by comparison with other relevant potential influences. Neither the student's age nor sex correlates with ideology to any great extent, the gammas being —.08 and .00, respectively. Even urban-rural residence is only weakly related (gamma = —.15). Once again, as in the case of partisanship itself, we observe that there is little direct impact of socioeconomic status on ideology (gamma = .03). Controlling for urban-rural residence results in the emergence of a fairly weak link (.17) between socioeconomic status and ideology among the urban teenagers, but not among their rural peers (.01).

Although these other factors have little or no *direct* influence on the teenagers' ideology as measured by the composite scale, they do affect the relationship between partisan support and ideology. Table 5-9 presents a summary of the correlations between party support and the ideology scale controlling for other factors.

The emphasis on the growth of cognitive capacities with age in the approach of developmental psychology to the emergence of ideology would lead us to expect an increase in the correlation between partisanship and ideology with the age or grade of the student. There is indeed an increase, but only a modest one—since even among the youngest the relationship is already quite strong. It is clear from the table that other factors have an even greater impact in specifying the correspondence of party and ideology. The correlation is much greater

Table 5-9

Partial and Conditional Gammas between Students' Party Support and Ideology Scale with Other Factors Controlled

Control	Partial Gamma[a]	Conditional Gamma[b]		
Grade	.50	8 .46	10 .45	12 .58
Sex	.51	Boys .61	Girls .35	
Urban-Rural	.49	Urban .53	Rural .43	
SES	.52	Low .30	Med .67	High .39
Media Exposure	.50	Low .27	Med .48	High .66

[a]Partial gamma = overall value of gamma between party support and ideology scale when the effects of the control variable are held constant.

[b]Conditional gamma = value of gamma in each category of the control variable.

among boys than girls, and somewhat greater among urban than rural children. These differences reflect, indirectly perhaps, the same influence on the development of ideology that is more explicit in the case of media exposure. The more the student reads magazines and newspapers and watches television programs about politics, the closer the fit between his party support and his ideology, as the term is used here. One obvious reason for this is that in following politics in the media, the student increases his information and knowledge about the symbols and the positions associated with the party he supports and with those he does not support.

The sex difference reflects this same point, because politics in Japan is a man's world; there are literally no more than a handful of women political leaders, none of them being well known. Moreover, women in Japan generally show less interest in politics and express fewer political opinions than men.[16] Girls, then, receive markedly less impetus toward political interest than do boys.

Similarly, the urban teenager comes in daily contact with more political stimuli than the rural teenager as a function of the constant presence of intense and fairly pervasive partisan conflict that is missing or muted in the village, where nonpartisanship and an overwhelming predominance of conservatism stifle the flow of partisan and especially ideological stimuli.[b]

In short, it seems evident that insofar as the fit between party support and ideology is concerned, the frequency and strength of relevant stimuli seem more important than age in influencing the ideological development of the Japanese teenager. To account for the development of ideology, in the simple sense that we have been using that term to mean the set of reactions to symbols and labels associated with the classic left-right, socialist-capitalist continuum plus a set of attitudes and beliefs about how other values relate to these symbols, it is not enough to look to the emergence of cognitive capacities. Richard Merelman has theorized that such cognitive development would be of central importance in the creation of ideology only in the absence of strong and unambiguous ideologically related stimuli in the environment. In Japan, the ideological nature of much of partisan politics provides a basis for such a stimulus in the very process of party identification and that stimulus is accentuated and reinforced by factors associated with increased political interest.[c]

---

[b]A substantial part of the explanation for the curvilinearity of the party-ideology relationship when SES is controlled is due to the same factors. The low SES group, a substantial part of which is made up of rural youngsters, is less politically interested and less politically stimulated than youngsters from the white-collar, urban families that make up most of the middle and upper SES groups. In the upper SES group, on the other hand, as I noted in the preceding chapter, there is a high proportion of youngsters who intentionally abstain from partisanship.

[c]Bradley Richardson, in a secondary analysis of the University of Michigan survey on Japanese voting behavior, reports that in Japan strength of party identification is highly related to political interest (gamma = .405 as compared to .040 for the 1968 Survey Research Center's sample of American adults). Unfortunately, my data do not permit direct measurement of the strength of party identification, but there is a clear parallel between this finding about adults' partisanship with the evidence in the data here that political interest increases the fit between party and ideology among teenagers. See Bradley M. Richardson, "Party Loyalties and Party Saliency in Japan," *Comparative Political Studies* 8:1 (April 1975), Table 6, p. 45.

Conclusion

The frequency and intensity with which ideological symbols and rhetoric are employed in Japanese politics give to ideology a significant place in the political learning of Japanese teenagers. From their mid-teens, most conceive of their country as primarily capitalist and only secondarily democratic. At the beginning of adolescence their conceptions of capitalism are ill-formed and nebulous, while socialism appears more readily and clearly grasped. By age fifteen or so, however, the great majority appear to understand the fundamental characteristics of both these "isms." But neither evokes the widespread positive reaction accorded to peace and democracy. Nevertheless, a substantial proportion, on the order of one-half those in the study, reacted affectively to the terms, either negatively or positively. There was widespread agreement among teenagers and parents alike on the merits and faults of the two systems: on the superiority of capitalism in promoting liberty and democracy and on the superiority of socialism in advancing equality and diminishing poverty and the "gap between rich and poor."

Analysis of the consistency with which teenagers held attitudes relevant to the left-right ideological continuum revealed moderate overall correlations. The degree of correspondence in such attitudes did appear to increase with age, in keeping with the model of the development of political thought as dependent on a process of progress from one stage of cognitive capacity to another. But the increases in consistency were not uniform across all attitudes, nor were they generally large in magnitude. The evidence on the relationship between party support and ideology suggested that for Japanese teenagers, the acquisition of an ideology is closely linked to the acquisition of partisanship, and that age and developing cognitive capacities are less important determinants than in situations where salient and potent external stimuli are lacking. This finding parallels the tentative finding of Richard Merelman, cited earlier, that American adolescents develop modes or styles of political thought characterized by consistency and argument from broad principles not so much as a function of increased cognitive capacity but as a response to powerful and unambiguous stimuli from the political environment.

In the preceding chapter, we found that "cultural" factors, in particular urban and rural residence, lie at the root of partisan cleavage. In this chapter, we have witnessed the emergence in adolescence of an ideological cleavage paralleling and overlapping that partisan cleavage and deriving from it. How that politico-ideological cleavage interacts with other lines of cleavage and with cultural factors to influence adolescents' support for the institutions of democratic politics as well as orientations affecting the political self is the question to which the chapter that follows must address itself.

Notes

1. Philip E. Converse's well-known essay is the seminal work on the role of ideology among the mass of Americans; see his "The Nature of Belief Systems in Mass Publics," in David E. Apter, ed., *Ideology and Discontent* (New York: The Free Press, 1964), pp. 206-61.

2. See especially the work of Joseph Adelson and his various associates and students: Joseph Adelson and Robert P. O'Neill, "Growth of Political Ideas in Adolescence: The Sense of Community," *Journal of Personality and Social Psychology* 4:3 (1966), 295-306; Joseph Adelson, B. Green, and Robert O'Neill, "The Growth of the Idea of Law in Adolescence," *Developmental Psychology* 1 (1969), 27-32; Judith Gallatin and Joseph Adelson, "Individual Rights and the Public Good: A Cross-National Study of Adolescents," *Comparative Political Studies* (July 1970), 226-42. See also Richard M. Merelman, "The Development of Political Ideology: A Framework for the Analysis of Political Socialization," *American Political Science Review* 53:3 (September 1969), 750-67, and the same author's "The Development of Policy Thinking in Adolescence," *American Political Science Review* 55:4 (December 1971), 1033-47.

3. Merelman, "The Development of Political Ideology," provides a useful introduction to this literature in both the text and the notes. See also Robert D. Putnam, "Studying Elite Political Culture: The Case of Ideology," *American Political Science Review* 55:3 (September 1971), especially pp. 655-56.

4. Converse, "The Nature of Belief Systems in Mass Politics," p. 208.

5. Ibid., p. 211.

6. See the works cited in note 2.

7. See Merelman, "The Development of Policy Thinking in Adolescence."

8. See Tokei Suri Kenkyujo Kokuminsei Chosa Iinkai, *Nihonjin no Kokuminsei (Japanese National Character)*, (Tokyo: Shiseido, 1961), pp. 503-04; and *Dai-ni Nihonjin no Kokuminsei (Japanese National Character: Second Study)*, (Tokyo: Shiseido, 1970), pp. 443-44. Also see *Asahi shinbun*, July 23, 1969, where figures are reported from a survey of young members of the All Communications Employers Union showing that 44 percent would prefer to reform capitalism as opposed to 36 percent who believe that Japan should become socialist. A 1962 survey showed that fewer of those in their teens than adults believed that things would improve if a progressive party took power. See Bando Satoshi and Iwai Sadao, eds., *Seinen-ron (On Youth)*, (Tokyo: San'ichi Shobo, 1963), p. 174.

9. Converse, "The Nature of Belief Systems in Mass Publics," p. 218.

10. See Richard M. Scammon and Ben J. Wattenberg, *The Real Majority* (New York: Coward-McCann, 1970), p. 72, and *Mainichi Shinbun*, March 23, 1975.

11. See the citations listed in note 2 for this chapter, especially Adelson and O'Neill, "Growth of Political Ideas in Adolescence."

12. Fred I. Greenstein, *Children and Politics* (New Haven, Conn.: Yale University Press, 1965), p. 70. Herbert Hyman came to a similar conclusion in summarizing the findings of a variety of studies; see his *Political Socialization* (Glencoe, Ill.: The Free Press, 1959), p. 46.

13. Elia T. Zureik, "Party Images and Partisanship Among Young Englishmen," *British Journal of Sociology* 25:2 (June 1974), 198.

14. Robert D. Hess and Judith V. Torney, *The Development of Political Attitudes in Children* (Garden City, N.Y.: Anchor Books, 1968), pp. 19-22.

15. Merelman, "The Development of Political Ideology," p. 755.

16. See, on this point, for example, Yasumasa Kuroda and Alice K. Kuroda, "Aspects of Community Political Participation in Japan: Influences of Education, Sex and Political Generation," paper delivered at the American Sociological Association Annual Meeting, San Francisco, August 1967, p. 8.

The Political Self: Social and Psychological Influences

Introduction

So far this study has concentrated mainly on *what* Japanese teenagers learn about politics. But an equally important question is *how* they acquire their political beliefs and values. One answer of obvious importance is that they may acquire them from other people with whom they interact; the family, the school, and the peer group are all socializing agents that communicate political ideas and values. That is an avenue of approach I explore fully in the next chapter.

A second answer is that they may also acquire them by virtue of their own identities—that is, by being members of categories of people, social strata, sexes, or generations, for instance. A great part of the body of social science literature on politics is concerned with the effects of such sources of identity on political beliefs and behavior. In this chapter then, I examine how belonging to an important set of such categories affects the political values and beliefs that Japanese teenagers acquire. Specifically, the question is how basic social and personal background characteristics—sex, age, urban or rural residence, and family socioeconomic status—affect the development by Japanese teenagers of three political orientations that are important as elements both of theories of democratic political culture and of competing models of political man among adult Japanese. These three orientations are political interest, political efficacy, and political trust, here broken into input support and output support categories.

Because democracy is predicated upon the participation of citizens in the political process, theories of the attitudinal and other psychological sources of support for democracy, or of democratic political culture, usually place great emphasis on the importance of political participation and the attitudes associated with it. The ideal-typical model of the participant democrat is one who takes an active part in politics as the result of his interest in events in the political realm; he is confident that his voice and his action can influence both the process and the outcome of decisions and is essentially optimistic about the responsiveness and the general fairness and morality of the actors, institutions, and processes involved in politics—though with a healthy skepticism of, and independent attitude toward, authority.[1]

Now any observer of politics in the real world will recognize that this is indeed an ideal, and idealistic, image of the actual attitudes and behavior of citizens in a democratic system. Many people are apathetic, many feel powerless, many are cynical, many never participate at all. And indeed in Japan there are two alternative ideal typical models of political man that are widely supposed to be more accurate representations of actual adult political attitudes and behavior. These are called here the "mobilized traditional man" and the "alienated mass man."

Traditionally, politics in Japan was the domain of the privileged, the elite, the influential; it was not for the common man. The political participation of ordinary people was the result of mobilization by local influentials; it relied on the traditional social norm that valued participation for its own sake and manifested itself as a social pressure to participate, rather than spontaneous political interest on the part of the individual. Political interest was usually low to nonexistent. The ordinary man was not likely to feel influential in a political system that emphasized the exaltation of the officials and the degradation of the people (*kanson minpi*). The citizenry were basically oriented to the output side of politics, trusting in and bowing to the superior wisdom of government and officials while being wary of and skeptical about the motives and interests of the political parties and other actors involved in the input process.[2] The converse of the "subject" orientation of the mobilized traditional man is that of the alienated mass man. He is likely to be interested in politics, but not in participation, at least not within the established framework of participation. He has lost faith in the morality of the actors and institutions in the political process and in his ability to have his voice heard in that process. Much of the most visible politics of youth in Japan, as well as of the Japanese left in general, appears to fit many of these descriptive indicators of alienation.[3]

Now it will be noted that these two alternatives to the democratic participant model of political man in Japan are closely linked to some important social and personal differences, in particular urban-rural residence, sex, and generation. Rural residents, women, and the prewar generation tend to be associated in Japanese political stereotypes with the mobilized traditional model; urbanites, men, and the postwar generation are associated with the image of alienated man. These stereotypes reflect also another dimension of assumptions about the sources of political attitudes and behavior, namely, that two general kinds of influences are at work.

The first type includes cultural or rather psychocultural influences, in which, in the case of the mobilized traditional man, traditional Japanese culture allegedly inhibits both his political interest and his general sense of efficacy and ultimately therefore throws a pall on his view of the input aspects of politics, all by creating in him a sense of self-suppression, subordination to the group, and loss of autonomy. The culture is also alleged to discourage sociability beyond the limits of the immediate group and thus to engender distrust in others, which in turn contributes to distrust of the remote and impersonal world of politics as well as skepticism about the possibility of being able to affect decisions taken there. To determine whether such traditional psychocultural factors continue to affect the way in which the political self is formed this chapter takes as one objective comparing the impact on today's teenagers' political interest, efficacy, and trust, of measures of ego-autonomy and social trust, described at the outset of the analysis, with other intervening influences.

Principal among the other intervening influences that will also be investigated are those in the second set of factors related to the models of mobilized and alienated men; these derive from social and ideological cleavage. Urban-rural residence, as we have seen,[4] is a major source of both partisan and ideological differences among Japanese adults and teenagers as well. But to what extent the urban-rural social and cultural gap operates as a direct source of differences among young Japanese with respect to feelings of efficacy, interest, and trust about politics—and to what extent its influence works through the intermediate effects of party and ideology—constitutes another main focus here.

The overall approach of the chapter, therefore, is to examine the relationships between the independent personal and social background variables, the intervening psychocultural and cleavage factors, and the dependent variables—the teenagers' political orientations—with the aim of developing several multivariate models of the sources and structure of those aspects of the emerging political self that are relevant to the democratic participant ideal type of political man. These models will make use of the technique of path analysis, a variety of causal modelling.

Intervening Psychocultural Influences on the Political Self: Ego-Autonomy and Social Trust

An important strain in modern democratic theory has emphasized that for democracy to flourish it requires support in the culture of the society it serves and in the personalities of its citizens. The current conception of a political culture of democracy, composed of patterns of specifically political attitudes and values plus other psychological orientations clearly relevant to such political attitudes and values, is the outgrowth of a long history of theories of how culture and personality affect politics. Chapter 1 presented a synopsis of the numerous criticisms of the logic and the method of such psychocultural studies of national character. But while the flaws of the psychocultural approach must be acknowledged, it is equally important to recognize that the approach does direct our attention to factors that may lie deeper and endure longer than attitudes and that by affecting more specifically political orientations, may be important links in the causal chains leading to adult political behavior.

Ego-autonomy and social trust are two psychocultural characteristics that play leading roles in both theories of democratic personality and theories of the Japanese national psyche. Let us look at each in turn.

The democratic personality, to use Robert Lane's phrase,[5] or the democratic character, to use Harold Lasswell's, is a man in control of himself and confident of his ability to deal with the environment. Lasswell's notion of character strength, a basic component of democratic character enabling the individual to "maintain the self-system despite environing conditions which are adverse,"[6] or, in Greenstein's more direct phrasing, "to withstand environmental pressure adverse to one's values,"[7] is particularly apposite in the context of a study of Japan. The subordination of the individual to the group, the coercive character of consensual decisions, and the use of shaming as a principal technique for inducing conformity are all commonly asserted to be characteristic elements of traditional Japanese culture.[8]

What then of contemporary Japanese? Do they exhibit this alleged cultural characteristic of personal incompetence? In a comparative study of American and Japanese grade school children, an American anthropologist found the Japanese to be "other-directed" and dependent on the group in comparison to the self-directed, autonomous Americans.[9] But a study of conformity among Japanese college students revealed that not only did many of the students make judgments independent of those of the group, but about a third of them even disagreed with the group when the group judgment was correct. Robert Frager, the author of the study, called this assertion of one's opinion against a correct majority opinion "anti-conformity" and argued that since it constituted a reaction against the group it was in effect another variety of group-controlled behavior.[10] Nevertheless, it can also be interpreted as evidence of a self-assertiveness that is hard to square with the characteristics of the weak ego. Similarly, the finding that Japanese blue-collar workers are likelier than American workers to resist an order from a superior that they consider illegitimate does not bespeak a culturally based inability to withstand pressures opposed to the values of the individual in contemporary Japan.[11]

In order to tap this particular psychological dimension, the survey used in the present study included five items relating to the respondent's ability to cope with an adverse environment. Table 6-1 presents these ego-autonomy items with a comparison of the responses to each item of both teenagers and parents. As is evident, there is little generational difference, with more students than parents choosing autonomous response on two of the items, and fewer doing so on the other three. Although our primary interest here is with the effects of ego-autonomy on teenager's political orientations rather than with its causes, it is noteworthy that among the four background factors—age, sex, urban-rural residence, and socioeconomic status—only the latter two show significant, though weak, correlations with the teenagers' scores on a summary scale of ego-autonomy based on their responses to the five items shown. And when, since these two sociological factors are strongly intercorrelated (gamma = .71), the partial correlations between each and ego-autonomy controlling for the effects of the other are computed, the strength of the association with area of residence

Table 6-1

Ego-Autonomy Scale Items with Responses, by Generation

(Percentages of students and parents choosing autonomous and nonautonomous responses)

Survey Items:	Students		Parents	
	Aut.	Nonaut.	Aut.	Nonaut.
A. "When your friends and others belittle a movie or TV program that you liked as 'dull' or 'stupid,' it is best to keep silent and say nothing."	67	14	47	40
B. "Do you often lose confidence when many of your friends and others disagree with you?"	50	50	64	35
C. "When you make plans do they often work out as you planned?"	36	64	57	42
D. "When you have disagreements with others do you often get your own way?"	45	55	40	60
E. "When you have made up your mind about something do you often change your mind if someone tries to argue you out of it?"	60	40	74	25

Note: Neutral responses (don't know) to Item A and nonresponses to all items are omitted from the table. Responses coded autonomous are Item A = "disagree" plus "disagree strongly"; Items B and E = "not very often" plus "hardly ever"; Items C and D = "very often" plus "often."

declines sharply (from gamma = .17 to .10), while that with SES declines only moderately (from gamma = .17 to .13). Thus, if traditionalism is a cause of low ego-autonomy, it would appear that it is a traditionalism that derives more from low social status—probably from the low educational level of the family—than from rural life per se and that the link between rural residence and low autonomy is due in large part to the presence of a high proportion of families with low educational levels among the rural group.

The second of the psychocultural intervening variables in the analysis, social trust, is also one that plays a leading role in conceptions of democratic man. Two of the three components of the self-system of the democratic character in Harold Lasswell's classic model are related to the capacity for trust in other people. Democratic man, Lasswell postulates, is characterized by "deep confidence in the benevolent potentialities of man" and the "maintenance of an open as against a closed ego" in which the individual's attitude toward other human beings is "warm rather than frigid, inclusive and expanding rather than exclusive and constricting...."[12] Almond and Verba likewise accord to the sense of social trust the status of one of the foundations of the democratic political culture.[13]

Few observers have asserted that cynicism or misanthropy is a major element in the Japanese national character. There appears to be little of the corrosive cynicism and the "associational incapacity" claimed to characterize the French or of the "amoral familism" of the southern Italians.[14] It is clear that the Japanese have traditionally been capable of civic cooperation and of forming highly effective and durable groups. Nevertheless, it has been asserted that the group life of the Japanese tends to be dominated by a single, intimate group whose closed boundaries play a significant role in determining the individual's social self. Nakane Chie has argued that the Japanese divide the world into *uchi* (we) and *yoso* (they), one of the consequences of which is a degree of suspicion about others not part of one's group. There is, she has asserted, an implied "moral censure" when a Japanese says that a person is a member of a group other than the speaker's own.[15] A second consequence is that multiple group membership and sociability with those in other groups are inhibited by the nature of group formation with its emphasis on "total emotional participation" and "sense of group oneness."[16] Ezra Vogel has made a similar observation about the prevalence of single-group membership among even urban middle-class individuals.[17]

In the present study, the questionnaire included four items relating to trust in people to see what role, if any, general cynicism plays in the attitude structure of Japanese youth. The items are given in Table 6-2, with responses by generation. On the whole, the teenagers appear somewhat less cynical than their parents, which finding would not be surprising except that, as we saw in Chapter 2, they were substantially more cynical about some aspects of politics than were their parents.

Table 6-2
Social Trust Scale Items and Responses, by Generation
(Percentages of students and parents choosing trusting and cynical responses)

Survey Items:	Students		Parents	
	Trusting	Cynical	Trusting	Cynical
A. "Given the chance, most people will try to take advantage of you."	26	50	44	35
B. "Most people can be trusted."	31	31	28	33
C. "It is necessary to take adequate precautions when dealing with people."	33	35	17	59
D. "Other people can't be depended upon. When you get right down to it, the only one you can rely on is yourself."	41	34	14	62

Note: Neutral responses (don't know) and nonresponses to all items are omitted from the table. Responses coded trusting are Items A, C, and D = "disagree" plus "disagree strongly"; Item B = "agree" plus "agree strongly."

It is striking to note that when the background factors are correlated with the teenagers' scores on a composite social trust scale based on a summary of their responses to the four items, only sex has any appreciable influence (gamma = .19), with boys more trusting than girls (32 percent to 23 percent high in trust, respectively). A similar weak positive relationship between sex and the social trust scale is observed among the adults in my sample as well (gamma = .12). This may be the effect of the widely noted deprivation of the woman in Japanese life, whose traditional role has been to serve men—the father and the eldest son in particular.[18] Nationwide surveys have shown that many more Japanese women would prefer to be men than to be women again if they could be reborn, and that most women believe that men have much more pleasure in life.[19] Many fewer high school girls go on to college, and the future life opportunities of a young woman tend to be much more restricted than those of her male peers. It is no wonder then that women, young and old, tend to be somewhat more cynical than men.

Ego-autonomy and social trust, then, are only weakly related to the social and personal bases of identity among Japanese teenagers. Nevertheless they are important because, as we shall see, each has a direct effect on several of the political orientations of Japanese teenagers and each also specifies the indirect impact of an independent background variable on those political orientations.

**The Dependent Variables: The
Teenagers' Political Self**

Political Efficacy

The norms of democratic ideology not only prescribe that the individual citizen should participate in political life but that his participation should be based on the belief that he is capable of influencing the course of events in politics. This concept, political efficacy or political competence, has been the subject of a large body of research on adult political attitudes and behavior. As Easton and Dennis have pointed out, several important studies of the political attitudes of adults, such as *The Voter Decides* and *The American Voter*, have concluded that political efficacy is an orientation of a deeper and more stable variety than most political attitudes—one approaching the status of a personality component.[20] In their view, this suggests that political efficacy "is likely to begin to form in childhood, when personality development is at its peak."[21] They concluded that their data on American children confirmed this thesis, as they found substantial evidence of the development of political efficacy as an attitude with coherence and structure from as early as third grade.[22] The data from the present study include evidence that is directly comparable to theirs and, as will be shown, tends to corroborate this finding. Table 6-3 presents the political efficacy items

Table 6-3

Political Efficacy Scale Items and Responses by Generation

(Percentages of students and parents choosing efficacious and nonefficacious responses)

Survey Items:	Students		Parents	
	Eff.	Noneff.	Eff.	Noneff.
A. "What ordinary people like my family say has no effect on what the government does."	42	37	29	42
B. "Ordinary people have no opportunity to get their views reflected in politics."	36	49	40	38
C. "What the government does is like the weather; ordinary people can't do anything about it."	45	30	39	33
D. "Things like politics and government are so complicated that people like myself can hardly understand how they work."	38	38	31	33

Note: Neutral responses (don't know) and nonresponses to all items are omitted from the table. Responses coded efficacious for all items are "disagree" plus "disagree strongly."

used in the survey and the overall responses of students and parents to each item.

The students appear to be slightly more efficacious than their parents, but the edge though consistent on three of the four items (all but B) is slight. Both generations appear to be quite evenly split into politically efficacious and inefficacious groups. Since it is often asserted that Japanese traditional political culture relegated ordinary citizens to the role of subjects or supplicants vis-à-vis the powers that be, the nearly equal proportions of efficacious and inefficacious respondents in the older generation as in the younger indicates that the characterization may be less generally applicable than in the past.

Turning to the way in which youngsters differ in this orientation, however, let us begin with the question of the influence of age. Easton and Dennis found, upon performing factor analyses on the responses of children in each grade of their American sample to the political questions in their questionnaire, that the items they used as individual indicators of political efficacy converged to form a separate identifiable attitudinal dimension by as early as third grade and that the factor loadings (correlations of responses to individual items with the factor) remained quite constant from grade to grade.[23] A factor analysis of the responses to the political questions in the present survey of the Japanese eighth graders also produced a distinct political efficacy factor, on which only the four items shown in Table 6-3 loaded at above .50. What is more, the three items (A,B, and C in the table) which were identical (within the limits of colloquial translation equivalence) to those used in the American survey, had factor loadings among the Japanese eighth graders that were also nearly identical to those among the American eighth graders; for Japanese and American young-sters, respectively, the loadings were: Item A = .70 and .71; B = .61 and .71; C = .59 and .59.[a] This striking degree of similarity in the outcomes of the factor analyses performed in the two cultures not only provides strong corroboration that political efficacy emerges as a distinct component of the individual's structure of political attitudes by at least the beginning of adolescence, it also suggests that the concept of political efficacy, although the product of American thought and culture, may be a measurable component of "political personality" that is *culture-free.*

Having established that political efficacy is an identifiable dimension of Japanese youngsters' political attitude structures by eighth grade, let us return to the question of how those youngsters differ among themselves with respect to it. Table 6-4 presents a summary of the correlations of the independent background variables and intervening psychocultural and cleavage variables with a cumulative scale of political efficacy based on the teenagers' responses to the four items in

Table 6-4
Correlates of Teenagers' Political Efficacy
(Gammas)

	Political Efficacy Scale (high efficacy/med/low)
Background Factors:	
Grade (12/10/8)	.07
Sex (boys/girls)	.20
Residence (urban/rural)	.02
Socioeconomic Status (high status/med/low)	.06
Psychocultural Factors:	
Ego-Autonomy Scale (high autonomy/med/low)	.15
Social Trust Scale (high trust/med/low)	.34
Cleavage Factors:	
Party Support (LDP/DSP/Komei/JSP/JCP)	.04
Ideology Scale (pro-cap'st/neut/pro-soc'st)	.03

Note: Parentheses show direction of variables; variables labeled "scales" are trichotomized cumulative indices based on multiple items from the questionnaire.

[a]Item d, which was not used in the American survey, loaded at .64. The factoring procedure employed here was identical in every detail to that used by Easton and Dennis, except for the use of product-moment rather than tetrachoric correlations. After performing a principal components analysis, the components that emerged were put through a varimax orthogonal rotation by taking an eigenvalue of 1.0 as the minimum criterion for rotation.

Table 6-3. Turning first to the impact of age, we see that there is but a slight increase in the efficacy of the older youths. Thirty-eight percent of the tenth graders as opposed to 30 percent of the eighth graders scored high on political efficacy, but there was no further increase among the twelfth graders. Thus, although Easton and Dennis found a substantial and consistent rise with age in efficacy among the American primary school children so that three times as many eighth graders as third graders scored high on the variable,[24] the Japanese data suggest that if the variable does indeed lie at a deeper level of the psyche, its direction may become fairly set by age fifteen or so.

One basis on which American, European, and Japanese adults have all been observed to differ with regard to their belief in their ability to have an impact on politics is sex—almost without exception, women have been found to feel less politically competent than men. However, Easton and Dennis found no difference in the political efficacy of the boys and girls in their sample of American children, but they were loath to accept the finding at face value since girls were markedly lower than boys in such other areas of political involvement as political interest and participation.[25] No such anomaly is present in the case of Japanese teenagers; the boys are appreciably more efficacious, with 42 percent of them versus 29 percent of the girls scoring high and 29 percent of the boys scoring low as opposed to 35 percent of the girls to produce the correlation of .20 shown in the table.

Despite the implied link between rural residence and low efficacy contained in characterizations of traditional Japanese as incapable of dealing with political authority as "citizens" rather than as "subjects," there is little evidence of any correlation between urban-rural residence and political efficacy among adult Japanese. Neither Watanuki Joji[26] nor Bradley Richardson found any such difference, although Richardson found evidence that urban adults were somewhat more efficacious with respect to national politics while rural adults felt more capable of influencing local politics.[27] As the table makes clear, the teenagers in the present study also do not differ in efficacy by place of residence; nor do they differ consistently by family socioeconomic status. While 40 percent of the upper-status but only 31 percent of the lower-status youngsters scored high on efficacy, the proportions scoring low were nearly identical at 31 percent and 32 percent, respectively, which accounts for the weak correlation. This again mirrors findings showing a lack of any socioeconomic status—based differences in efficacy among Japanese adults,[28] but contrasts markedly with Easton and Dennis's data on American youngsters, which showed a moderate and consistent relationship between the two variables (Pearson's *r* ranging from .16 to .22).[29]

Perhaps the most striking finding in Table 6-4 is the degree to which the two psychocultural variables are associated with the teenagers' efficacy. The preadult's belief that ordinary people like his family and himself when he becomes an adult exert some control over politics is clearly affected by his own sense of himself and of the environment. If he feels incapable of dealing with the world immediately around him and of influencing the course of his own life, he is unlikely to feel influential over the more remote, complex, and harder-to-understand realm of politics. Similarly, if the world is peopled with unscrupulous and threatening strangers, then politics, which for the Japanese youngster, as we have seen, is often associated with strangers out for their own interests and nonresponsive to ordinary folk, should be beyond the capability of people like himself or his family to influence. As the table makes plain, each of these two psychocultural variables does have an effect on teenagers' political efficacy. Nearly half again as many of those scoring high on ego-autonomy as those scoring low are politically efficacious (43 percent to 30 percent) but the correlation is fairly weak. In comparison, the effect of social trust is markedly greater, with twice as many of the trusting youngsters being efficacious as those who are cynical (52 percent to 26 percent) and nearly three times as many of the latter as the former (46 percent to 17 percent) scoring in the lowest rank on efficacy. Clearly, then, how ready teenagers are to place their trust in other people has an important bearing on their sense of ability to influence politics.

In contrast to the psychocultural variables, the cleavage factors of partisanship and ideology have no significant general impact on the teenagers' political efficacy. Those teenagers who identify with the progressive parties are no less efficacious than those who identify with the conservatives, nor are those who favor socialism less efficacious than those who prefer capitalism. Thus, the near permanent minority position of the progressive parties in national politics appears not to be a source of feelings of political impotence among youngsters who support them (indeed, the JCP identifiers were the *most* efficacious of any party supporters among the students). Perhaps the growing strength of the progressives on the local level, especially in the big cities, enables the youthful opposition supporters to feel that politics on that level are accessible and capable of being influenced.

In this connection it is significant to note that the Komeito supporters are an exception to the general finding; among all the student party supporters, only they had a larger proportion (40 percent to 29 percent) who were nonefficacious than those who were efficacious. This is intriguing because of widespread belief in Japan that Soka gakkai adherents, who form the overwhelming bulk of the Komeito's supporters, are a variety of mass man, beset with feelings of alienation, distrust, and powerlessness that make them prey to the appeals of an all-encompassing "true religion." And indeed, the Komeito supporters were also significantly more likely than other teenagers to score low on the social trust scale, although not on the ego-autonomy scale.

In general, then, Japanese teenagers' feelings of political efficacy vary little with social and political sources of cleavage (with the exception noted) and tend to be associated more with psychocultural or personality characteristics as well as with sex. Social trust was found to be the strongest correlate of efficacy among the variables in the analysis, followed by sex and ego-autonomy. But political efficacy itself, if we treat it as part of the political personality, should play a role in influencing other aspects of the political man emerging within each of our teenagers. One obvious and important such aspect is that of political interest.

Political Interest

Interest in what happens in politics—a concern with following the course of political events—is a pivotal variable not only in the conception of democratic man, but in stereotypes of the varieties of political men in Japan. The participant democrat's political participation is sparked by his political interest; the alienated mass man's high political interest either never materializes in political action or else is associated with extra-system participation—violence, mass demonstrations, and other sorts of anomie; the mobilized traditional man's participation in the established modes is not due to his own inherent interest in politics, but to social pressures to participate. The measure of political interest employed here is based on the four items given in Table 6-5, which, as usual, shows the responses of both students and parents to each item.

Not surprisingly, the teenagers are lower on each of the individual measures of political interest than their parents. It is noteworthy that newspapers are as frequently the media through which youngsters report following politics as television is, and this roughly equal reliance on these two media is true

Table 6-5
Political Interest Scale Items and Responses by Generation
(Percentages of students and parents choosing high interest and low interest responses)

Survey Items:	Students		Parents	
	High Int.	Low Int.	High Int.	Low Int.
A. "Are you interested in politics?"	51	49	60	39
B. "Do you often read articles about politics in the newspaper?"	60	40	73	27
C. "Do you often watch TV programs or listen to the radio about politics?"	58	42	78	21
D. "Do you often read articles about politics in weekly and monthly magazines?"	35	65	54	45

Note: Nonresponses to all items are omitted from the table. Responses coded high interest are Item A = "very interested" plus "somewhat interested"; Items B and C = "every day" plus "sometimes"; Item D = "often" plus "sometimes."

throughout the teenage years. But, in taking professed interest and the items on following politics in the various media together as a scale of political interest, how do the teenagers differ among themselves? Table 6-6 presents the correlations between each of the independent and intervening variables that we have been examining up to now, plus political efficacy, with the teenagers' scores on a political interest scale based on items given in Table 6-5.

As the table makes clear, a number of factors appear to affect the teenagers' interest in politics. Age, to begin with, has a clearcut and moderately strong impact, with twice as many twelfth graders as eighth graders (44 percent to 21 percent) scoring high on interest, while the proportion of youngsters with low interest drops substantially (to 24 percent from 38 percent). This increase with age in interest in political affairs accords with the expectation that as the maturing teenager becomes increasingly aware of stimuli from beyond his immediate sphere of existence, his interest in what is happening in the wider world, and his consciousness of politics as affecting him, will expand. The comparative evidence, however, is not as clearly supportive of this expectation as the Japanese data is. Hess and Torney's data on American elementary school children, for instance, showed an increase in discussions about political affairs among youngsters in the upper grades as compared to those in the early grades, but a decline in the children's self-reported interest in government and current events.[30]

Table 6-6
Correlates of Teenagers' Political Interest
(Gammas)

	Political Interest Scale (high interest/med/low)
Background Factors:	
Grade (12/10/8)	.25
Sex (boys/girls)	.28
Residence (urban/rural)	.12
Socioeconomic Status (high status/med/low)	.09
Psychocultural Factors:	
Ego-Autonomy Scale (high autonomy/med/low)	.31
Social Trust Scale (high trust/med/low)	.05
Cleavage Factors:	
Party Support (LDP/DSP/Komei/JSP/JCP)	−.21
Ideology Scale (pro-cap'st/neut/pro-soc'st)	−.08
Political Personality Factors:	
Political Efficacy Scale (high efficacy/med/low)	.25

Note: Parentheses show direction of variables; variables labeled "scales" are trichotomized cumulative indices based on multiple items from the questionnaire.

The impact of sex on the Japanese teenagers' political interest is likewise clear and moderately strong: nearly twice as many boys as girls scored high on interest (41 percent to 22 percent), with a somewhat smaller gap in the opposite direction in the proportions falling into the low-interest group (28 percent of the boys versus 37 percent of the girls). This finding is in keeping with the great bulk of the evidence on adults, both in Japan[31] and in the United States,[32] which has shown women to be significantly less politically interested than men. The same pattern has likewise been noted among American children. Greenstein reported that whenever there were differences between the boys and girls in his sample, the boys were "invariably" more political.[33] Hess and Torney also found that the elementary grade school girls in their sample were less likely than the boys to be politically interested and to discuss political issues.[34]

Just as we found in the case of political efficacy, the teenagers' political interest is generally unaffected by the sociological factors of urban-rural residence and family socioeconomic status. Despite the claim of modernization theory that greater interest in political affairs is a concommitant of urbanization, and the stereotype of the traditional rural Japanese as politically apathetic, the rural teenagers in the sample were only slightly (and statistically insignificantly) less likely than their urban fellows to be interested in politics: 29 percent of the rural group versus 34 percent of the urbanites scored high on the interest scale while 36 percent versus 29 percent, respectively, scored low, thereby accounting for the very weak correlation. This absence of a link between political interest and urban-rural residence has also been found to be true among Japanese adults.[35]

Among both Japanese and American adults, those in the upper-status groups—with better education, more income, and in the white-collar, mental labor rather than physical labor occupations—tend to be better informed and more interested in politics.[36] But no differences in political interest based on family status levels were discovered among the American children in the Hess and Torney study,[37] nor, as Table 6-6 indicates, does family status have any significant impact on the political interest of Japanese teenagers. True, more upper-status than lower-status youngsters do score high on interest (35 percent to 26 percent) and fewer score low (30 percent to 35 percent). But the relationship is too weak to be statistically significant. In Japan as in the United States, the political socialization process does not produce fixed class-based boundaries of political consciousness or quiescence. The striking similarity in the levels of intergenerational social mobility in the two societies is matched by their equal potential for intergenerational mobility in levels of political involvement.

While social cleavages do not affect the teenagers' political interest, it is apparent from the table that one of the political cleavage factors, partisanship, does. If the intense interest in politics of the leftist students whose own special kind of political participation has been so visible in postwar Japan and who are clearly one important variety of the alienated mass man can be taken as a guide, we would expect that among the young, left party support (and left ideology) would be associated with political interest. And, indeed, the direction of partisanship does show a general relationship to level of interest; the Communist Party supporters are the most interested (48 percent scoring high), followed by the Socialist (44 percent) and Democratic Socialist (42 percent) teenagers. Bringing up the rear are the Liberal Democrats (29 percent) and the Komeito supporters (26 percent). The low level of interest of the Komeito group is of particular interest since, as we have already seen, they were also the least politically efficacious of any of the party supporters among the teenagers.

Overall, then, the direction of partisanship has a moderate impact on teenagers' political interest, while that of ideology is much weaker and disappears when party support is controlled, which indicates that the weak zero-order correlation that does exist reflects in large part the indirect influence of partisanship.

The strongest correlate of the teenagers' political interest is not one of the aspects of social or political cleavage, however. Rather, it is the internal, psychocultural dimension of ego-autonomy. As Robert Lane has suggested, the individual with a sense of personal control and mastery of the environment is likely to take an active interest in the control processes of his society.[38] And indeed, among our teenagers, those with a high sense of ego-autonomy were markedly more likely than those who felt less personally competent to be interested in politics (44 percent versus 20 percent, respectively, scoring high on the scale, and 22 percent versus 43 percent scoring low). In view of this fairly strong link with political interest and the weaker but still significant link with political efficacy, ego-autonomy appears to play something of a central role as a personality or psychocultural source of an important side of the political man emerging within Japanese youths in adolescence. The absence of any association between social trust and political interest, on the other hand, is rather surprising in view of the major impact trust has on political efficacy.

Finally, we would expect greater political interest among those youngsters who feel that they or their parents can make their voices heard in politics than among those who feel politics is beyond their understanding and influence. This hypothesis seems all the likelier in view of the dual linkage of feelings of personal competence to both political efficacy and political interest. And, as Table 6-6 shows, these two "political personality" components are related to one another. Nearly twice as many politically efficacious youths are highly interested in politics as those who feel politically powerless (42 percent versus 25 percent). The overall relationship, though only moderate in absolute terms, is fairly strong in comparison with the average strength of the relationships among Japanese teenagers' attributes and attitudes.

*Teenagers' Political Efficacy and
Political Interest: A Path Analysis Model*

The preceding discussion has presented the relationships between four personal and social background variables, four intervening psychocultural and political cleavage variables, and two political orientations. As a means of both summarizing the discussion and of establishing how each of these variables fits into the emergence of the political self among Japanese teenagers, they have all been put into a path analysis model of the development of political efficacy and political interest. Path analysis is a variety of causal modeling in which the direct effect of each antecedent variable on a succeeding variable is calculated with the effects of all other antecedent variables affecting the succeeding variable held constant.[b] The particular utility of path analysis in the present case is to reduce the complexity of the many interrelationships among the independent and intervening variables to a set of meaningful links in a causal pattern that explains why some Japanese youths are more politically efficacious or politically interested than others. As will be evident in the model, moreover, path analysis permits us to rank the correlates of the dependent variable by the strength of the direct impact on it of the independent variables and to view both the direct and the indirect paths between causes and effects, which characteristic is especially useful when the objective is to show the developmental relationship between "sociological" characteristics like urban-rural residence or socioeconomic status (or biological ones like sex) and "psychological" characteristics, such as social trust, ego autonomy, and party support in an explanation of political attitudes.[39] Figure 6-1 presents the path analysis.

Examination of the specifics of the model reveals that political efficacy is directly affected by only three factors: sex and the two psychocultural variables, ego-autonomy and social trust. Social trust is the single most influential of these determinants, while sex exerts both a direct effect and an indirect effect through

---

[b]Strictly speaking, path analysis requires one to make five assumptions about his data: that the variables are measurable on an interval scale, that their relationships are linear, additive, and asymmetric, and that the other causes of each of the variables in the model are uncorrelated with the other variables in the model. Social scientists routinely make the first assumption even when using ordinal or nominal level data. The data used here are, of course, mainly ordinal level cumulative indices. In the three models presented in this chapter, the causal sequence of the variables is, in most instances, not problematic, social and biological characteristics earliest in the sequence, "personality" level orientations next, and political orientations last. The ordering of the political orientations is of course arbitrary but, I believe, reasonable, and the absence of relationships between the political cleavage variables on the one hand and the psychocultural variables avoids any problem on that score. The assumption that is probably least well-founded is additivity, since as might be expected in a study of teenagers' developing political orientations, there is a certain amount of interaction, especially on the part of age. But the interaction effects are mild and scattered and do not produce major changes in the main effects. A clear and useful introduction to the social science use of path analysis is Otis Dudley Duncan, "Path Analysis: Sociological Examples," reprinted in Hubert M. Blalock, Jr., *Causal Models in the Social Sciences* (Chicago and New York: Aldine-Atherton, 1971), pp. 115-38.

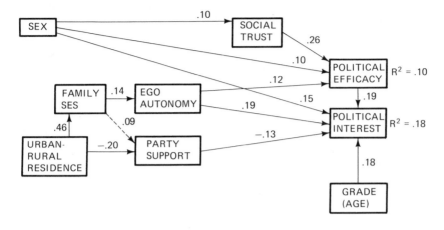

Note: Coefficients shown are path coefficients (standardized partial regression coefficients) between linked variables in the indicated direction of causality with all antecedent variables controlled. The coefficients were calculated on the uncollapsed cumulative indices of the scale variables; sex and urban-rural residence were treated as dichotomous "dummy variables." See Table 6-6 for the direction of each variable.

Figure 6-1. Path Analysis Model of Japanese Teenagers' Political Efficacy and Political Interest.

social trust. The impact of ego-autonomy, though slightly greater than that of the direct effect of sex, is substantially weaker than that of social trust. Taken together, these three factors account for only 10 percent of the variance in Japanese teenagers' feelings of political competence, and it is clear that other influences on this important dimension of teenagers' political orientation will have to be sought out. The examination of family influence in the next chapter probes one such potential source.

Political interest is affected directly by five of the variables; in order of their respective impact, they are: ego autonomy and political efficacy, grade (or age), sex, and the direction of party support. Whereas political efficacy was largely unrelated to the social and political cleavage factors in the analysis, being linked only indirectly through ego-autonomy (which is related to socioeconomic status), political interest is clearly the outcome of both psychocultural *and* cleavage factors, as well as maturational influences. But the impact on interest of the cleavage elements in the model is not great, as will become apparent by comparison with the models of input and especially output support that will be presented later. Most of the influence on political interest involves the psychocultural and personality characteristics of the youngsters. It is noteworthy, nonetheless, that while there are essentially two streams of causal links, one psychocultural and one relating to cleavage, both streams are related to urban-rural place of residence, which is a sociological difference but also, as Watanuki Joji has emphasized, ultimately a cultural one.[40] As we shall see again in the case of political trust, urban-rural differences play a consistent role in the genesis of political differences among Japanese youngsters; but it is in how that influence is mediated—whether directly or through its effect on the personality-related variables, or through its influence on partisanship and ideology—that a major part of the differing causal patterns of individual orientations develops.

The Nature and Sources of
Political Trust: Input and
Output Support

A pervasive sense that politics is corrupt—that politicians are dishonest, that the processes through which decisions are made are under the influence of special interests, that the rules of the game are disregarded or flaunted or "fixed"—are some of the elements of the phenomenon known as political cynicism. On the opposite end of the spectrum is implicit trust in government, deference or even awe toward political leaders, and a spirit of submissiveness and obedience toward the authorities that was said to have characterized the ordinary Japanese before 1945. Somewhere in the gulf between these two extremes, the ideal-typical democratic citizen steers his course. On the one hand, he needs a fundamental belief that democratic political institutions and processes as well as the men who engage in politics are essentially moral and concerned with and responsive to the needs and desires of ordinary citizens. On the other, he must feel able to deal with government not in awe and obedience but with confidence in himself and his rights as a citizen.

Japanese teenagers' attitudes toward the figures and institutions of Japan's democratic regime, we saw in Chapter 2, appear in some instances negative and cynical, while in others, positive and supportive. This led to the conclusion that there appeared to be a general patterning of such attitudes into two clusters depending on whether the figure or institution was involved in the authoritative, "output" side of government or in the "input" side of the political process, through which citizen participation in politics is mediated. One straightforward test of the validity of this interpretation of the prevailing structure of the teenagers' trust in or support for political institutions would be to correlate their attitudes toward the various institutions and ascertain whether two distinct clusters of related attitudes did emerge. Table 6-7 presents the matrix of correlations between summary indices of support for all of the figures, institutions, and processes discussed in this context in Chapter 2.

It is readily apparent that two such attitude clusters do indeed exist. Attitudes toward the prime minister, Diet, and government intercorrelate strongly with each other, but correlate with attitudes toward the other

Table 6-7
Matrix of Institutional Support Scale Correlations
(Goodman and Kruskal's Gammas)

Support for:	P.M.	Diet	Government	Party System	Elections	Popular Participation
Prime Minister	1					
Diet	.70	1				
Government	.73	.74	1			
Party System	.33	.36	.33	1		
Elections	.27	.29	.35	.36	1	
Popular Participation	.04	.09	.06	.63	.57	1

institutions at sharply lower levels. Support for party system, elections, and popular participation also correlate with each other more strongly than with the first three, but the coherence of these attitudes is somewhat lower than that of the other group. It would appear that to a certain extent attitudes toward the political parties are less distinctly separate from output attitudes than are those toward elections and popular participation. This somewhat ambiguous status of the parties in the attitude structure of Japanese youth is understandable, of course, since in some respects the parties, especially the LDP, do play "output" roles as well as input roles. Nevertheless, the strength of the correlation between attitudes toward the parties and party system and those toward popular participation (.63) makes it clear that the former belong, on balance, to the dimension of input support.

The correlations in Table 6-7 provide firm evidence, then, that input and output support exist as separate dimensions of political evaluation for young Japanese. To ascertain how these two kinds of support differ in origin, a summary index of each has been created: output support as used hereafter will refer to the scale created by summing the prime minister support, Diet support, and government support scales; input support will represent a similar summary of scores on party system, election, and popular participation support. These scales do correlate (gamma = .44), but are clearly separate dimensions of political evaluation; less than half (47 percent) of the sample fall into the same ranks on both variables when each is trichotomized.

Given then that these two dimensions of political trust exist among Japanese youngsters, what accounts for the differences among the youngsters on each dimension? Table 6-8 presents a summary of the correlations between the youngsters' input and output support and the various factors—background, psychocultural, cleavage, and political personality—that we have been exploring up to now.

Table 6-8

Correlates of Teenagers' Input and Output Support

(Gammas)

	Input and Output Support Scales (high support/med/low)	
	Input Support	Output Support
Background Factors:		
Grade (12/10/8)	.07	−.36
Sex (boys/girls)	.08	−.08
Residence (urban/rural)	−.22	−.53
Socioeconomic Status (high status/med/low)	−.08	−.19
Psychocultural Factors:		
Ego-Autonomy (high autonomy/med/low)	.02	.00
Social Trust (high trust/med/low)	.21	.25
Cleavage Factors:		
Party Support (LDP/DSP/Komei/JSP/JCP)	.16	.42
Ideology Scale (pro-cap'st/neut/pro-soc'st)	.15	.33
Political Personality Factors:		
Political Efficacy (high efficacy/med/low)	.42	.26
Political Interest (high interest/med/low)	.10	−.13

Note: Parentheses show direction of variables; variables labeled "scales" are trichotomized cumulative indices based on multiple items from the questionnaire.

To begin by eliminating those factors that are unrelated to either dimension of the teenagers' political trust, we note that sex, ego-autonomy, and political interest are all either completely uncorrelated or very weakly correlated with them. Since we noted earlier that these variables are themselves intercorrelated, it would appear that political interest and its sources constitute an aspect of the political self among Japanese adolescents that lies in another sphere from that of political trust.

For those factors that are related to either or both dimensions of political trust, it is instructive to note how the correlates of the two dimensions differ. Let us begin with the background factors. Age in particular shows a dramatically different effect on the two types of support: a very weak positive relationship with input support, and a much more substantial negative relationship with output support. This reflects the finding of Chapter 2 that a persistent decline in support for the prime minister, government, and Diet occurred with age, while the level of support for elections, the party system, and popular politics remained generally constant or slightly increased. In short, then, the political cynicism that emerges during adolescence is mainly directed toward the output institutions rather than toward the input institutions and processes.

The distinction between input and output support is equally salient when we consider the impact of place of residence on teenagers' political trust. The stereotype of the traditional Japanese, whose support for political institutions was based on deference and uncritical acceptance, is often associated with rural culture. That of the politically alienated and cynical mass man is equally closely associated with urban life. Bradley Richardson found on the basis of a large number of surveys that urban adults were consistently less positive than rural adults about the morality and the responsiveness of politicians and political institutions.[41] As we observe in Table 6-8, urban teenagers are more negative than their rural fellows toward both input and output institutions. But the impact of urban-rural residence is substantially greater on output support than on input support. Since the output institutions, particularly the prime minister and the government, have a partisan coloration, this is not surprising, since conservatives predominate among the rural group and opposition party supporters among the urbanites.

Family socioeconomic status also appears to have a moderate association with output support and a much weaker one with input support. Youngsters from upper status families are more cynical about both aspects of politics. This parallels findings by Greenstein, Hess and Torney, and others that lower-status American youngsters are more positive about the president and other aspects of politics than are their more advantaged fellows.[42] But in Japan, the relationship between teenagers' socioeconomic status and their political trust disappears when urban-rural residence is controlled. Among urban youngsters, there is almost no difference in either input or output support by family status, and the same holds true among rural youngsters as well (the partial gammas are .03 for input support and −.04 for output support). Thus, the prevalence of political cynicism among upper-status Japanese teenagers is due not to the inherently alienating effects of higher status but rather to the effects of urban residence, which is the major determinant of social status. The absence of any clear and consistent differences based on educational attainment—a component of social status—in the political cynicism of Japanese adults that is observed in data reported by Richardson is corroborative in this regard.[43]

Of the basic personal and social characteristics of the teenagers, then, only urban-rural residence has a major impact on both input and output support, while age affects only output support. Turning from these predetermined characteristics to the inner man, let us examine the impact on political trust of the psychocultural variable of social trust. Distrust of politics and politicians has been widely linked to personal cynicism, as a particular manifestation of a deep-seated, general distrust of others. Such a relationship between personal cynicism and political cynicism has been documented in a number of studies of American and European adults as well as of American teenagers.[44] Thus, the finding shown in Table 6-8 that Japanese teenagers' general trust in other people affects their political trust comes as no surprise, but does add corroborative data to the accumulating store of evidence that this personality—or psychocultural— characteristic has a significant impact on political man. As shown earlier, trust in people is also related to political efficacy among Japanese teenagers. But the particularly noteworthy fact about the impact of their social trust on political trust is that the relationship is *equally* strong in the case of both input and output support. The other correlates of political trust, both those already discussed and those to be presented below, differ significantly in the strength of their relationships to the two kinds of political support. That social trust correlates with each almost equally indeed does suggest that a portion of political cynicism is an extension of personal cynicism unrelated to the political institution, figure, or process to which it attaches.

The unusual nature of social trust's impact on political support is well illustrated by the markedly different levels of association that the political cleavage factors have with input and output support, as shown in Table 6-8.

It is of course to be expected that support for political institutions will be greater among conservative supporters than among supporters of the opposition parties. And it is also to be expected that the disparity between right and left supporters should be greatest with regard to the output institutions, which, as already pointed out, have continued to be dominated by the Liberal Democratic Party. The input side of politics is much less closely identified with any single party; thus, substantial numbers of teenagers who support the opposition parties are able to feel trust and respect for one major part of the regime even though they reject another part thereof. The percentages by party support of those scoring high on input support (LDP, 44 percent; DSP, 48 percent; Komei, 29 percent; JSP, 34 percent; and JCP, 37 percent) contrast with those scoring high on output support (LDP, 47 percent; DSP, 40 percent; Komei, 15 percent; JSP, 22 percent; and JCP, 14 percent) and drive the point home. Twice as many or more Komeito and JCP supporters, and half again as many JSP supporters are highly supportive of the input institutions as of the output ones.

It is again noteworthy that the Komeito youths are the most cynical of all the party identifiers on both dimensions of support. Although more Komeito supporters score high on input than on output support, in both cases the largest proportion falls into the low support category (46 percent and 53 percent for input and output support, respectively). The only other group of young partisans of whom this is true are the JSP supporters, with 41 and 46 percent low, respectively. The Communist party identifiers, on the other hand, are the clearest case of a group that is overwhelmingly negative toward the authoritative, output side of politics (52 percent low versus 14 percent high), while tending on balance to support the input side (37 percent high to 33 percent low). This moderately high level of input support among the JCP identifiers may be a reflection of the party's extensive activity in the creation of organized "movements" including both partisan and suprapartisan adult "citizens' movements" and a large youth organization (popularly known as *Minsei*, the "Democratic Youth League").

The impact of political cleavage on teenagers' political support is also evident in the relationship between ideology and the two varieties of support. We would anticipate that youngsters favorable to capitalism would tend more than those favorable to socialism to support the output institutions, and this they do (45 percent of the pro-capitalists scoring high on output support versus 20 percent of the pro-socialists). And for reasons enunciated earlier, the smaller gap in support for the input side (40 percent versus 30 percent, respectively, scoring high) is consistent with our expectations and with the data on partisanship and support.

Finally, if as appears to be the case, political efficacy lies deeper in the personality than most other political orientations, it can and probably should be considered as a potential influence on political trust, as it was earlier considered a potential influence on political interest. As the figures in Table 6-8 make clear, political efficacy is indeed related to both kinds of support, but its effect is particularly marked on input support. This makes perfectly good sense, intuitively, since while we would expect whether one feels capable of influencing politics to affect his feelings of how concerned and especially how responsive government is (and vice-versa, of course), we would expect it to be even more important in shaping whether one believes that citizen politics and the whole process of making demands on the system is worthwhile and estimable or useless and suspect. Such is the case, and indeed not only does political efficacy correlate more highly with input support than with output support; it is the only variable that does so, as well as being by far the strongest correlate of input support.

Teenagers' Input and Output
Support: Path Analysis Models

The foregoing discussion has examined the relationship to the two varieties of political support or trust of an extensive number of factors. As in the case of political efficacy and political interest, path analysis models of input and output support will serve to summarize and clarify the multivariate causal influences on these two aspects of political trust. Figures 6-2 and 6-3 present the two models.

Seen adjacent to each other in graphic form, the differences in the patterns associated with each of the two kinds of political support are distinct. Once again, as in the case of the model of political efficacy and political interest, a psychocultural causal stream, now including political efficacy as well as social trust and the antecedents of both, and a social and political cleavage stream comprising urban-rural residence and party support are involved in each case. But there is a striking difference in the relative weight of the causal streams in the two models. The dominant stream in the case of output support is the cleavage stream, reflecting, as we have said, the partisan hue of the output institutions. Urban-rural residence plays a pivotal role in this stream not only by

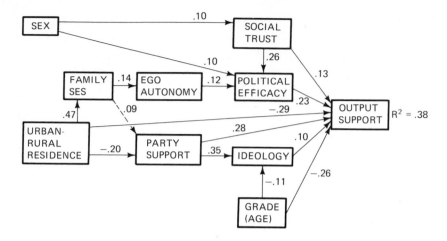

Note: Coefficients shown are path coefficients (standardized partial regression coefficients) between linked variables in the indicated direction of causality with all antecedent variables controlled. The coefficients were calculated on the uncollapsed cumulative indices of the scale variables; sex and urban-rural residence were treated as dichotomous "dummy variables." See Table 6-8 for the direction of each variable.

Figure 6-2. Path Analysis Model of Japanese Teenagers' Output Support.

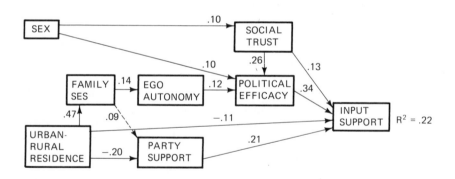

Note: See the note to Figure 6-2.

Figure 6-3. Path Analysis Model of Japanese Teenagers' Input Support.

having the strongest direct impact on output support of any variable but also by exerting substantial indirect influence through partisanship (which itself has the second strongest direct impact) and ideology. The psychocultural stream, in comparison, is relatively less influential, even though political efficacy has a fairly substantial impact. In addition to these two streams, age also has a marked, and negative, effect on output support. All told, the model accounts for nearly two-fifths of the variance in Japanese teenagers' output support, which though far from a complete causal account seems fairly impressive in view of the fact that it is the attitudes of teenagers still in their formative years that are being accounted for.

The balance of causal forces in the case of input support, however, is quite different. Not only does the influence of age disappear, but the dominant causal stream is the psychocultural one. Ideology drops out of the cleavage stream of influences, and both urban-rural residence and party support have less impact than on output support. The main influence affecting Japanese youngsters' support for the process and institutions of popular politics is political efficacy, supported by trust in others, and a sense of personal competence and autonomy. The model accounts for a good deal less of the variance in the teenagers' input support than did the model of output support. But that reflects both the fact that the inner man is less accessible to measurement, and the fact that the psychic dimensions along which individuals differ are far more diverse and idiosyncratic in their effects than are the external, socially related ones, especially among teenagers undergoing the inner battles and ambivalences of adolescence.

In Chapter 2, it was argued that teenagers' tendency to be relatively supportive of the institutions and processes mediating citizen participation in politics builds into the emerging Japanese political culture an avenue of support for democratic politics that counters the predominant stream of cynicism toward authority and government. Here, the evidence is that this input support is also relatively immune, in comparison with output support, to the influence of the cleavages—the two cultures of city and countryside, and especially the gulf between left and right—that divide the Japanese socially and politically. In effect, it can be argued, this provides a sound support for an important element of the democratic regime that both transcends those cleavages and lessens their corrosive effect on political trust when, for the supporters of the left, the government and the authorities are controlled by the opposition.

Conclusion

This chapter began by asking *how* the Japanese teenager acquires his political orientations, and more specifically to what extent each youngster's political self derives from his personal and social characteristics. As the analysis has shown, each of the four basic characteristics is indeed involved in one way or another in molding the emerging political man. It is appropriate now to summarize the overall effects of each of these characteristics.

Sex, that most elemental human difference, is also among the most pervasive sources of difference in the political attitudes and behavior of people everywhere. Among Japanese teenagers, as we have seen, its effects are relatively muted. Its greatest impact comes on political interest, boys being markedly more interested and thus prefiguring one of the major sex role differences in the political lives of adults. A similar but less strong direct effect is true also of feelings of political efficacy, where again boys, like men, are more efficacious. In both cases, the influence of sex is also felt indirectly through the greater tendency of girls toward personal cynicism, which in turn contributes to lowered efficacy and lowered interest. And it is only indirectly through this effect on social trust and on political efficacy that sex has any effect on input or output support.

Age, like sex, affects some political orientations more than others. Its most marked effects are to diminish support for output institutions and to increase political interest. Twelfth graders are notably more interested in politics and notably more cynical about government than the eighth graders. Age affects that cynicism indirectly as well by nudging the teenager to the left, ideologically, as he matures.

The effects of age per se on the other political orientations dealt with here are negligible. But it would understate the role that increasing age plays in molding the teenager's political self if we were to ignore a different kind of age-related effect. In a few instances, age either increases or decreases the impact of one of the other factors on a political orientation. An increase with age in the strength of the relationship between partisanship and output support is a case in point. So is a decrease in that between social trust and output support. But these interaction effects of age with the other variables are relatively few and do not alter the main effects shown in the path analysis.

Of all the background variables, however, that of greatest interest with respect to its effects on adolescent political man in Japan is, of course, the urban-rural dimension. At the outset, it was pointed out that Japanese political stereotypes identify rural residents as "mobilized traditional men" essentially not motivated toward playing the role of the participating democratic citizen; while urbanites are seen as alienated. As the analysis in this chapter has shown, the urban-rural dimension does indeed play a role in the background of Japanese youths' political selves. To begin with, it explains almost all of the effects of socioeconomic status on youngsters' political orientations. But its own direct impact is limited to those spheres that are tinged with political cleavage—party support, ideology, and support for the authoritative institutions. While it does play a role as one source of the other main causal stream identified in this chapter, that of the psychocultural influences, that role is unexpectedly small and indirect. The image of the village as the perpetuating source of the subordination of the individual to the group appears to be of declining validity, if we judge by the fact that the urban-rural dimension has only an indirect effect on ego autonomy. Although ego autonomy itself does have an impact on both of the two orientations most directly tied up with the nature of democratic participation, political efficacy and political interest, in each case its impact is relatively small.

In short, then, despite the greater tendency for rural youngsters to support the conservatives and the output institutions and for urban youngsters to reject both, the overall differences between them across the broader range of political characteristics are too small for us to accept as valid a classification of the emerging Japanese political culture as broadly divided into urban and rural subcultures. And it is most definitely not the case that the pattern of differences accords with the stereotypes of rural apathy and mobilization versus urban alienation and political withdrawal. Politically interested and efficacious youngsters exist in both the countryside and city in proportions that differ only insignificantly, and nearly as many urban as rural youngsters support the input processes and institutions of popular politics.

It would appear, on balance, that maturational and personal factors, including what has been termed "psychocultural" influences are more important sources of difference among Japanese teenagers when it comes to the main indices of the democratic self versus apathy or alienation. It is thus particularly noteworthy that only one readily identifiable group of youngsters clearly and consistently manifested an overall rejection of the major characteristics of democratic man; the supporters of the Komeito scored low on political interest, political efficacy, and on both kinds of political support, and on trust in other people as well. It may be that the elements of both mass alienation and traditional apathy and authoritarianism converge in the culture of the Soka gakkai and Komeito. Happily for most other Japanese youngsters, where one aspect of the political self may be caused by external cleavage or the internalized legacy of past culture to reject the democratic participant model, the other elements of the political self usually embrace it.

Notes

1. See footnotes b and c in Chapter 1 for the sources on which this description of the ideal-typical democrat is based.

2. The best statement of the assumptions and hypotheses from which this model derives may be found in Watanuki Joji, "Social Structure and Political Participation in Japan," Report No. 32 (Iowa City: University of Iowa, Department of Political Science, Laboratory for Political Research, May, 1970), especially pp. 2-3.

3. The literature on alienation is vast but diffuse. An excellent introduction to the subject can be found in Joel D. Aberbach, "Alienation and Political Behavior," *American Political Science Review* 63:1 (March 1969), 86-99. See also Ada W. Finifter, "Dimensions of Political Alienation," *American Political Science Review* 64:2 (June 1970), 389-410. James White, "The Political Implications of Cityward Migration in Japan," unpublished manuscript (University of North Carolina, Department of Political Science, 1971), presents an

excellent review of the literature on the city as a source of alienation. His *The Sokagakkai and Mass Society* (Stanford: Stanford University Press, 1970) also discusses the applicability of theories of mass man and mass society, notably that of William Kornhauser, to an important group of contemporary Japanese adults.

4. See the discussion of these points in Chapters 4 and 5.

5. See Robert E. Lane, *Political Ideology* (New York: The Free Press, 1962), p. 412.

6. Harold D. Lasswell, "Democratic Character," in *The Political Writings of Harold D. Lasswell* (Glencoe, Ill.: Free Press, 1951), p. 503.

7. Fred I. Greenstein, "Personality and Political Socialization: The Theories of Authoritan and Democratic Character," *The Annals of the American Academy of Political and Social Science* 361 (September 1965), p. 95.

8. See among others: Ruth Benedict, *The Chrysanthemum and the Sword* (Boston: Houghton Mifflin, 1946); Geoffrey Gorer, "Themes in Japanese Culture," reprinted in B.S. Silberman, ed., *Japanese Character and Culture* (Tucson: University of Arizona Press, 1962).

9. Mary Ellen Goodman, "Values, Attitudes, and Social Concepts of Japanese and American Children," *American Anthropologist* 59:6 (December 1957), pp. 979-99.

10. Robert E. Frager, "Conformity and Anticonformity in Japan," *Journal of Personality and Social Psychology* 15:3 (1970), pp. 203-10.

11. See Arthur Whitehill and Shin'ichi Takezawa, *The Other Worker* (Honolulu: East-West Center Press, 1965), pp. 184-87.

12. Lasswell, "Democratic Character," pp. 495-502.

13. Gabriel Almond and Sidney Verba, *The Civic Culture* (Princeton, N.J.: Princeton University Press, 1963), p. 287.

14. See, on France: Laurence Wylie, *Village in the Vaucluse* (New York: Harper & Row, 1964), and Sidney Tarrow, Fred I. Greenstein, and Mary F. Williams, "Associational Incapacity in French Children: Some Evidence from a Study of Political Socialization in France and England," unpublished manuscript (Yale University, Department of Political Science, and Wesleyan University, Department of Government, 1971); on Italy: Edward C. Banfield, *The Moral Basis of a Backward Society* (Glencoe, Ill.: Free Press, 1958).

15. Nakane Chie, "Nihonteki Shakai Kozo no Hakken" (The Discovery of a Japanese-style Social Structure), *Chuo Koron* (May 1964), 60 and 64.

16. Ibid., p. 61.

17. Ezra Vogel, *Japan's New Middle Class* (Berkeley and Los Angeles: University of California Press, 1963), p. 118.

18. See Richard K. Beardsley, "Personality Psychology," in John W. Hall and Richard K. Beardsley, eds., *Twelve Doors to Japan* (New York: McGraw-Hill, 1965), pp. 378-79.

19. See Tokei Suri Kenkyujo Kokuminsei Chosa Iinkai, *Dai-ni Nihonjin no*

Kokuminsei (Japanese National Character: Second Study) (Tokyo: Shiseido, 1970), pp. 436-38 and 111-24.

20. David Easton and Jack Dennis, "The Child's Acquisition of Regime Norms: Political Efficacy," *American Political Science Review* 61:1 (March 1967), 33.

21. Ibid.

22. Ibid.

23. Ibid., p. 30, Table 1.

24. Ibid., p. 33. A general increase in political efficacy with age is also reported for British, Italian, and German children and teenagers, as well as Americans, in Jack Dennis, Leon Lindberg, Donald McCrone, Rodney Stiefbold, "Political Socialization to Democratic Orientation in Four Western Systems," *Comparative Political Studies* 1:1 (April 1968), 79.

25. Easton and Dennis, "The Child's Acquisition of Regime Norms," p. 37.

26. Watanuki Joji, "Social Structure and Political Participation in Japan," p. 5, Table 1.

27. See Bradley M. Richardson, "Urbanization and Political Participation: The Case of Japan," *American Political Science Review* 67:2 (June 1973), Table 5, p. 440.

28. Watanuki Joji, "Social Structure and Political Participation in Japan," Table 1, p. 5.

29. Easton and Dennis, "The Child's Acquisition of Regime Norms," p. 36.

30. Robert D. Hess and Judith V. Torney, *The Development of Political Attitudes in Children* (Garden City, N.Y.: Anchor Books, 1968), Figure 14, p. 80, and Figure 15, p. 82.

31. See Watanuki Joji, "Social Structure and Political Participation in Japan," Table 1, p. 5, and Yasumasa Kuroda and Alice K. Kuroda, "Aspects of Community Political Participation in Japan: Influences of Education, Sex, and Political Generation," paper delivered at the American Sociological Association Annual Meeting, San Francisco, August 1967, p. 23.

32. See Robert E. Lane, *Political Life* (New York: The Free Press, 1959), pp. 209-16, for a good summary of sex-related differences in political attitudes and behavior, based mainly on American data.

33. Fred I. Greenstein, *Children in Politics* (New Haven, Conn.: Yale University Press, 1965), p. 115.

34. Hess and Torney, *The Development of Political Attitudes in Children*, pp. 214-216.

35. See Watanuki Joji, "Social Structure and Political Participation in Japan," Table 1, p. 5. See also Bradley M. Richardson, *The Political Culture of Japan* (Berkeley and Los Angeles: University of California Press, 1974), Table 6-5, p. 152. Richardson found that urban adults tended to be more interested in national politics than rural adults who, conversely, were the more interested in local politics.

36. See Lane, *Political Life*, pp. 230-34, and Watanuki Joji, "Social Structure and Political Participation in Japan," Table 1, p. 5.

37. Hess and Torney, *The Development of Political Attitudes in Children*, p. 174. Interestingly, the American children's reports of their own political interest did not differ by family status level but their reports of their *parents'* interest did vary directly with status.

38. Robert E. Lane, *Political Ideology* (New York: The Free Press, 1962), p. 412.

39. See Fred I. Greenstein, *Personality and Politics* (Chicago: Markham, 1969), pp. 36-40. Greenstein points out that it is essential to recognize that sociological and psychological characteristics are often related developmentally as intrinsic parts of a causal sequence affecting some third variable rather than being competing explanations of that variable. The mediation of the effects of the sociological or biological variable by the psychological one is of obvious concern when one is trying to depict the process through which political man emerges in adolescence.

40. See Watanuki Joji, "Patterns of Politics in Contemporary Japan," in S.M. Lipset and S. Rokkan, eds., *Party Systems and Voter Alignment* (New York: The Free Press, 1967), pp. 447-66, especially pp. 456 ff.

41. Richardson, *The Political Culture of Japan*, Table 6-6, p. 158.

42. See Greenstein, *Children in Politics*, pp. 101-02, and Hess and Torney, *The Development of Political Attitudes in Children*, p. 154. But a study of New York teenagers found no relationship between family status and a political cynicism scale. See Sandra J. Kenyon, "The Development of Political Cynicism Among Negro and White Adolescents," paper delivered at the American Political Science Association Annual Meeting, New York, September 1969.

43. Richardson, "Urbanization and Political Participation: The Case of Japan," Table 7, p. 443.

44. See Morris Rosenberg, "Misanthropy and Political Ideology," *American Sociological Review* 33 (December 1956), 650-95; Robert E. Agger, Marshall Z. Goldstein, and Stanley A. Peart, "Political Cynicism: Measurement and Meaning," *Journal of Politics* 23 (August 1969), 495-99; Edgar Litt, "Political Cynicism and Political Futility," *Journal of Politics* 25 (May 1963), 312-22; and Kenyon, "The Development of Political Cynicism."

7

Sources of the Political Self: The Role of the Family

Introduction

Preceding chapters have detailed both the patterns of Japanese teenagers' political orientations and the ways in which social, cultural, and psychological factors affect them. The major remaining question concerns the sources of those orientations. *Where* do Japanese teenagers acquire their attitudes, values, and beliefs about the political world? This chapter deals with the major agents that may influence the political orientations of young Japanese and in particular with the diverse ways in which one principal agent of political socialization, the family, affects the development of political man.

The maturing individual is exposed to a variety of potential socializing agents. These may be face-to-face relationships with people such as the teacher or one-to-one contact with others within a primary group context such as the peer group. Other agents that are more impersonal and formal include the mass media and the school and its social studies curriculum. While we shall deal to some extent with the impact of such agents, particularly the students' personal relationships with teachers and the peer group, the primary focus of the chapter is on the role of the family in the political socialization of the Japanese youngster.

The family occupies a central position in theories about the development of political man and also in well-known interpretations of Japanese society and politics. The old familiar saw that "the hand that rocks the cradle rules the world" reflects a view that has been long and widely held—that is, the family is preeminent among the forces that mold political man. The fundamental nature of family ties does confer on the family a special influence over the values and attitudes the child learns. Moreover, the family's role in the life of the individual is at its height in his early years when he acquires very basic attitudes, values, and identifications, which are apt to become more deeply rooted and enduring than others acquired later, and which therefore are likely to become elements of a political screen through which later learning is likely to be filtered. As the child matures, he will come into contact with other agents: the school, the peer group, mass media, and so forth. From these he will also acquire political values and beliefs; but the foundations of his political self will have been laid within the family, and the later learning will be heavily influenced thereby. Such, in general, are the outlines of a widespread picture of the role of the family in the molding of political man.

155

The role of the Japanese family that is commonly depicted in interpretations of Japanese society and politics, and particularly in psychocultural or "national character" analyses, parallels and extends this view. For many writers the family has been the sole key, sufficient in and of itself, to an understanding of Japanese behavior and institutions. The authoritarian "family state" of the pre-1945 "emperor system" reflected the paternal authoritarianism of the family. Submissiveness to political authority was forthcoming as a result of submissiveness learned in the family toward paternal authority. Even such aspects of politics as the factionalism of the postwar parties have been explained as consequences of the nature of affective relationships between superiors and subordinates first learned in the parent-child context.[1]

This chapter attempts to provide firm evidence on the role played by the Japanese family in the development of political man by considering family influence from several different perspectives. At the outset, the family is dealt with comparatively to assess the degree to which it prevails over other sources of political learning, particularly the school, in the person of the teacher, and the peer group. The view that, as Hyman put it, the family is "foremost among agencies of socialization into politics,"[2] has been challenged by several recent empirical studies of American youngsters. In a study involving a detailed comparison of the political attitudes of pairs of grade school age siblings with matched pairs of unrelated children, Hess and Torney found little evidence for family preeminence. While noting that "in early years the family's role is to promote attachment to country and government,"[3] their overall conclusion was that "the family transmits its own particular values in relatively few areas of political socialization and that, for the most part, the impact of the family is felt as only one of several socializing agents and institutions."[4]

A second challenge to the belief in the family's preeminent role in political socialization came from the results of a study of the political attitudes of American high school seniors and their parents by Jennings and Niemi. After finding that the degree of correspondence between parents' and children's attitudes was, with the exception of party identification, low to moderate at best, Jennings and Niemi concluded that it is "clear that any model of socialization which rests on assumptions of pervasive currents of parent-to-child value transmissions of the type studied here is in serious need of modification."[5] The second section of this chapter, therefore, is devoted to an analysis of the degree to which parents' political orientations are transmitted to Japanese teenagers. We examine parent-child correspondences over a broad spectrum of political orientations that range from partisanship and ideology to output and input support and political interest and efficacy.

In this second section of the chapter, the analysis is shaped around several general hypotheses. One of these is the prediction of a decrease in parent-child correspondence as the age of the child increases. In addition to the effects of age, the discussion also considers the effects of a number of factors that might be expected to lower the congruence in political orientations of parent and child. One central issue revolves around the political role of the mother versus that of the father. Conventional wisdom has long portrayed the father as the dominant political model for the child, both as authority figure and as political opinion leader. But the alleged political dominance of the father has been shown to be illusory in studies of American and Jamaican families.[6] Thus, a major concern of the chapter is with determining which parent is more effective in transmitting political values to the child and in identifying those factors that work to intensify or to blunt paternal and maternal political influence.

In addition to considering the transmission of specific political orientations from parent to child, this chapter also considers the political role of the family in a broader sense—one that centers on the view that the structure of affect and authority in the family serves as the prototype for the political system. The analysis of this variety of family influence takes several emphases. The first is on patterns of contact and affection between parent and child and their political impact. The second emphasis is on the patterns of authority and decisionmaking in the family. Is the family still an authoritarian partiarchy where the father rules by fiat? An opposing view suggested by some writers is that the father has withdrawn from involvement in the family. Which view more accurately represents the prevailing patterns of authority and decision-making in the contemporary family?

An additional question dealt with here is that of the nature and extent of political rebellion against parents on the part of Japanese teenagers. One persistent hypothesis in this regard has been that youngsters from authoritarian families, forced to conform and obey at home, will seek autonomy by rejecting their parents' political views. Such a view is echoed in the recurring interpretations of the radical student movement in Japan as essentially a manifestation of rebellion against the authoritarian family.

The "family writ large" view has witnessed something of a renaissance in studies of political socialization at least in so far as the conception of generalization is concerned. Almond and Verba and others have argued that with particular regard to the feeling of political efficacy, the individual who experiences a family decision structure open to his efforts to exert influence on decisions affecting himself will be more likely, *ceteris paribus*, to believe that he will be able to make his voice heard in the political process as well. This chapter investigates the evidence bearing on this hypothesis.

The final element of the analysis continues the focus on generalization, again in the context of the "family writ large" view of politics, this time by concentrating on the generalization of affect from parent to political authority figure. One major element of the theory of the benevolent leader discussed in Chapter 2 is that the leader gains much of his emotional significance from being invested by the child with the qualities of a parent. The analysis of family influence ends with a consideration of the diverse ways in which Japanese teenagers' images of and reactions to the prime minister parallel their affective responses to their parents.

The Family in the Wider Nexus of Socializing Influences

By the time a child enters his teens, the near monopoly over his social and political learning that the family enjoyed during his youngest years has given way to a situation in which there are various institutions and agencies to which he has been exposed. He is likely to have learned both cognitive and affective orientations about politics at school, from his friends, from the newspapers, from television, and so forth.[a] To what extent do these sources of political learning supplant the family? Table 7-1 presents evidence bearing on the question in the form of teenagers' responses to four items in the survey questionnaire related to the political aspects of their relationships with their parents, their teachers, and their friends.

Table 7-1
Teenagers' Perceptions of Political Aspects of Parents, Teachers, and Friends
(Percentages of students by grade choosing indicated reply)

Survey Items:	Grade	Father	Mother	Teachers	Friends
1. Most respected political opinion	8	36	10	19	16
	10	34	5	22	18
	12	26	2	20	18
2. Discuss politics "often" plus "sometimes"	8	35	24	13	34
	10	39	26	11	41
	12	47	25	10	66
3. Political opinions "very similar" plus "fairly similar"	8	32	30	16	44
	10	27	25	13	47
	12	29	21	7	58
4. Know party identification	8	59	55	37	37
	10	67	67	46	43
	12	79	80	53	55

Note: Items 2, 3, and 4 asked respondents about each agent separately. The percentages shown here include only those students responding as indicated in the item description with regard to each agent and do not include those who chose other responses. Thus the percentages in the case of these items do not total to 100 percent.

[a]A full-scale analysis of the impact of agents outside the family is beyond the scope of the available data. However, the data do include indirect evidence on some important aspects of the role played by these agents in the political socialization process.

The first item asked the students to choose among the four agents (plus "other") in response to the question: "When you don't yet have an opinion about some political or social problem and want to clarify what you think, whose opinion do you most respect and take into account?" It is apparent that while the parents' preeminence declines with age, the father, at least, continues to be the preferred source of advice over both teachers and friends even among the twelfth graders. Not shown in the table, however, is the fact that among the oldest students, the largest group (30 percent) chose the open-ended category of "other," in which the predominant write-in response was "myself."

The small number of youngsters who report respecting their mothers' political opinion most, and the sharp decline of this figure with age, presents our first evidence that early in their teenage years Japanese youngsters discern the political role differences between their parents. The finding parallels Greenstein's finding that American children named their fathers more frequently than their mothers as the person whose advice they would seek in regard to voting.[7]

It is interesting to note that there is little change with age in the proportion of youngsters who look for advice to the extra-family sources of teacher and friends. While there is only scant comparative evidence, from the eighth graders in Greenstein's study, it would appear that the teacher's role as source of advice is not strikingly different; Greenstein found that 11 percent of the eighth graders from higher-status families and 15 percent from the lower-status families would seek the teacher's advice on how to vote, in comparison with the 19 percent of the Japanese eighth graders who most respect the teacher's opinion.[8]

The strong showing of the teacher in this rather hypothetical situation, however, should be contrasted with the substantially smaller number of teenagers who report they actually discuss political and social issues with their teachers as compared to those who discuss such issues with their parents and friends. This may reflect the fact that civic education is supposed to be neutral, and there is thus little room for the teacher to discuss political and social questions individually with students.

The trends in the figures on the youngsters' discussions with the other agents are interesting and revealing. The father contends with friends for the discussion partner most often chosen among the eighth and tenth graders. But by twelfth grade friends are cited substantially more often; indeed, fully two-thirds of the high school seniors report discussing political and social issues with their peers, which signals the emergence of a new crop of political men who now are beginning to relate—politically—primarily with one another rather than to their parents. Strikingly, while there is a rise with age in those reporting discussing politics with their fathers as well as with friends, no such rise occurs vis-à-vis discussions with mothers, which reflects once more the low salience of the mother as a political role model for most children.

The third item changes the focus slightly from the frequency of youngsters' political contact with the various agents to their knowledge of the political opinions of the four agents and their identification with them. Here, the peer group, "friends," stands out from the rest of the agents. Markedly more students report their friends share their opinions than report any of the other agents do. Moreover, this perception of the political similarity of one's friends increases with the student's age, while in the other three cases there takes place a decrease. By twelfth grade, twice as many students feel a sense of political identification with their friends as with their fathers, the agent next most frequently picked as having the same opinions. (It is noteworthy that the perception of political difference from others increases with age in the case of all of the agents, even friends. This parallels the finding noted earlier that there is a marked increase with age in those who say they would rely only on themselves in forming a political opinion.)

The first three items in the table, based on the youngsters' general reactions to the four agents as political role models and opinion leaders, seem to establish a hierarchy in which father and peer group occupied the positions of greatest influence. Teachers were important mainly only in the hypothetical case of a need for political advice but not in actual political contact with the youngsters. And mothers played the least central role, one which decreased severely in significance as the youngster's age increased. The fourth item, however, does not support such a picture of paternal and peer group dominance. There is no significant difference in the proportion of youngsters who can name paternal and maternal partisanship. Those proportions are much higher than in the case of the two extra-family agents. Even when taking into consideration the misperception of parental partisanship discussed in Chapter 4, the fact remains that when asked about an important specific political characteristic, many more of the students felt able to identify their parents' position than were able to do so for the majority of their teachers and especially for the majority of their friends. Moreover, it is equally significant that the increase with age in the proportions of youngsters able to name their parents' partisanship also outpaces that in the proportions naming the partisanship of friends and teachers. Thus, it would appear that the increase with age in teenagers' orientations toward the peer group and away from the family manifested in their responses to the items on political discussions and the sharing of political opinions represents not a diminishment of the actual flow of political communications within the family but rather an increase in extra-family contacts accompanied by a tendency for older youths to give themselves in their own eyes a greater sense of autonomy and independence from the family by overstating their political differences with their parents.

It is also likely that the peer group may come to have a substantial impact on some political attitudes and values but not on others. In particular, as analysis of peer group influence on the political attitudes of American high school seniors has indicated, the peer group may be able to influence "short-term" opinions such as reactions to political candidates and particular issues but be much less able to sway more basic and enduring orientations such as party identification.[9]

The relatively high proportion of teenagers at all grade levels who are unable to name the party preference of most of their teachers is a finding that reinforces the image created by the previous findings of the teacher as being of low political salience to most youngsters. While this no doubt partly reflects the taboos on the overt intrusion of teachers' political opinions into the classroom, the teacher does carry out a number of important activities relevant to political socialization: the teaching of cognitive skills and knowledge regarding politics, the nature of democracy, the meaning of capitalism, socialism, and communism, to name some. But while the specific teaching about such political phenomena may be neutral, discussions with Japanese teachers tended to reinforce the impression that many believe their responsibility involves imbuing Japanese youngsters with a critical awareness of the gap between political ideals and political reality coupled with a critical attitude toward authority. A thorough assessment of the impact of the school—texts, curricula, and teachers—on the political socialization of Japanese teenagers is regrettably beyond the scope of the present study; but it is clear that the school plays a major role in the transmission of cognitive learning about politics in Japan and serves, as well, to instill in many youngsters a focus on the flaws and problems in the political system.

On the whole, then, it would appear that the increase in the transmission of political cues from beyond the boundaries of the family that accompanies and stimulates the rising political interest of Japanese adolescents does not entail a general diminishment of the family's political influence. But it does appear that one aspect of the family's role is affected as the teenager matures: the mother becomes increasingly less salient as a perceived source of political opinions. I say as a "perceived" source because, as Table 7-1 suggests, she may continue to be an important source of political learning, but one whose influence is unrecognized by the teenager, who no longer regards her as a model for his own political opinions and behavior.

Fathers versus Mothers as Political Role Models

We have seen that only one eighth grader in ten and one twelfth grader in fifty names his mother as the person whose political and social opinions he would take most into consideration in determining his own opinion on some question and that 60 percent of teenagers at all grade levels claim not to know their mothers' opinions, while substantially fewer students report discussing politics with their mothers than with their fathers or friends. The reasons for this low salience of the mother in the political consciousness of youth are well known. As pointed out in Chapter 6, women in Japan as elsewhere are much less involved in politics than are men. They tend to participate less, to be less interested, and to have fewer opinions. Politics, in short, at both elite and mass levels, is a man's game.

The mothers of the students in the sample are no exception to the general rule. Only 34 percent of them report that they discuss political and social questions with their friends, as opposed to 71 percent of the fathers who do so. In regard to participation, only 24 percent of the mothers as opposed to 41 percent of the fathers had attended a political speech or assembly in the previous three years. On each of five other measures of political participation, substantially fewer mothers than fathers reported having taken part. The sex differences in parents' reported political interest follow a similar pattern. Four times as many fathers as mothers (45 percent to 12 percent) say they read newspaper articles about politics on a daily basis, and nearly three times as many (34 percent to 13 percent) say that they watch television programs about politics every day. Altogether, over three-fourths of the fathers (76 percent) say that they are interested in politics as against less than half of the mothers (44 percent). This systematic difference in political interest is reflected in a consistently lower level of mothers who express political opinions. In 51 of 58 relevant items in the parent version of the questionnaire, for instance, more mothers than fathers replied "don't know" or did not respond; the mean difference between the percentage of mothers without opinions and fathers without opinions was 7 percent.

That Japanese youngsters early become aware that their mothers and fathers play different political roles is clear in Table 7-2, which presents students'

Table 7-2
Students' Perceptions of Parents' Political Interest
(Percentages of students by grade choosing responses shown)

Students Grade	Very; Somewhat		Not very; Hardly at all	
	Father	Mother	Father	Mother
8	68	46	8	19
10	72	35	8	33
12	71	30	13	43
Parents' Report of own Interest	75	44	24	56

Survey Item:
"Do you think your father and mother are interested in politics?"

perceptions of their parents' political interest. As we see, from as early as eighth grade, far more Japanese youngsters view their fathers as politically interested than view their mothers as such. Strikingly enough, while there is little change in the proportion of youngsters in the higher grades reporting paternal interest in politics, a sharp decline takes place in the number reporting that their mothers are interested. This parallels the same trend that we observed in Table 7-1. It would seem likely, then, that the mother's political influence would be less than the father's and would decline as the teenager matures.

But it would be premature to accept any such hypothesis simply on the basis of children's images of their parents as political role models. In the first place, there is the seeming anomaly that the proportion of youngsters who report knowing their mother's party identification is as high as the number who report knowing their father's and that both proportions increase with the age of the child. Moreover, as we discussed in Chapter 4, the youngsters' own party identifications correlate almost as highly with their mothers' as with their fathers' identifications and the mother-student correlation shows as substantial a rise with the age of the student as does the father-student correlation. This one area of partisanship might of course be one in which the mother is uniquely influential, which possibility shall be explored shortly. But there is also substantial alternative evidence to suggest why the mother might be expected to play at least as large a part in transmitting political orientations to the child as the father. The nature of that evidence lies in the fact that Japanese teenagers have substantially more contact on a daily basis with their mothers than with their fathers. Thus, more students in the survey reported having frequent talks about things in general with their mothers (34 percent) than with their fathers (21 percent). And these reports were corroborated by the parents; 41 percent of the mothers report frequent talks with their children as opposed to only 23 percent of the fathers. The manifest importance of these figures is that they indicate the persistently greater exposure to the mother that most youths have. What is only implicit here, however, is that greater exposure to the mother in general may also very often mean a greater exposure to her political orientations.

We saw earlier that substantially more teenagers reported discussing political and social questions "often" or "sometimes" with their fathers than did so with their mothers. But we have just seen that the reverse was true when the question asked only about discussions in general. This discrepancy is illuminating in the light of a further datum: when the parents were asked how often they discussed politics with their children, *more mothers than fathers (44 percent to 38 percent) responded positively* (i.e., "often" or "sometimes"). In short, then, there are two processes at work during adolescence that appear to bear on the relative potential capacities of the father and mother to transmit their political orientations to the child. On the one hand, teenagers appear to be early and increasingly aware of the apolitical tendencies of their mothers and to ignore or reject them as political role models. But at the same time they are in much more frequent contact with their mothers and with their mothers' ideas and attitudes than with their fathers'. Yet because they see the father as the salient political role model and political opinion leader, they tend to magnify their political interaction with him and to diminish in their own minds the equally frequent or perhaps even more frequent political interactions they actually have with the mother.

Parent-Child Agreement on Political Orientations

Having set the stage with the preceding discussion, it is time to see just how Japanese mothers and fathers compare in their ability to transmit political orientations to their youngsters. The discussion in Chapter 4 established that despite reasons to expect otherwise, Japanese parents were nearly as effective in transmitting partisanship to their children as British and American parents and that the Japanese mother compared very favorably with the father in this regard. What about the broader spectrum of political orientations? How successful are Japanese parents in imbuing their children with the broad range of their political values and beliefs, and does the mother possess widely equivalent influence to that of the father? Table 7-3 presents the correlations between students and

Table 7-3
Parent-Student Agreement on Six Political Orientations
(Gammas by sex of parent, for students by grade and as a whole)

Correlation	Party I.D.	Ideology	Output Support	Input Support	Political Interest	Political Efficacy
With Father: Grade						
8	.32	.17	.19	.18	.21	.16
10	.40	.13	.23	.12	.02	.17
12	.66	.20	.25	.10	.21	.20
Total	.45	.15	.20	.13	.15	.18
With Mother: Grade						
8	.25	.32	.29	.11	.22	.17
10	.40	.23	.40	.29	.04	.04
12	.61	.10	.38	.09	.30	.22
Total	.42	.21	.36	.17	.17	.14

fathers and mothers on six important political orientations for both the students as a whole and by grade. Let us look first at the overall correlations between student-father and student-mother pairs and reserve discussion of the effect of the student's age until later.

As we see, partisanship is the area in which both parents are most effective at passing on their political characteristics to their children. Only the student-mother correlation on output support is at all close to the strength of the associations on partisanship. This accords with the findings of Jennings and Niemi on American high school seniors and those of the Kubota and Ward pilot study of Japanese fifteen to nineteen year olds.[10]

As to the relative influence of the two parents, there appears to be little difference. The father's slight overall advantage in transmitting partisanship is duplicated in the case of political efficacy. But, at least in the case of partisanship, even the slight paternal advantage is negated when, rather than looking at the overall figures, one considers only those cases in which parents disagree on party support. In those instances, slightly more students agree with their mothers' than their fathers' partisanship (25 percent to 22 percent, respectively) as was also found to be the case among American teenagers.[11] Moreover, on four of the orientations in Table 7-3, we observe that the overall mother-student correlations surpass the father-student ones. However, only in the case of output support is there a difference of more than 10 points in the gamma coefficients.

Although the Japanese father is more politicized than the mother and is widely perceived by teenagers as the more salient adult political role model, his actual influence, as measured by the correlations between parents' and students' political orientations, is not generally higher than that of the mother. The American and Jamaican evidence on parent-child political correspondences indicated a clear rejection of the hypothesis of paternal dominance and indeed showed a clear advantage to the mother.[12] The Japanese data confirm the rejection of the paternal dominance hypothesis but also indicate a balance between the influence of the two parents. This finding that neither parent clearly prevails in the transmission of political orientations to the child is supported by Kubota and Ward's study of fifteen- to nineteen-year-old Japanese youths in which they found that in the first wave of their multiwave study the father-student correlations on partisanship were higher than the mother-student ones, while on the second wave the reverse was true.[13] In sum, then, Japanese parents seem to have roughly equal levels of political influence on their children. That influence, however, is far from extensive; it centers mainly, as in the American family, on the creation of students' party identifications.

Under what circumstances is the correspondence in political opinions and values between parents and children likely to be at its highest? Do the circumstances that intensify the correlations between fathers and students operate in the same direction and to the same degree as those between mothers and students? There are a number of plausible hypotheses as to the factors that may stimulate students to absorb the political orientations of their parents, or of one parent. Two factors that seem most likely to make a difference in the effectiveness with which parents transmit their values are the age and the sex of the child.

As we saw earlier, the older the child the more likely he was to be aware of extra-family opinion sources, such as the peer group. It was likewise clear that older youths turned away from their mothers as political role models. Two obvious hypotheses emerge from these trends: first, parent-child correlations on political orientations will decline with the age of the child; second, the decline will be greater in the case of mother-child correlations than father-child correlations. Table 7-3 also presents evidence bearing on both of these hypotheses in the form of the correlations by grade.

Clearly, the first hypothesis is rejected outright. In only three of the twelve cases is there a decline in the size of the correlations from eighth to twelfth grade. And in most (eight) cases, the trend is actually the reverse of that predicted by the hypothesis. Second, controlling for student age does not save the paternal dominance hypothesis. Among the oldest students, father-student correlations are higher than mother-student correlations on three of the orientations, but lower on the other three. Moreover, the influence of the mother appears actually to increase rather than decrease as the student's age increases. The magnitude of the mother-student correlations is higher among the twelfth graders than among the eighth graders in four of the six cases.

If age is the first obvious factor, sex is the second. The hypothesis that suggests itself is that sex role patterning may occur: boys will be more like their fathers and girls more like their mothers. Table 7-4 presents the relevant

Table 7-4

Parent-Student Agreement on Six Political Orientations, by Sex Both of Students and Parents

(Gammas)

Correlation	Party Identification		Output Support		Input Support	
	Boys	Girls	Boys	Girls	Boys	Girls
With Father	.50	.47	.21	.18	.14	.12
With Mother	.41	.51	.33	.39	.13	.22

Correlation	Ideology		Political Interest		Political Efficacy	
	Boys	Girls	Boys	Girls	Boys	Girls
With Father	.06	.27	.15	.18	.15	.19
With Mother	.09	.32	.18	.15	.13	.14

evidence. The data here are intriguing, because of the differences between the parents' "pull" for sons as opposed to daughters. In half the cases (party identification, output support, and input support), boys are more like their fathers than girls are; but in the other three cases, the girls correlate more highly with their fathers. So there seems no systematic sex similarity in the case of father-child pairs. But in the case of the mothers, daughters are more like them than sons are on five of the six orientations, while the mother-daughter correlations tend, in four of the six cases, to be the strongest parent-child correlations. Thus, daughters and sons tend to be equally like their fathers; but daughters tend to be more like their mothers than sons do. These findings generally corroborate those from the study of American teenagers, although American daughters were found to be slightly more similar to their fathers than were the sons.[14]

The urban-rural difference is another obvious factor that might bear on the capacity and effectiveness of parents to transmit their political values. Rural parents might be less effective because they are likelier than urban adults to retain older attitudes and opinions from which younger Japanese have been turning and which other agents like the school and the mass media contradict in their socialization. On the other hand, the urban child is likely to be more fully exposed to a range of extra-family influences that might run counter to parental attitudes and values.

However, a breakdown of the correlations between parents and children by urban-rural residence reveals only slight and inconsistent differences that do not warrant tabular presentation. Neither urban or rural parents are generally more effective at transmitting their political orientations to their children. But it is worth mentioning that the correlations on partisanship were higher among urban children and their parents, especially fathers (gamma = .52 versus .42 for rural father-child pairs). This is due in large measure to the high desertion of children of rural supporters of the Japan Socialist Party from their parents' party to the Liberal Democrat Party, which, of course, is the party that predominates in their communities. Rural JSP fathers lose 41 percent to the Liberal Democrats as compared with only a 24 percent loss to the LDP among urban JSP supporters. The percentage losses among urban LDP families to the JSP are, conversely, only very slightly higher than among rural LDP families (17 percent to 16 percent). This suggests that pressures for conformity to the norms of the community may still be more potent in the village than in the city. However, the difference is substantially smaller in the case of the mother-child correlation on partisanship (only 9 percent greater losses among rural than urban JSP mothers). Moreover, rural parents on the other hand were slightly more effective than urban parents in transmitting several of the other orientations. In general, then, urban-rural residence cannot be said to have a systematic impact on the degree of parent-child congruence in political attitudes.

It seems plausible that the degree to which the child is aware of his parents' political orientations should affect his own orientations and their congruence with those of his parents. Jennings and Niemi found that this hypothesis of greater parent-child political congruence where there is greater political cue-giving in the family was only partially supported in the case of the American teenagers. Taking the frequency of student-parent political conversations and of husband-wife political conversations as two measures of the extent of such cue-giving, they found that only correspondences in parent-child political cynicism were affected by both measures while partisanship was affected by parental conversations but not by parent-child discussions. None of the four other orientations was affected by either measure.[15] Table 7-5 presents the Japanese evidence on the effects of family participation on parent-child political congruences.

Looking first at the effects of father-mother political discussion, we see that there is no general increase in parent-child political congruence produced by increases in the frequency with which the parents discuss politics with each other. Such an effect can be seen only in the case of father-child correlations on ideology. In the cases of partisanship of both father-child and mother-child pairs, the correlations are indeed highest when the parents report discussing politics often, but do not decrease uniformly as the reported frequency of discussions diminishes. Indeed, the father-child relationship correlation is very high (.67) in families where the father reports himself hardly ever discussing politics with his wife.

The effects of parent-child political discussion on the correlations are equally indistinct. In so far as father-child political congruence is concerned, the correlations on partisanship and political interest do show a uniform increase with the frequency of discussions. But none of the other father-child correlations are so affected. Moreover, the mother-child correlations show a rather strange pattern in several instances—partisanship, ideology, and political interest, in particular. The strength of the correlations increases in linear fashion as discussions increase from "hardly ever" to "sometimes," but then decreases in the highest category of frequency of mother-child political discussions. One possible explanation for this may be that the youngster motivated to discuss politics frequently with his mother will also be frequently discussing politics with fathers and friends who, as we saw earlier, are more often perceived as appropriate opinion sources than is the mother. Hence, the drop in the mother-child correlation may be the result of the mother's lesser "pull" on the politically interested youngster in comparison with that of father and friends. In any event, however, the fact that family politicization does not have a general and uniform impact on the degree to which Japanese teenagers absorb their parents' political perspectives is significant because, particularly in view of the corroborating data from the American study, it would seem to disconfirm one widely held assumption about how the family transmits political orientations. In the words of Jennings and Niemi, "students with highly politicized backgrounds do not necessarily resemble their parents more closely than students from apoliticized families."[16]

Table 7-5

Parent-Student Agreement on Six Political Orientations, by Two Measures of Family Politicization

(Gammas)

By Father-Mother Political Discussions:

Correlation	Party I.D.	Ideology	Output Support	Input Support	Political Interest	Political Efficacy
With Father:[a]						
Often	.73	.39	.24	−.23	.02	.14
Sometimes	.42	.24	.10	.18	.07	.18
Not very often	.40	.10	.22	.07	.27	.23
Hardly ever	.67	−.22	.60	.39	.29	.14
With Mother:[b]						
Often	.74	.45	.54	.16	.38	.18
Sometimes	.39	.15	.30	.11	.13	.10
Not very often	.47	.22	.42	.30	.20	.22
Hardly ever	.39	.16	.28	.12	.15	.18

By Student-Parent Political Discussions:

Correlation	Party I.D.	Ideology	Output Support	Input Support	Political Interest	Political Efficacy
With Father:[c]						
Often	.63	.06	.26	.01	.64	.18
Sometimes	.58	.17	.03	.16	.18	.10
Not very often	.40	.20	.37	.14	.01	.16
Hardly ever	.29	.06	.16	.11	−.10	.22
With Mother:[d]						
Often	.33	.32	.21	−.31	.07	−.12
Sometimes	.77	.35	.35	.12	.16	.07
Not very often	.50	.18	.49	.26	.09	.23
Hardly ever	.14	.09	.21	.20	.00	.08

[a]By father's report of father-mother discussions.

[b]By mother's report of father-mother discussions.

[c]By student's report of student-father discussions.

[d]By student's report of student-mother discussions.

We have seen that the degree to which students take on the political characteristics of their parents varies with the nature of the political orientation. But the analysis of potential intervening variables that would explain the circumstances under which parental effectiveness at transmitting political orientations is maximized has been notable mainly for its negative findings. Neither sex, urban-rural residence, nor family politicization had a substantial, uniform effect on the degree of parent-child political congruence. Only the age of the student had a consistent and marked impact. But there is another dimension of family life, not yet discussed, that has often been alleged to play a major role in shaping the political nature of the young individual. That is the character of the patterns of authority and affection in the relations between parents and child.

Affection, Authority, and Family Political Influence

Two stereotypes of the structure of authority and affection predominate in discussions of the Japanese family. The older of the two portrays the Japanese family as essentially a microcosm of arbitrary authority, in which a stern father rules without constraint and in which there is little expression of paternal affection for the child. To some extent such a situation of ultimate and arbitrary paternal authority, it has been argued, persists even in such modern families as those of the urban middle class.

The second and more recent stereotype is one in which Japanese fathers have, in the view of such writers as Robert Lifton, withdrawn into ineffectual noninvolvement in the life of the young Japanese. In this new family, Lifton argues, the mother remains as the primary source of affection for the child. But in consequence of the father's emotional absence from the family, Japanese youths seek strong extra-family identifications and release from anxiety by engaging in mass demonstrations and radical student movements.[17]

To get at the empirical evidence for these stereotypes, the survey included several items on the patterns of authority and affection in the family. Let us look first at the parents' decision roles. The parents were asked: "In your family who usually makes the decisions about family matters?" Both parents were reported as taking part in decisions in two-thirds of the families, with 39 percent of the parents responding that "both parents discuss and decide on everything together," and another 27 percent indicating that "the husband makes some of the decisions while the wife makes others." In 26 percent of the families, the husband was reported as being the sole decision-maker, as opposed to only 7 percent where the wife was so described. In contrast, when asked "In your family, who takes care of raising the children?" only 5 percent of the parents responded "the husband alone" as against 39 percent who named "the wife alone" and 54 percent who replied "both parents." Thus, most families appear to have shared parental participation in decision-making and in child rearing. But in a substantial minority of cases, the father's role appears to be that of an authority who steps in only to make the decisions but who otherwise plays little role in the day-to-day rearing of the children.

One implication of the patterns of parental authority and emotional involvement is that Japanese teenagers are likely to feel more distant from their fathers than from their mothers. The student respondents in the survey were asked two questions in this regard: "Do your father and mother understand you?" and "Do you think your father and mother are concerned about you and take good care of you?" The great majority of the students, ranging from two-thirds to seven-eighths, responded positively (i.e., chose "very well" or "somewhat") about each parent on each question. But somewhat more felt that their mothers understood them very well than felt that their fathers did (by 31 percent to 23 percent), and substantially more that their mothers cared very much about them (by 53 to 35 percent). Thus, the mother is clearly more often perceived as benevolent than is the father, as might be expected, and as has been found to be true of American youngsters' feelings toward their parents as well.[18] Nevertheless, those children who seem fairly close to their fathers and reasonably content with their relationships with them far outnumber those whose negative responses indicate marked estrangement.

Still, since one major part of the alleged political rebellion syndrome is that the child who is estranged from his parents emotionally will be likely to reject them politically, it is important that we examine the evidence at hand. Testing the hypothesis by examining the effects on parent-child correlations on the six political orientations of a scale of the child's closeness to each parent (based on the understanding and caring items just mentioned plus the frequency of general discussions with each parent) revealed that the hypothesis is not supported by the Japanese data. The child's emotional closeness to his parents made no consistent or significant difference in the degree to which he agreed with their political attitudes. Once again, the Japanese evidence corroborates the American finding: Jennings and Niemi found an equal lack of support for the hypothesis in the American case.[19]

Another perspective on the impact of family affection and authority patterns that has enjoyed wide currency stresses the child's feelings about his own influence in the family. The stereotype of the decision process in the traditional Japanese family portrays the child as having to obey his parents', particularly his father's, rules without complaint. The new norms of democracy, however, were meant by their Occupation authors to penetrate even the authoritarian family. Table 7-6 provides the evidence on how far such democratic norms have entered family decision processes in the form of students' and parents' replies to two items asking about children's influence on family decisions affecting them.

As the patterns of responses in both generations make clear, the Japanese family no longer appears to be an authoritarian microcosm. Very few youngsters, especially among the oldest students, feel they have little or no influence on the decisions that affect them; and a majority, which increases to nearly three-fourths among the twelfth graders, believe they can affect decisions already made. In each case, the proportions of parents giving the same replies seem to bear out the students' predominant feeling of efficacy.

Table 7-6
Family Efficacy: Students' and Parents' Replies to Two Items on the Child's Influence in the Family
(Percentages of students by grade, and parents as a whole, giving each response)

Survey Item:

Student version: "When some decision concerning you (such as going on to the next level of school, etc.) is made in your family, how much does your opinion count?"

Parent version: "In your family, how much do you listen to your child's opinions when you are making a decision concerning him?"

Grade	Very much	Somewhat	Not very much	Hardly at all	N.R.	Total
8	21	59	18	1	1	100%
10	46	46	6	2	0	100%
12	51	41	7	1	0	100%
Parents	61	35	3	0	1	100%

Survey Item:

Student version: "When you disagree with some decision made at home, how much effect do you think it would have to complain?"

Parent version: "In your family do you ever change decisions you [the parents] have made concerning your child if he objects to the decision?"

Grade	A lot (often)[a]	Some (sometimes)	Not much (not very often)	Hardly (hardly ever)	N.R.	Total
8	5	47	39	8	1	100%
10	11	54	30	5	0	100%
12	15	59	21	5	0	100%
Parents	11	62	24	2	1	100%

[a]Parents' response categories in parentheses.

Another, more recent variation on this theme, which also must be considered, has a peculiar significance in contemporary Japan. Here the emphasis shifts away from arbitrary parental authority to pervasive parental interference in the child's use of his time. The parent, especially the mother, concerned that her child should succeed in the fierce competition of Japan's "examination hell" nags and pesters the youngster to study hard and keeps a close watch on how much time he spends at play and with his friends. Various writers have blamed the tiresome nagging of the *kyoiku mama* ("education mama") for the numerous social pathologies that afflict Japanese high school and college age youth. The youngsters in the survey were asked about this kind of family interference in two items: "Do you think your parents interfere too much in such things as whom you become friends with and when you go out to play?" and "Do your parents nag too much about studies?" Apparently the assertion of tiresome family interference fits in only a very few cases, as the proportions responding "too much" amounted to only 8 percent in the first item and 7 percent in the second, compared with 26 percent and 24 percent, respectively, who felt "some" interference, and an overwhelming 66 percent and 69 percent who felt "little" or "hardly any at all." And the proportions who did feel some or too much interference or nagging declined in each case with the age of the child.

Thus, in whichever version, the old or the new stereotype, family suppression of teenagers' autonomy does not seem to be prevalent in the families in the present sample. Moreover, in the case of both dimensions of family authority, the proportion of youngsters expressing dissatisfaction decreases as age increases. In short, the Japanese family appears to make it possible for most youngsters by the time they reach the age of high school seniors to feel able to control a large part of their own lives.

Nevertheless, some teenagers clearly do feel freer and more autonomous from family authoritarianism and interventionism than others. How does this affect the relative degree to which each group is likely to adopt its parents' political values? The hypothesis operative here is that the youngster burdened down by a compelling parental authority that yields him no autonomy or influence will react by rebelling against parental values, including those in the political realm. Conversely, the family that does afford the child a sense of self-determination gives him an incentive to accept and identify with its values and beliefs. Table 7-7 offers the relevant evidence here by showing parent-child correlations on the six political attitudes controlling for the student's score on a composite family efficacy scale, based on his responses to the two items shown in Table 7-6, and for his score on a family interference scale, based on his responses to the two items just discussed on parental interference and nagging.

While it is apparent that there is no consistent and uniform effect of family autonomy upon the parent-child congruence, there are several noteworthy instances of a patterning of differences in the predicted direction. Agreement on party identification is the clearest example: father-child agreement increases as the child's autonomy increases on both measures, which is also true of father-child agreement on political interest. Mother-child agreement on partisanship increases with increased family efficacy, but is not affected by changes in the degree of family interference. In spite of the overall negative outcome of this test, as of the test of the impact of most of the other intervening variables, the patterning of the parent-child correlations on partisanship is in the predicted direction.

This outcome raises something of a dilemma for any interpretation of the value of the hypothesis that the authoritarian family produces political rebellion. The dilemma stems from the fact that the major area of the family's direct political influence is indeed affected by family authoritarianism, but other dimensions of political orientation are not. On the whole, it was also congruence on partisanship that was most consistently affected by the variables discussed earlier. Partisanship is a more concrete and visible political characteristic than almost any other. Thus, the parent's partisanship becomes the clearest target toward which the child can express either his ire or his identification. In this sense, then, it would be unwarranted to simply dismiss the political rebellion hypothesis or indeed the family politicization hypothesis. Clearly, both hypotheses have some validity in regard to the most important area of family political

Table 7-7

Parent-Student Agreement on Six Political Orientations, by Two Measures of Family Interference with Student's Autonomy

(Gammas)

By Student's Sense of Family Efficacy:

Correlation	Party I.D.	Ideology	Output Support	Input Support	Political Interest	Political Efficacy
With Father:						
High	.52	.11	.07	−.03	.25	.18
Medium	.52	.13	.37	.21	.15	.12
Low	.38	.21	.12	.20	.05	.22
With Mother:						
High	.59	.00	.27	.18	.03	.21
Medium	.46	.30	.51	.14	.22	.12
Low	.27	.31	.23	.18	.24	.09

By Student's Feeling of Family Interference:

Correlation	Party I.D.	Ideology	Output Support	Input Support	Political Interest	Political Efficacy
With Father:						
Low	.62	.10	.24	.15	.21	.17
Medium	.46	.16	.20	.13	.14	.20
High	.42	.17	.15	.12	.14	.13
With Mother:						
Low	.51	.03	.39	.11	.09	.02
Medium	.39	.18	.33	.18	.17	.20
High	.49	.45	.37	.18	.23	.11

influence. But the vagaries of the process whereby teenagers adopt or reject other political characteristics of the family mean not only that the family's influence as the source of specific political orientations is limited, although admittedly to a basic sphere, but that the factors that may maximize or minimize the success with which the family transmits its political values are likewise operative almost exclusively within that sphere.

"The Family Writ Large": Generalization from the Family to the Polity

Aside from possibly affecting the strength of parent-child political congruence, family authority patterns have an additional potential effect on the political development of the child. The psychoculturalists often drew heavily on family authoritarianism as the explanation, by analogy, of political authoritarianism. While rejecting this "family writ large view" in any simple form, students of political culture, notably Gabriel Almond, have argued that the individual's experiences with authority in the familiar institutions and setting of personal life may serve as the source of one's expectations of political authority, particularly if the personal experiences tend in the same direction. If the individual finds himself able to exert an impact on the making of decisions in the family, the classroom, and the job, he is likely to expect to be able to influence decisions in the political process as well.[20]

The evidence from the present survey permits us to test one important part of this particular hypothesis, namely, that feelings of efficacy in the family decision process will be reflected in feelings of efficacy about politics. Cross-tabulating the students' scores on the family efficacy scale with their scores on the political efficacy scale, however, produces a very weak correlation (gamma = .10). Clearly, there is very little relationship between the two feelings. Whatever the factors affecting the teenager's belief that he can exert influence on the political system, his experience in influencing family decisions is not prominent among them. The finding of Almond and Verba that experiences in later decision systems, such as the job and the school, tended to override those in the family suggests that age might be an intervening factor here, with younger children being likelier than older ones to generalize from the family. But there is only a slight drop in the size of the correlation, from .09 among the eighth graders to .05 among the twelfth graders.

The concept of generalization is not confined to such projection of feelings of family efficacy into the political realm, however. Among the most important and best known specific hypotheses based on the notion of generalization is that in which the political authority figure becomes a "parent writ large." The discovery of the "benevolent leader" syndrome in young American children's views of the president led some early researchers to suggest that children tended to project their images of primary authority figures, especially the father, onto secondary authority figures beyond their direct experience, among whom the president was the most visible and most significant.[21] The notion of the leader as "parent writ large" is of course particularly resonant with the traditional (i.e., prewar and wartime) imagery of the emperor's role in the Japanese nation. How apt is it now that the emperor has been displaced from the center of national political salience by the prime minister? The highly negative character of Japanese youngsters' imagery about the prime minister makes the question of whether those images are generalized from children's images of their parents especially intriguing.

The questionnaire included items asking the teenagers about similar aspects of both their parents and the prime minister. In particular, they were asked whether they thought the prime minister cared about the problems of ordinary Japanese and tried to help them; they were also asked, as mentioned earlier in this chapter, whether their parents understood them and cared for them. Table

7-8 presents the correlations between the teenagers' responses to these two parental concern items and the prime minister concern item, broken down by age to permit us also to test the likely corrolary that the younger the child the more probable generalization from parent to political authority is. Indeed, the corrolary is of more direct interest, since the hypothesis itself originated in studies of younger children and its applicability to high school age teens may be questionable.

The results are notable not for the strength of the overall correlations, but for the clearcut way in which the gammas diminish with the student's age. Clearly, generalization does occur among the eighth graders, and just as clearly it disappears as a basis for evaluation of the prime minister among the high school seniors. By seventeen or eighteen years of age, teenagers have on the whole become sufficiently interested in politics to be able to hold more information-ally (and/or ideologically) based political views and to absorb the overt and manifest transmission of evaluations of political figures from a variety of sources. But a significant proportion of the younger children apparently base their views of the prime minister's concern or benevolence on their feelings toward their parents.

That the Japanese data does provide evidence that supports the generalization hypothesis, even if only weakly, is significant in view of the sparse confirmatory evidence found in other studies. What corroborative evidence there has been has tended to be weak indeed,[22] and there is even evidence that no such generalization takes place. Jaros and his associates, for example, reported that in a study of rural children from Kentucky, a comparison of the children's feelings about parents and the president on three similar measures revealed "no evidence at all to support the hypothesis that evaluations of family authority figures are directly projected onto remote political ones."[23]

While direct projection of parental image onto the political figure is one version of the generalization hypothesis, there is an alternative hypothesis

Table 7-8

Correlations of Students' Image of Prime Minister's Concern for the Ordinary People with Two Measures of Parental Concern for the Child

(Gammas)

Prime Minister's Concern	Father's Concern for the Child	Mother's Concern for the Child	Father's Understanding	Mother's Understanding
Grade:				
8	.15	.22	.20	.33
10	.08	.11	.18	.21
12	.08	.09	.09	.04
Total	.09	.13	.16	.19

linking children's feelings toward their parents with their feelings toward the political figure. It is a view that portrays the child's endowment of the political authority figure with benevolence as a reaction formation, in which the child seeks a positive authority figure either to compensate for specific negative experiences with parental authority or in reaction to his general feeling of vulnerability in the face of authority. Such a mechanism, it has been argued, is particularly apt to be the case among Japanese. Doi, for example, states that "...the Japanese are always prepared to identify themselves with, or introject an outside force, to the exclusion of other ways of coping with it."[24]

A full explanation of the degree to which these two hypotheses fit Japanese children is beyond the scope of the present analysis. But inspection of the cross-tabulations of the two measures of parental concern with that of prime minister's concern suggests that direct projection is a more common pattern than that of reaction formation.[b] In most cases, the principal factor producing the correlation was the high proportion of youngsters who felt their parents didn't care or didn't understand and who also believed that the prime minister didn't care. Among the youngest teenagers in the sample, those who were positive about their parents also tended to be positive about the prime minister. But this positive-positive link tended to disappear among the older youths. In nearly every instance, however, those who felt negative toward their parents and positive toward the prime minister constituted the smallest proportion in the table. The reaction formation hypothesis thus finds little support. In short, the principal way in which Japanese teenagers link parents' images with images of the prime minister appears to be by converting negative feelings toward parents into negative feelings toward the leader.

Conclusion

The magnitude and the pace of the changes that have taken place in Japanese society since the end of the war have led many observers to conclude that the family's role in shaping and molding the values of youth would inevitably become attenuated and atrophied. In this chapter, we have seen that while it is true that the Japanese family is far from having a monopoly of influence over the political development of the teenager, it nevertheless continues to have an appreciable effect on the politics of youth in a variety of ways.

[b]This accords with an interesting interpretation of the role played by the teacher in Japan in the tendency of some teenagers to political alienation, proposed by Christie Kiefer. Kiefer argues that the teacher is seen as a "motherly father" who fills the role of an affectionate male authority figure left empty by the distance of the father from the child in Japanese society. Those teenagers who continue to have hostile feelings toward authority project "bad father" images onto political leaders and other secondary authority figures. See Kiefer, "The Psychological Interdependence of Family, School, and Bureaucracy in Japan," *American Anthropologist* 72:1 (February 1970), p. 73.

In the first part of the analysis, the focus was on the family's political role in the wider nexus of socializing influences, especially the school and the peer group. It was evident that for the most part, a great increase takes place during adolescence in the *salience* of one major extra-family source of political orientations and interaction, the peer group, but not in another, the teacher. At the same time, the family's role does not suffer a general decline, as the father continues to be a salient opinion source.

But Japanese youngsters early become aware of the political role differences between their parents, and particularly of the low level of political involvement of their mothers. The mother's perceived salience, already low among even the eighth graders, declines to nearly nothing among the oldest youngsters. This does not, however, reflect a decline in her actual influence on the child's political attitudes. The evidence on parent-child correlations over a broad range of political orientations showed not only that the mother's orientations were as likely or more likely than the father's to be absorbed by the teenager, but that as in the case of the father-child political agreement, the strength of maternal influence actually increases with the age of the child, especially in the case of the family's most important contribution to the developing political man, party identification. The commonplace image of adolescence as a time in which a political gap develops and widens between parent and child is contrary to fact. The evidence shows that parents and child—and even, most unexpectedly, mother and child—grow *closer* politically.

The seeming anomaly between the teenager's low and still decreasing orientation toward the mother and her apparent equality of influence with the father on the child's political orientations (which increases just as the child supposedly is turning away from her) is due, it was argued, to two closely related factors. Children spend more time with their mothers than their fathers, and thus are more often exposed to their mothers' political values and beliefs. Moreover, they very often fail to realize how frequently they discuss political and social questions with her. She is a constant but unrecognized influence on their developing political attitudes and values.

The analysis of the family as the source of specific political attitudes and values thus established three major conclusions: first, that that influence tended to concentrate on the sense of partisanship, as it does in American families. Second, that such family influence was as much *maternal* as it was paternal in origin; and third, that such influence tended on the whole to increase with the age of the child. What the analysis did not show was that the child's sex, his closeness to his parents, or the urban-rural residency dichotomy made any consistent difference in the degree to which the child adopted his parents' political outlook.

The final section of the analysis turned from the family as a source of specific political attitudes to the family as prototype for the polity. We saw that the stereotypical authoritarian patriarchy no longer prevails in contemporary families and that indeed in the majority of families both parents and children themselves report that the child has a voice in, and influence over, family decisions affecting him. But the teenagers gave no evidence supporting the "family writ large" extension of feelings of efficacy at home onto feelings of efficacy in politics; nor, on the whole, did the data show consistent support for the hypothesis that adolescent political rebellion against the political views of the parents occurs as a result of resentment against an authoritarian family. But if the latter effect was inconsistent, its appearance in the case of the congruence between parents' party support and that of the child was significant, because of the weighty role of partisanship in the family's legacy to the child. The data do appear to confirm that the authoritarian family creates a political rebel, in the sense of a child with a party allegiance at odds with that of the parents.

The final section of the analysis in this chapter provided another significant piece of evidence on the indirect political role of the family, because contrary to expectations we found that a substantial number of the youngest respondents in the sample did invest the prime minister with the same characteristics as those of their parents. If the overall tenor of the evidence was contrary to the theory of the political system as the "family writ large," the finding of correspondences between the eighth grader's images of the benevolence of their parents and of the prime minister suggested that one element of the theory, that of the political authority figure as "parent writ large," does indeed describe a major component of the influence of the family in the early political life of the child.

Finally, however, the most important conclusion to be drawn from the analysis of family influence must involve the transmission of partisanship. While we have laid little emphasis on the acquisition of cognitive learning about politics, it seems clear that the school bears the brunt of much of the transmission of this, and it is seconded by the mass media. The peer group becomes an increasingly salient source from which the Japanese youngster may acquire opinions and attitudes. But as we have seen, it does not appear to be a major factor in the creation of partisanship. That role belongs to the parents, in Japan as in the United States, which is a fact of no small significance. In serving as the source of the young Japanese' partisanship, his parents not only provide him as an individual with an orientation that becomes a basic filter through which he views politics and evaluates issues, but also provides the democratic regime with a psychological foundation for one of its most important elements— the party system—and thus also one basis for political stability.

Notes

1. Frank Langdon, *Politics in Japan* (Boston: Little, Brown, 1967), p. 207.
2. Herbert Hyman, *Political Socialization* (Glencoe, Ill.: Free Press, 1959), p. 69.

3. Robert D. Hess and Judith V. Torney, *The Development of Basic Attitudes and Values Toward Government and Citizenship during the Elementary School Years*, Part 1, Office of Education Cooperative Research, Project No. 1078 (Chicago: University of Chicago Press, 1965), p. 191.

4. Ibid., p. 193.

5. M. Kent Jennings and Richard G. Niemi, "The Transmission of Political Values from Parent to Child," *American Political Science Review* 62:1 (March 1968), 183.

6. See ibid., and Kenneth Langton, *Political Socialization* (New York: Oxford University Press, 1969), especially pp. 52-83.

7. Fred I. Greenstein, *Children and Politics* (New Haven, Conn.: Yale University Press, 1965), p. 119.

8. Ibid.

9. Susanne K. Sebert, "Friend and Peer Influences on the Politics of the High School Senior," paper delivered at the American Political Science Association Annual Meeting, New York, September 1969.

10. See Jennings and Niemi, "The Transmission of Political Values," and Akira Kubota and Robert Ward, "Family Influences and Political Socialization in Japan," *Comparative Political Studies* 3:2 (July 1970), p. 152.

11. Langton, *Political Socialization*, p. 65.

12. Ibid.

13. Kubota and Ward, "Family Influences and Political Socialization in Japan," Table 4, p. 160.

14. Jennings and Niemi, "Transmission of Political Values," p. 180.

15. Ibid., p. 182.

16. Ibid.

17. Robert J. Lifton, "Youth and History: Individual Change in Postwar Japan," in Erik H. Erikson, ed., *The Challenge of Youth* (Garden City, N.Y.: Anchor Books, 1965), p. 268.

18. Langton, *Political Socialization*, p. 68.

19. Jennings and Niemi, "The Transmission of Political Values," p. 181.

20. Gabriel A. Almond and Sidney Verba, *The Civic Culture* (Princeton, N.J.: Princeton University Press, 1963), especially pp. 326 ff.

21. David Easton and Robert Hess, "The Child's Political World," *Midwest Journal of Political Science* 6:3 (August 1962), p. 242.

22. See, for instance, the correlations between indices of American children's affect toward their fathers and toward the president reported by David Easton and Jack Dennis in *Children in the Political System* (New York: McGraw-Hill, 1969), p. 366.

23. Dean Jaros, Herbert Hirsch, and Frederick J. Fleron, Jr., "The Malevolent Leader: Political Socialization in an American Subculture," *American Political Science Review* 62:2 (June 1968), 573.

24. Doi Takeo, "Amae: A Key Concept for Understanding Japanese Personal-

ity Structure," in Robert J. Smith and Richard K. Beardsley, eds., *Japanese Culture: Its Development and Characteristics* (Chicago: University of Chicago Press, 1962), p. 137.

8 Summary and Conclusions

Reflecting on the occurrence in rapid succession of the imposition of martial law in South Korea, Thailand, and the Philippines during the previous year, a writer in Japan's best-known daily newspaper column "Tensei Jingo" of the *Asahi Shinbun* was moved to remark:

Taking a look around us, we can't help feeling that Japan today may be a rarity in Asia. For whatever reason, she is stable, and we are free to assemble and free to speak. . . . Throughout the long-tension-filled period of the postwar period, Japan has come through without ever once having to resort to martial law or to calling out the troops. This makes us part of a rare group of nations, not just in Asia, but even in comparison with Western Europe.[1]

What explains Japan's rare success in the contemporary world at establishing and maintaining a viable new democratic regime? This central question has been the impetus and guide to this study, and the approach taken here to deal with it has been an investigation of the formation of democratic roots in the Japanese political culture since these constitute resources on which the regime can draw for support.

In the preceding analysis we attempted to assay to what extent the political socialization process operates in contemporary Japan to create such resources. Now it is time to draw together the results of the analysis and to consider the implications of the findings, both for the continued vitality of democratic politics in Japan and for the role of the political socialization process in a new democracy.

The Findings

Sources of Diffuse Support: Personal, Institutional, and Ideological Legitimation

1. Japanese youngsters have no "benevolent leader." The first major finding to emerge from the early studies of political socialization in the United States was that the president plays the role of "benevolent leader" in the eyes of American children. The initial section of this study addressed itself to the question of whether a "benevolent leader" exists in today's Japan who, like the American president or British queen, would serve as the agent through which Japanese children are bound to their country's political regime. The data revealed that the emperor, once a "benevolent leader" *par excellence*, has become for most children a figure of little salience and little emotional appeal, a "peripheral monarch." As striking as the emperor's decline in the hierarchy of expressive symbols in the political culture of Japanese youth is, however, the prime minister's place in that culture is equally noteworthy. We saw that Japanese children from the early years of elementary school not only do not have an image of the prime minister as an omniscient and omnipotent "benevolent leader," but indeed tend to have a negative image of him as unlikeable and untrustworthy. The incidence of such negative feelings among children rises so sharply with age that by as early as age thirteen more Japanese children were found to have negative feelings toward the prime minister than did their parents, which is a dramatic reversal of the American findings. The available comparative evidence from England and other European countries likewise made it apparent that markedly fewer Japanese youngsters than youngsters in other lands feel positive toward their national leader.

But the dislike and mistrust of the prime minister does not, we found, betoken a wholesale rejection by Japanese youngsters of political authority figures. Comparison of the prime minister's image with that of the local leader—for example, a mayor or governor like Tokyo's Minobe Ryokichi—makes it clear that Japanese teenagers show a persistent positive reaction to the local leader. This difference can be attributed to several factors, particularly the nonpartisan nature of local politics that absolves the local leader of the stigma of being a "politician" at the same time as it enhances the importance of personality as a factor in his leadership and as a factor that contenders for the role of local leader use in their appeal to the electorate.

2. Japanese youngsters' "diffuse support" for political institutions is selective and directed heavily toward the input institutions and processes of democratic politics. The analysis showed that Japanese youngsters' cynicism toward the prime minister does not constitute part of an undifferentiated cynicism toward the institutional structure of the regime, but rather a limited negativism directed against the authoritative output institutions of government. If the "missing leader" was the most important negative finding of the second chapter, the relatively widespread supportive feelings of Japanese teenagers with regard to elections, parties, and popular participation in politics was the most important positive finding. Such support for the institutions and processes through which the citizenry take part in the democratic process reflects, we concluded, the existence in the political culture of Japanese youth of an important basis of institutional legitimation for the democratic regime, one particularly appropriate in a society that has rejected an authoritarian *ancien regime* founded on the personal legitimation of a sanctified monarch.

One theme running through the study has been that of the question of generational continuity or change in political culture. The finding that Japanese youngsters tend to be more negative than their parents toward the authoritative output institutions of politics is matched in significance by the fact that they also tend to be more positive than their parents toward the participatory input institutions. Accordingly, this constitutes a major redirection of Japanese political culture, away from one in which the prevailing pattern was for the individual to relate to politics mainly or exclusively as a subject, oriented primarily toward the authorities, to a pattern in which the individual perceives politics as a process in which he has a stake and a voice, and a right to have that voice heard.

3. A synthesis of the symbols of democracy and peace has become the core of consensus in the emerging political culture as well as a defining element of Japan's national identity in the eyes of Japanese youth. Chapter 3 turned from the potential personal and institutional bases for regime legitimation to the role democracy itself might play as concept, value, and symbol—as the vehicle of its own legitimation. After establishing the prevalence of a Lincolnian popular sovereignty interpretation of the meaning of the concept, the analysis showed that democracy has become a strongly positive symbol among the overwhelming majority of both Japanese youngsters and adults. But the analysis also found that the traditional Japanese preference for decision by consensus rather than by majority rule continues to predominate even among the young. The rules of the game in the adaptation of democracy preferred by Japanese youth emphasize achieving decisions that are fair to all and do not ignore or override the dissent of the minority. In this new amalgam of democracy and consensus, the traditional emphasis on harmony has been retained, but the intolerance of dissent that the principle of consensus used to entail is no longer legitimate.

Perhaps the most unusual finding on democracy's role in the political culture of the young is that it is closely linked to the value and symbol of peace. One influential element in many Japanese youngsters' conception of democracy is an emphasis on the right of the people to live in peace. The analysis showed that peace stands at the pinnacle of the hierarchy of social values among young Japanese and surpasses even democracy. And the evidence suggests that many Japanese youngsters seem to find Japan's national identity in her unique role of a democracy constitutionally committed to peace. This synthesis of the two symbols appears to serve as a major source of ideological legitimation of the contemporary regime for Japanese youth.

Symbols of Dissensus: Partisanship and Ideology

In Chapters 4 and 5, the focus of inquiry shifted from symbols of consensus and legitimacy to symbols of dissensus and cleavage.

4. The Japanese party system has established extensive roots in the political culture of Japanese youth as well as in the adult culture. One of the major ways in which the individual citizen in a democracy relates to the political process is through his identification with a political party. Party affiliation serves not only as a guide and a mediator to much of the individual's political activity but also as a filter through which the complexities of politics can be screened and political issues interpreted. From the point of view of the stability of the political system, moreover, widespread durable affiliations to the existing parties among the electorate are a means to insure against the kind of recurrent swings in political loyalties and the consequent turmoil that pervaded pre-de Gaulle France. It seems clear that the socialization process in contemporary Japan, like that in Britain and in the United States and unlike that in France, is creating substantial numbers of Japanese youngsters allegiant to one or another of the five parties. Japanese youngsters appear to form party identifications in proportions only slightly less than American youngsters and from an equally early age. Moreover, they acquire their partisanship as their main political legacy from the family; they share their parents' partisanship to a degree that approaches that to which American youngsters do. Thus, despite the recency of the Japanese party system, it appears to have developed a set of allegiances among Japanese that reach from one generation to the next and in so doing provide a basic element both of generational continuity in the political culture and of support and stability for the democratic regime.

One additional significant aspect of the findings on partisanship among Japanese teenagers is that the social factors that influence party affiliation continue to be dominated by the urban-rural dichotomy that has figured in so many analyses of the social bases of Japanese politics. Despite the class conflict rhetoric of the opposition in Japan, the impact of socioeconomic status and class continues to be less significant than that of the "cultural" differences of city versus countryside.

5. The high density of ideological stimuli in Japanese politics (compared to the United States) means that ideologically based symbols and labels play a significant role in the political learning process, one which is reinforced by the nature of partisan cleavage. Like most other industrial nations and many of the developing countries, but unlike the United States, Japan is a nation whose principal political cleavage is based on an ideological split: a classic conflict between a conservative, capitalist establishment and a Marxian, socialist opposition. Much of the political rhetoric is thus infused with the terminology and conceptual framework of Marxism. The evidence showed, to begin with, that this permeation of politics by ideological symbols and rhetoric makes an impact on the way in which Japanese youngsters perceive their society. For a substantial majority of the older teenagers, capitalism takes precedence over democracy as the principal defining characteristic of Japan. The basic characteristics of capitalism and of its opposite, socialism, are understood by most youngsters by about age fifteen. But neither term or symbol has the positive appeal to young Japanese of the symbols of democracy and peace; and although attitudes toward capitalism tend to be more negative than those toward socialism, the difference is generally slight, with about half of the students being neutral in each case.

The analysis also investigated attitudes toward the two symbols from the perspective of ideology considered as a style of thought characterized by consistency and reasoning from causal principles. Here the most significant finding was that partisanship in Japan appears to offer a powerful and clearcut stimulus to ideological development, with the acquisition of an ideology being closely linked to the acquisition of a party identification for many teenagers. This process is facilitated, and the ideology made readily salient and comprehensible, by the extensive use of simple ideological labels like "capitalist" or "socialist," which may in turn become familiarly linked with the political parties. Thus, the lines of political cleavage are drawn where party and ideological symbols coincide, and the simplicity of the symbols and their similarity to party labels, makes it possible for ideology to penetrate mass politics and the political learning process to a much greater degree than in the United States.

Influences on the Developing Political Self

The two final analytic chapters, 6 and 7, both dealt with the factors affecting the overall development of the teenager's political self. Chapter 6 focused on the multiple influences on political orientations of a youngster's social situation and his own psychological characteristics. Chapter 7 investigated the impact of potential agents of socialization, especially the family.

6. The relative impact on the teenager's political orientations of psychocultural factors and that of cleavage-related factors varies with the degree to which the orientation is linked with partisan divisions. The multivariate analyses of the social and psychological influences on the various dimensions of the political self (partisanship and ideology, political interest, political efficacy, and input and output support) are too intricate to be summarized in detail here. But the principal results can be summarized broadly as indicating that essentially four main streams of influence are at work in affecting the political development of the teenager. The first are maturational factors associated with increased age. The second stream includes psychocultural influences deriving from culturally determined aspects of personality. In the present analysis, these have been ego-autonomy and social trust. The third stream of influence is linked to the basic social cleavages that divide Japanese society, notably urban versus rural residence and socioeconomic status. Finally, sex constitutes an additional factor that impinges on the Japanese teenager's political development.

The major finding in this respect is that the nature and balance of forces working to increase or diminish Japanese teenagers' support for political institutions varies markedly from output to input institutions. The main correlates of teenagers' support for output institutions are factors involved with the basic social and political cleavages of Japanese society: urban-rural residence and party support. These factors, especially the urban-rural dichotomy, play lesser roles in affecting input support. In this context, we concluded that the relative immunity of support for the input institutions and processes to the influence of the social and ideological cleavages was further evidence that those elements of the democratic regime involved with popular political participation play an important legitimizing role that is able to bridge the gap between city and country and even, to some extent, between left and right. The overall character of the evidence, moreover, led to rejection of the validity of any classification of the political culture of Japanese youth as broadly divided into an urban and a rural subculture, since only with respect to partisanship and output support was the direct influence of the urban-rural difference strongly present. Significantly, the pattern of urban-rural differences among Japanese teenagers failed to support urban and rural political stereotypes. Neither urban nor rural youngsters were significantly more politically interested or politically efficacious, on the average, than the other. And while substantially more rural than urban teenagers were supportive of the output institutions, the difference was much smaller with regard to input support.

7. The family makes its main direct political impact on the child by influencing his partisanship; direct paternal and maternal influence, as measured by parent-child agreement on political values, are roughly equal and in each case tend to increase with the child's age. Over the course of adolescence, the family's monopoly of political influence over the child recedes, at least as measured by the rise in the *salience* of other agents to the child, and in his reported exposure to other agents such as friends, the mass media, and so forth. But strikingly enough, despite the increased exposure that the young child has to extra-family sources, the congruence of parents and child on political attitudes rises with the age of the child, particularly in the case of party identification. Equally striking is the fact that despite the mother's severe decline as a political role model, her actual influence increases at the same pace as that of the father. In large part, this anomaly appears due to the mother's unrecognized political contact with the child within the broader context of more frequent overall contact with the child by the mother than by the father.

8. The Japanese family no longer fits the image of an authoritarian patriarchy; teenagers and parents both reported a family decision process in which the child can exert influence. The consequences of family authority structure on the child's political orientations are intriguing. The "family writ large" hypothesis of an extension of experiences with family decision processes into expectations about feelings of influence in the political realm was not supported; there was no correlation between youngsters' feelings of family efficacy and political efficacy. The evidence on the transmission of parental partisanship to the child did show that those teenagers from the most "democratic" families tended to resemble their parents most closely and those from the most authoritarian families to resemble theirs the least. Thus, in the case of partisanship the hypothesis that the authoritarian family breeds political rebellion was upheld by the Japanese data.

The data also provided a certain degree of corroboration for a related hypothesis, namely, the child's affective response to the political authority figure is a generalization of his response to his parents. But, as was also predicted, the correspondence on parent and political figure images is appreciable only among the youngest students in the sample and declines in linear fashion as the student's age increases. Thus, the Japanese family operates as an agent of political socialization not only by directly transmitting parental political values, but by the parents' serving as prototypes for the leader. Moreover, of course, the family also influences the child's political development indirectly by giving him a social identity that has political consequences. In the case of Japan, that means most importantly by making him an urban or a rural resident.

Some Remaining Questions

Despite its length, this study has not begun to plumb the depths of political socialization in Japan. Some major areas are in need of further exploration if the process and its results are to be more fully understood. One obvious area in need of further analysis is that of the extra-family agents of socialization. We have not been able to deal here with the influence of the school, mass media, and peer group fully and systematically. The fact that the Japanese family, like the American family, transmits its political values primarily within the realm of partisanship leaves open a whole host of developing political attitudes and values on which the other agents may have a significant impact. Clearly this is the case with regard to the impact of the school on the child's cognitive orientations toward politics. But even in the cognitive realm, it would be desirable to be able to specify and assess the nature of the school's influence in comparison with that of the mass media, for example.

A second major question involves the life cycle. The evidence on changes in the partisanship of age-cohorts in Japan suggests that changes in important political values of young Japanese adults may occur during their late twenties and early thirties and that these changes may constitute a resocialization away from values acquired in pre-adult socialization.[2] In a political system like Japan, where the regime is still young, the political culture is in a continuing state of flux that makes it difficult to sort out age-related change from generational change. But if there is significant age-related change during adulthood on such basic elements of the political self as partisanship, then the influence of the family in the socialization of Japanese political man may be even more restricted than the present analysis has indicated.

A third question that remains to be investigated has to do with what may be the major pattern of social change in contemporary Japan—that is, urbanization. During the past two decades, the proportion of people living in the cities in Japan has seen a vast increase, with a parallel decrease in the proportion living in the country. These urban immigrants have had their political values and beliefs formed in the countryside, which as we have seen, tends to be the major continuing source of support for the output institutions of politics, as well as for the ruling Liberal Democratic Party. The question arises as to how the political values and attitudes that the children of these immigrants develop will differ from those of their parents. From the perspective of Japanese political culture this is an important and problematic question because if a "second generation effect" of rejection of parental values in the face of contradictory social pressures occurs, the consequence is likely to be a further diminishment of support for output institutions coupled with a sharper decline in the conservative dominance of the distribution of party loyalties than is already occurring. From the perspective of political socialization theory, the question is interesting because of the additional stress placed on the family's ability to communicate its political values and, consequently, because of the competition of extra-family agents, especially the peer group, in the family's major area of political influence, partisanship.

Political Socialization and the
Future of Japanese Political Culture

Unquestionably, the most important general finding of the study has been of a profound shift in Japanese attitudes toward authority. Japanese youngsters do not link themselves to the political regime by developing an emotional bond to the authority figure. There is no benevolent leader in Japanese culture now, despite the long history of intensely emotional leader-follower relations; nor do young Japanese defer to political authority. Today's teenagers' posture toward politics—contrary to that of their parents—is that of the confident popular sovereign who is supportive of the institutions and processes that convey popular demands and mediate participation. Toward the authoritative institutions, young Japanese are cool, skeptical, and even mistrustful. Toward the decision process, they are equally sensitive to the undesirable possibility of coercion or suppression of dissent.

What is the likelihood that this change will endure as a major shift in emphasis in Japanese political culture? To some extent, as the remarks above would suggest, part of the apparent generational difference in attitudes related to authority may be actually a function of age. But there is evidence of a steady and substantial decline over the twenty years since 1953 in the proportion of respondents in the sample of the quintennial survey of Japanese national character who choose the authoritarian response to an item on "leaving politics to leaders."[a] Moreover, both culture and cleavage contribute to making it likely that a large part of this shift will endure as a principal component of Japanese political culture: culture, because the new antiauthoritarianism coincides with a traditional preference for harmony and solidarity; cleavage, because the tension between opposition and establishment—progressive and conservative—is likely to continue to play a central role in politics. From that continuing confrontation, the notion of democracy as resistance to wrongful authority[3] has taken hold of one segment of Japanese society and is unlikely to disappear so long as the confrontation continues, and that is apt to be for the foreseeable future. Moreover, that segment is found in the urban areas where, if the "second generation" effect discussed earlier should occur among the children of the new urban immigrants, it is likely that the antiauthoritarian emphasis would become even more predominant than it is among today's youth.

But while it seems most unlikely that the basic substance and thrust of the change away from deference toward authority will be reversed, the reemergence of expressive leadership at the national level seems equally likely, though not of the pre-1954 variety. Such expressive leadership is already common at lower echelons of politics, as in the case of Governors Minobe and Yara on the left, the late Mishima Yukio on the right, and Ikeda Daisaku in the Sokagakkai. It seems apparent that many Japanese, old and young—as we saw in the youngsters' quotes in Chapter 2—alike, desire more human and approachable leaders. But during the postwar period the supply of potential expressive leaders at the national level was effectively reduced to nil. Those were the years in which the primary national political figures, the emperor and the prime minister, were in effect kept in quarantine away from the emotional leader-follower relation that had been the hallmark of the discredited *ancien regime* to which they themselves retained links. From now on, however, a new generation of national leaders, men wholly of the present without any links to the older, repudiated forms of expressive leadership, are beginning to emerge. It seems probable that if the present emperor should pass away in the next few years and a young new

[a]In 1953, 43 percent of the sample agreed, as opposed to 38 percent which disagreed with the statement that "if we get good political leaders the best way to improve the country is for the people to leave everything to them rather than for the people to discuss things among themselves." By 1968 the proportion agreeing had fallen to 30 percent while those disagreeing had risen to 51 percent. See Tokei Suri Kenkyujo Kokuminsei Chosa Iinkai, *Dai-ni Nihonjin no Kokuminsei* (Japanese National Character: Second Study), (Tokyo: Shiseido, 1970), p. 565; see also Table 2-9, p. 90.

emperor, one with a beautiful commoner wife and several handsome children, should ascend the throne, he would be able to evoke the same kind of popular affection that the Scandinavian monarchs enjoy. And a similar possibility may be open to the younger generation of partisan political leaders, like Ishihara Shintaro, the novelist turned conservative politician, or Oda Makoto, leader of the anti-Vietnam war group, *Beheiren*, who are wholly men of the contemporary era. But in either case, the popular affection these leaders might evoke would be unlikely to overcome the bases on which the other elements of the new antipathy toward authority depend. If Japan were to have a new benevolent leader, that leader's role would still be likely to be more constricted and restrained than in the United States, or England, let alone than in Japan's own past.

Finally, it is important to point out that the factors that intervene between the values and attitudes of the mass of men and the character of political systems are so many and so complex that democratic politics are not guaranteed by the existence of a democratic political culture. But if the democratic predispositions of the citizens are not a sufficient guarantee of democracy, they are surely a necessary condition. The nearly thirty years of democracy that Japan has enjoyed in the postwar era have been possible partly because of a redirecting of Japanese political culture. In this study, we have seen that the values and beliefs being acquired by Japanese children and teenagers in the socialization process are dominated by the elements of an emerging political culture of democracy that, in its selective emphases, accords with both the cultural and the cleavage aspects of Japanese political life.

Notes

1. *Asahi Shinbun*, October 19, 1972. Reprinted with permission.

2. For some interesting evidence on this question, see Ellis S. Krauss, *Japanese Radicals Revisited: Student Protest in Japan* (Berkeley and Los Angeles: University of California Press, 1974). The general applicability of Krauss's findings, however, is restricted by the nature of his sample.

3. See Shinohara Hajime, *Nihon no Seiji Fudo (Japanese Political Culture)*, (Tokyo: Iwanami, 1968), p. 53, where the argument is made that urban Japan is characterized by a combination of two types of democratic political culture, one emphasizing participation; the other, resistance to authority. The rural political subculture Shinohara protrays as dominated by obligation rather than real participation.

Appendixes

Appendix A:
Methodological Postscript

The basic details of the research on which this study is based are summarized in Chapter 1. The purpose of these brief remarks is to provide the reader with an account of some of the methodological considerations and constraints that governed the execution of the survey and the interviews.

The principal source of the data used in the study were self-completed questionnaires administered to 942 Japanese public school students and, through them, to their parents. The decisions to use self-completed questionnaires and to administer them to students in their classrooms were dictated both by economy and by the objectives of the study. One important objective was that the sample be broadly *representative* of Japanese families. The ideal way of assuring representativeness—drawing a national random sample of families perhaps stratified by size of locality—was ruled out because the costs of administration of the questionnaire to a sufficiently large sample of families to enable statistical analysis of the results would have been far greater than a modest research budget would allow. These limited resources, which would have allowed creating only a very small, statistically random sample that permitted little in the way of analysis, determined, instead, the choice of constructing a large sample whose principal demographic characteristics would be roughly representative of the population at large.

The schools where the survey was conducted, therefore, were selected so that the sample would have the same proportions of families as those in the population with respect to urban-rural residence, income and education levels, and occupational types. The Tokyo schools were located in the *shitamachi* ("downtown") area, a traditional section whose population consists largely of industrial workers and self-employed proprietors of small shops and businesses and their families, and in the *yamanote* ("uptown" or suburban) area, whose mainly white-collar families live in the huge concrete apartment complexes that are representative of "modern" Tokyo on the whole. The rural schools were located in Tochigi prefecture, a prefecture close to the national median on almost every demographic statistic. Of the small cities and farm villages, two—one of each—are located near the main railroad line of Japan's northeast, the Tohoku Trunk Line; the other city, a former castle town, as well as the other village are far off the main north-south highways and rail routes and are thus farther from the influence of Tokyo in some ways, although the near 100 percent diffusion of television in Japan now has lessened the significance of the difference. Table A-1 presents a breakdown of the sample by number of respondents, by category and by the principal demographic characteristics. Strictly speaking, of course, since the sample was purposely rather than randomly selected, it is representative only of itself. Nevertheless, in view of the

Table A-1
Basic Demographic Composition of the Sample

A.	Totals		
	students	942	
	fathers	802	
	mothers	835	
	father-mother pairs	752	
B.	By grade for students		
	Grade 8	282	
	Grade 10	334	
	Grade 12	326	
C.	By sex for students		
	boys	492	(52.2%)
	girls	450	(47.8%)
D.	By place of residence for students		
	Tokyo: central city	260	(27.6%)
	Tokyo: suburban	278	(29.5%)
	Tochigi: rural (small city and village)	404	(42.9%)
E.	By family occupation (father's report)		
	professional	45	(4.6%)
	administrative	150	(18.7%)
	owner of large shop or business	37	(4.6%)
	owner of small shop or business	131	(16.3%)
	clerical	85	(10.6%)
	skilled labor	122	(15.2%)
	unskilled labor	12	(1.5%)
	farm	184	(22.9%)
	Other and no response	36	(4.5%)

sample's fairly close demographic similarity to the population at large and in view of the fact that the method of sample selection is essentially the same as used in most of the other socialization studies with which the results of the present study are compared, it has been treated here as being representative of Japanese families generally.

One important consequence of conducting the survey in the schools was that it undoubtedly contributed to the high response rates of the parents. The procedure employed was to have the students take home a sealed envelope containing two copies of the parental questionnaire, to have these completed by their parents, and to return them to the school within several days. The fathers and mothers were explicitly requested to complete their questionnaires individually and without conferring with one another; inspection of the returned questionnaires revealed few cases of obvious mutual parental consultation, all of which were subsequently discarded from the sample. Almost 90 percent of the parental questionnaires were in fact returned, but a fair number had been only partially completed. Nevertheless, the final response rate after exclusion from the sample of any parent who answered fewer than 75 percent of the items was 85 percent (802) for the fathers and 89 percent (835) for the mothers. In 80 percent (752) of the cases, both parents responded. These are of course very high response rates, and it seems clear that they are due to the fact that the students were instructed to return their parents' questionnaires back *to the school*, which as an institution continues to occupy an influential and prestigious role in Japanese society.

A second major objective of the study is comparability. The political and other related attitudes of Japanese teenagers are compared both *cross-nationally* with findings about American and other adolescents' political beliefs and *trans-generationally* with their parents' beliefs. Thus, the fixed-choice format of the questionnaire was most appropriate because it permitted the gathering of data on a wide variety of attitudinal measures that are unambiguously comparable within the context of the Japanese sample itself, and whose cross-national comparability depends only on the semantic and linguistic comparability of the items used and the representativeness of the sample.

Every appropriate step was taken to insure that those items in the questionnaire relevant to Japanese teenagers' orientations that were to be compared with American or other youngsters' were as similar in their Japanese wording to the meaning of the original English version as it was possible to make them. Some of these items were taken directly or almost directly from the questionnaires used in American studies, notably the Jennings and Niemi work on American high school seniors,[1] and the various studies carried out by Dennis, Easton, Hess, and their associates.[2] The most important of these were the items used in the political efficacy, political interest, social trust, and ego-autonomy scales, which are discussed in detail in Chapter 6.

There are obviously great difficulties involved in capturing all of the connotations of a statement in English in as disparate and noncognate a language as Japanese. Some colloquial English phrases or expressions are not directly translatable into Japanese. Okamura's survey, for example, included an item meant to be comparable to one asked in the Easton and Hess study of American children that asked whether they thought the president was "doing a good job." The literal translation of this expression in Japanese is not colloquial and the item that Okamura finally used, as the closest Japanese approximation, was literally whether the youngster thought the prime minister was "carrying out his responsibilities."

To minimize this kind of difficulty, the questionnaire for this study was constructed via a lengthy series of steps. First, I myself wrote the original Japanese-language version of the questions, giving a literal translation of all items taken from English-language questionnaires. (Many of the questions were, of course, original and some were borrowed from Japanese surveys.) A Japanese sociologist and a political scientist and their students read the questionnaire and revised all items into correct colloquial Japanese. The linguistic clarity of this corrected version, as well as the level of cognitive difficulty of the questions, was then tested by discussing the meaning of each item, one by one, with a half a dozen thirteen- to fifteen-year-old children in a Tokyo neighborhood. As a final preliminary step, the questionnaire was administered to some ninety eighth graders at a middle school in Tokyo as a pretest of the instrument. After the patterns of responses were examined and the problem items identified, ten of the students who had taken the pretest questionnaire were interviewed to discuss the format of the instrument and the individual questions. As a result of these pretest steps, a number of questions were reworded or in a few instances discarded entirely. In short, the questionnaire was thoroughly tested to guarantee that teenagers as young as thirteen would clearly understand each item as it was meant to be understood and be able to complete the questionnaire in a reasonable period of time. (The time averaged thirty-five to forty minutes, or slightly less than a full class period.)

Despite the advantages of the fixed-choice questionnaire with respect to comparability, ease of answering for the respondent, and of coding for the researcher, as well as the variety of measures that could be included, there are obvious disadvantages. Most important, it does not permit the respondent to express his own ideas and images, and it thus may give a distorted picture that is more reflective of the researcher's interests than of the respondent's perspectives. In order to avoid this situation, in addition to the questionnaire, a series of loosely structured, taped interviews were conducted with forty of the students in the sample. These interviews lasted from forty minutes to an hour. I myself did most of the interviewing, but because Japanese have a strong consciousness of the differences between themselves and foreigners, several measures were taken to reduce the impact my foreign nationality might have on the interviews. First, several Japanese college students carried out a number of the interviews, the results of which could serve as a rough check on the effects of my presence versus that of a native interviewer. This tactic was also used in administering the questionnaires in the classrooms, where in half the classes I was present to explain the purposes and procedures of the survey and to answer any questions and in the other half my Japanese assistant was present. The results of both sets of interviews as well as the questionnaire results indicate there was no appreciable systematic difference in either case.

A second tactic I used in the interviews to diminish the alien atmosphere of my presence involved talking with two respondents in the same session. While this technique had the disadvantage of some obvious contamination of responses, several advantages made that a tolerable cost. The first was a lessening of the tension of the situation; for nearly all of the interviewees, I was the first foreigner with whom they had ever spoken, and in at least one of the rural areas, the first foreigner ever seen in the flesh. The presence of two students meant that each could feel reassured and fortified and thus less vulnerable to the mild *angst* produced by the experience of being interviewed by an adult male foreigner. The second advantage was that it facilitated stimulation, and then observation and recording of interchanges between the teenagers with respect to their images and beliefs about politics. This resulted in a more natural flow of discussion than would have been possible in the somewhat artificial setting of an individual interview. Often one student's remark or reply to a question would prompt an interesting contradictory remark from the second student, which is a most satisfying state of affairs from an interviewer's perspective.

Needless to say, the interviews with these youngsters were as enjoyable and rewarding to conduct as any research in the study of politics could possibly be. Talking politics with earnest and enthusiastic eighth graders, sophisticated urban high school seniors, and sometimes even more sophisticated rural youths leaves one with not merely a set of recorded interviews but a set of vivid images of individuals—in this case, individuals of remarkable diversity in some respects despite the ubiquitous navy blue school uniforms they all wore. It also left me with a feeling of deep optimism about the future of the democratic enterprise in Japan.

Notes

1. M. Kent Jennings and Richard G. Niemi, Student and Parent Questionnaires, High School Senior Study, Project 477, Survey Research Center, University of Michigan, Spring 1965.

2. See Robert D. Hess and Judith V. Torney, *The Development of Basic Attitudes and Values Toward Government and Citizenship During the Elementary School Years*, Part 1, Office of Education Cooperative Research Project No. 1078, Chicago, 1965, Appendix D; and Jack Dennis et al., Civic Concepts Survey Questionnaire, mimeo, n.d.

Appendix B:
Student and Parent
Questionnaire

Student Questionnaire (English Translation)

C1. What's your family's occupation? Please circle the one that applies:
   1. Professional occupation (doctor, teacher, lawyer, etc.).
   2. Managerial occupation (bureau chief or above in a company or government office).
   3. Self-employed A (owner of a large store or factory, etc.).
   4. Self-employed B (owner of an ordinary store, beauty shop, barber shop, grocery store, etc.).
   5. A—Clerical (office worker in a government office, company, or store, etc.); B—Sales or service (clerk or attendant in a store, beauty shop, grocery store, etc.); C—Security (policeman, fireman, member of the Self-Defense Forces).
   6. Skilled laborer or production process employee (machine operator, carpenter, mechanic, etc.).
   7. Simple labor (handyman, day laborer).
   8. Farming, fishing, forestry.
   9. Unemployed; other.
C2. How many children are there in your family including yourself?
C3. What number child are you in your family?
C4. Who lives with your family, aside from you and your brothers and sisters?
C5. How old is your father?
C6. How old is your mother?
C7. Which school did your father last attend: 1. Primary school; 2. Old higher primary, new middle school; 3. Old middle, new high school; 4. Old higher technical or normal, new junior college; 5. College; 6. Don't know.
C8. Which school did your mother last attend: 1. Primary school; 2. Old higher primary, new middle school; 3. Old higher girls, new high school; 4. Old higher technical or normal, new junior college;
   5. College; 6. Don't know.
Q9. What kind of country do you think Japan is? Pick the one that you think suits Japan best:
   1. A socialist country;

Items numbered Q9 through Q60 were identical in both the student and parent versions of the questionnaire and for that reason are omitted from the parent questionnaire reproduced here. Item Q61 differed only in the addition in the parent version of the phrase "during the past year or two." Items numbered C1 through C8 and C62 through C80 were asked only of the students, while those numbered P1 through P6 and P62 through P78 were asked only of the parents. The format of item responses has been edited to conserve space.

2. A capitalist country;
3. A dictatorship;
4. A democratic country;
5. Don't know.

Q10. Everyone would like to live in a peaceful and free country. But unhappily, not all countries are always peaceful and free at the same time. Suppose you had to live in one of the two countries given here. Which would you choose?

1. In this country, there is peace and its people don't have to worry at all about war. But this country's government severely restricts the liberty of the people. Hence the people of this country can live in peace but not in freedom.

2. In this country, there is freedom; fundamental human rights are guaranteed, so its people don't have to worry at all about tyranny. But this country is at war with another country. Hence the people of this country can live in freedom, but not in peace.

Q11. We all have hopes about the sort of society we'd like to make of Japan. Which of the following sorts of society is closest to your hope?

1. A society in which people can compete freely and men of ability can readily become wealthy, but where there are people who have a hard time earning a living.

2. A society where the government controls the economy, so one can't get very wealthy, but where a minimum standard of living is firmly guaranteed.

3. A society where able men become wealthy but where such people are highly taxed by the government to help look after the disadvantaged.

4. Don't know.

Q12. There are many opinions about democracy. From the following eight, pick in order the two that you think best express the essence of democracy and write their numbers in the two boxes.

1. All adults can vote in elections.

2. People can freely and safely criticize the government.

3. The nation's politics are decided by the opinions of the majority of the people.

4. Basic human rights, such as freedom of speech and assembly, are respected.

5. There is no poverty; the government attempts to make it possible for everyone to lead a life with minimum basic wealth and cultural standards.

6. Political parties, including those opposed to the government, can freely compete in elections to take office.

7. There is no discrimination; everyone has an equal opportunity to get the place to live, the education, and the job that he chooses.

8. The people have the right to live in peace.

Q13. Is your reaction favorable when you hear each of the following words [1. Very Favorable; 2. Favorable; 3. Can't say either; don't know; 4. Unfavorable; 5. Very Unfavorable]:

Pacifism;

Socialism;

Liberalism;

Capitalism;

Democracy;

Communism.

Q14. Do you think you find each of the following things more often in capitalist or in socialist countries [1. Much more in Capitalist; 2. More in Capitalist; 3. About same; don't know; 4. More in Socialist; 5. Much more in Socialist]:

Peace;

Poverty;

Democracy;

Inequality;

Justice;

Liberty.

Q15. How much do you think each of the following cares about the problems in the lives of an ordinary Japanese and tries to do something about them [1. Very Much; 2. Somewhat; 3. Can't say; don't know; 4. Not Much; 5. Hardly at All]:

Prime Minister;

Diet;

Government;

Political Parties.

Do you agree or disagree with the following opinions? [For each item, the response choices were 1. Strongly Agree; 2. Agree; 3. Can't say either; don't know; 4. Disagree; 5. Strongly Disagree.]

Q16. What ordinary people like my family say has no effect on what the government does.

Q17. Most Japanese politicians don't really believe in democracy; they only pretend to.

Q18. Things like politics and government are so complicated that people like myself can hardly understand how they work.

Q19. If we get good political leaders, the best way to improve the country is for the people to leave everything to them rather than for the people to discuss things among themselves.

Q20. Real democracy is impossible in a capitalist country.

Q21. Real democracy is impossible in a socialist country.

Q22. Japan is not really a democracy because the capitalists hold power. For Japan to become a real democracy the socialist forces must take power.

Q23. In a socialist country individuals do not have freedom so it is necessary to preserve capitalism in Japan.

Q24. Japan's democracy is not a real democracy, because it was forcibly imposed by foreigners.

Q25. Ordinary people have no opportunity to get their views reflected in politics.

Q26. The Prime Minister makes many public pledges but he usually doesn't intend to keep them.

Q27. When the Prime Minister decides on a policy, he pays a great deal of attention to what the people want.

Q28. The Prime Minister works hard for the sake of all the people, not just for himself and his party.

Q29. A good many people in the government are dishonest and involved in corruption.

Q30. The government's policies are increasing the gap between rich and poor, and work only for the benefit of the rich.

Q31. Over the long run, the government pays a great deal of attention to what the people want, when it decides on policies.

Q32. Since the same one party always wins, general election results don't really represent the will of the people.

Q33. Since there are always so many election law violations, it would be better if our representatives were chosen by some other means such as competitive examinations, instead of elections.

Q34. Elections make the government pay attention to what the people think.

Q35. It would be better if instead of all the present political parties, there were only one party which represented all the people and really did its best for the country.

Q36. The political parties play an important role in making the government pay attention to what the people think.

Q37. The political parties are all nothing more than groups of factions and influential men who think only of their own interests.

Q38. When it comes to deciding what to do in the Diet, most Diet members pay very little attention to the wishes of the voters who elected them.

Q39. Most Diet members are trustworthy, honest men, who do not get involved in things like graft.

Q40. In the Diet, the majority ignores the rights of the minority, and the minority impedes majority decisions, so I don't think it is carrying out its responsibility to the people.

Q41. In most cases, demonstrations and strikes cause a lot of trouble to ordinary people, so the government ought to take strong steps to control them.

Q42. Demonstrations and mass movements are better ways of making the government pay attention to what the people want than relying on the Diet and the political parties.

Q43. What the government does is like the weather; ordinary people can't do anything about it.

Q44. Let's suppose you belong to a certain group (such as a club, etc.). Suppose that group had decided to go on a trip. But there were some people who wanted to go to the mountains and others who wanted to go to the seashore. Circle which one of the three ways of deciding where to go that you think would be best:

1.   One person says that since the group's affairs have been put in charge of its leaders, you should rely on them and have them decide.

2.   Another person says that everyone should give his opinion, and discussion should be continued until all agree on one opinion.

3.   Someone else says that it should be decided by majority rule, even if there is a large minority.

Q45. Let's suppose that that group had decided to determine where to go by taking a vote. If there were 30 people in the group, how many should agree for the decision to be fair to everyone:

1.   Nearly everyone (27-30 people);

2.   About four-fifths (24 people or more);

3.   About two-thirds (20 people or more);

4.   About three-fifths (18 people or more);

5.   About half (16 people or more).

Do you agree or disagree with the following opinions? [For each item, the response choices were 1. Strongly Agree; 2. Agree; 3. Can't say either; don't know; 4. Disagree; 5. Strongly Disagree.]

Q46. When you're trying to decide something, if there is a relatively large number of people in the minority, those in the majority shouldn't insist on their opinion.

Q47. When you're trying to decide something, and only a very few people disagree, for those people to continue insisting on their opposing opinion should be condemned because it is selfish.

Q48. When your friends and others all make little of a movie or TV program that you liked, as "dull" or "stupid," it is best to keep silent and say nothing.

Q49. Given the chance, most people will try to take advantage of others.

Q50. Most people can be trusted.

Q51. It is necessary to take adequate precautions when dealing with people.

Q52. Other people can't be depended upon. When you get right down to it, the only one you can rely on is yourself.

[For each of the following items, the response choices were 1. Very Often; 2. Fairly Often; 3. Not Very Often; 4. Hardly Ever.]

Q53. Do you often lose confidence when many of your friends and others disagree with you?

Q54. When you have disagreements with others, do you often get your own way?

Q55. When you make plans do they often work out as you thought?

Q56. When you have made up your mind about something do you often change your mind if someone tries to argue you out of it?

Q57. Are you interested in politics: 1. Very; 2. Somewhat; 3. Not Very; 4. Hardly At All.

Q58. Do you often read newspaper articles about politics: 1. Every Day; 2. Sometimes; 3. Not Very Often; 4. Hardly Ever.

Q59. Do you often watch TV programs or listen to radio programs about politics: 1. Every Day; 2. Sometimes; 3. Not Very Often; 4. Hardly Ever.

Q60. Do you often read magazine articles about politics: 1. Often; 2. Sometimes; 3. Not Very Often; 4. Hardly Ever.

Q61. Have you ever done any of the following things in connection with politics and elections, or a citizen's movement or student movement:
A. Attended a speech or other meeting?
B. Made a donation (including to people soliciting in public places for a fund-raising campaign)?
C. Signed a petition?
D. Participated in a demonstration?
E. Yourself distributed handbills or collected donations or signatures?

Q62. Do you think your mother and father are interested in politics [1. Very; 2. Somewhat; 3. Don't Know; 4. Not Very; 5. Hardly at All] :
Father;
Mother.

Q63. Do you discuss political and social questions with the following people [1. Often; 2. Sometimes; 3. Not Very Often; 4. Hardly Ever] :
Your father;
Your mother;
Your teachers;
Your friends.

Q64. On political and social questions, do you think your opinions are the same as those of the following people, or different [1. Very Much the Same; 2. Fairly Similar; 3. Don't Know; 4. Fairly Different; 5. Very Different] :
Your father;
Your mother;
Your teachers;
Your friends.

Q65. When you don't yet have an opinion about some political or social problem and want to clarify what you think, whose opinion do you most respect and take into account: 1. Father; 2. Mother; 3. Teacher; 4. Friend; 5. Other ( ).

Q66. There are a number of political parties in Japan. Which party do you think each of the following persons supports? Put the number of that party in the box next to each person(s) [1. Liberal Democratic; 2. Japan Socialist; 3. Democratic Socialist; 4. Komeito; 5. Japan Communist; 6. Other; 7. Support no party at all; 8. Don't know] :

A. Yourself, if you could vote;
B. Your father;
C. Your mother;
D. Most of your teachers;
E. Most of your friends.

C67. Do you often have talks with your father and mother [1. Often; 2. Sometimes; 3. Not Very Often; 4. Hardly Ever] :
Father;
Mother.

C68. Do you think your father and mother understand you [1. Very well; 2. Fairly Well; 3. Not Very Well; 4. Hardly at All] :
Father;
Mother.

C69. When you have some worry or problem, with whom do you usually discuss it: 1. Father; 2. Mother; 3. Teacher; 4. Friend; 5. Other ( ); 6. Have no one to consult.

C70. Do you think your father and mother are concerned about you and take good care of you [1. Very; 2. Somewhat; 3. Not Very; 4. Hardly at All] :
Father;
Mother.

C71. Do you think your parents interfere too much in such things as whom you become friends with, and when you go to play, etc.: 1. Interfere Very Much; 2. Interfere Some; 3. Don't Interfere Very Much; 4. Interfere Hardly at All.

[For each of the following items, the response choices were 1. Very Much; 2. Somewhat; 3. Not Very Much; 4. Hardly at All.]

C72. When some decision concerning you (such as going on to the next level of school, etc.) is made in your family, how much does your opinion count?

C73. When you disagree with some decision made at home, how much effect do you think it would have to complain?

C74. Do you think your parents nag too much about study?

C75. Are you concerned about your school record and entrance examinations?

C76. Do you attend after-school classes, etc.?

C77. *During the past three years*, have you ever run for office in the student council, class council, or a club, etc.? If you have, please write the number of times you have run in the box.

C78. *During the past three years*, have you ever served as an officer in the student council, class council, or of a club, etc.? If you have, please write the number of times you have served in the box.

C79. *This year*, do you belong to any circles or clubs? If you do, please write the number of clubs to which you belong in the box.

C80. How far do you want to continue in school: 1. Middle school; 2. High school; 3. Junior College; 4. College and beyond.

Parent Questionnaire (English Translation)

P1. Are you the student's father or mother?

P2. What is your age?

P3. Which is the last school you attended: 1. Primary school; 2. Old higher primary, new middle school; 3. Old middle, new high school; 4. Old higher technical or normal, new junior college; 5. College.

P4. What is your family's occupation? Please circle the one that applies.
1. Professional occupation (doctor, teacher, lawyer, etc.).
2. Managerial occupation (bureau chief or above in a company or government office).
3. Self-employed A (owner of a large store or factory, etc.).
4. Self-employed B (owner of an ordinary store, beauty shop, barber shop, grocery store, etc.).
5. A—Clerical (office worker in a government office, company, or store, etc.); B—Sales or service (clerk or attendant in a store, beauty shop, grocery store, etc.); C—Security (policeman, fireman, member of the Self-Defense Forces).
6. Skilled laborer or production process employee (machine operator, carpenter, mechanic, etc.).
7. Simple labor (handyman, day laborer).
8. Farming, fishing, forestry.
9. Unemployed, other (   ).

P5. How many children do you have?

P6. Aside from yourself and your children, who is now living with your family (please omit servants, etc.): 1. Husband; 2. Wife; 3. Husband or wife's father; 4. Husband or wife's mother; 5. Husband or wife's brothers or sisters; 6. Other (   ).

[Questions 9-61 are identical to those in the student questionnaire and are omitted here.]

P62. How often do you discuss political and social questions with the following people [1. Often; 2. Sometimes; 3. Not Very Often; 4. Hardly Ever] :
Spouse;
Friends;
Children.

P63. Do you think your opinions on political and social problems are the same as your wife's (husband's) or are they different: 1. Very Much the Same; 2. Fairly Similar; 3. Don't Know; 4. Fairly Different; 5. Very Different.

P64. Which political party do you support: 1. Liberal Democrat; 2. Japan Socialist; 3. Democratic Socialist; 4. Komeito; 5. Japan Communist; 6. Other (   ); 7. Independent.

P65. There are various opinions about today's youngsters. Do you agree with the opinions about them expressed here [1. Strongly Agree; 2. Agree; 3. Can't say either; don't know; 4. Disagree; 5. Strongly Disagree] :
A.   They should respect their parents' opinions more.
B.   They have too much freedom; they need more discipline.
C.   They'll grow up at their own pace, even if their parents don't keep after them.
D.   They're too individualistic and don't care about others.
E.   They're too soft; they need stricter training.

P66. In your family, who generally makes the decisions about family matters:
1.   Husband makes almost all decisions;
2.   Wife makes almost all decisions;
3.   Both discuss everything and then decide together;
4.   Sometimes decisions are left to husband, other times wife makes the decisions.

P67. In your family, who takes charge of raising the children: 1. Husband; 2. Wife; 3. Both.

P68. Do you often discuss things with your children: 1. Often; 2. Occasionally; 3. Not Very Often; 4. Hardly Ever.

P69. When your child has a worry or a problem does he often discuss it with you: 1. Often; 2. Sometimes; 3. Not Very Often; 4. Hardly Ever.

P70. Do you pay a lot of attention to such things as whom your child becomes friends with, and where he goes to play, etc.; or do you let your child do as he likes: 1. Pay a Lot of Attention; 2. Pay Some Attention; 3. Generally Let Do as Pleases; 4. Nearly Always Let Alone.

P71. In your family how much do you listen to your child's opinions when you are making a decision concerning him: 1. Much; 2. Some; 3. Not Much; 4. Hardly At All.

P72. In your family do you ever change decisions you have made concerning your child if he objects to the decision: 1. Often; 2. Sometimes; 3. Not Very Often; 4. Hardly Ever.

P73. If you didn't keep after him, would your child study hard: 1. Would Study Hard; 2. Would Study Some; 3. Would Not Study Much; 4. Would Not Study at All.

P74. Are you satisfied with your child's school record and attitude toward the entrance examinations: 1. Very Satisfied; 2. Fairly Satisfied; 3. Somewhat Dissatisfied; 4. Very Dissatisfied.

P75. How far do you want your child to go in school: 1. Middle school; 2. High school; 3. Junior college; 4. College and beyond.

P76. Do you often attend PTA meetings: 1. Often; 2. Sometimes; 3. Not Very Often; 4. Hardly Ever.

P77. Have you ever held office in, or been on a committee of, the PTA?

P78. How much is your family's monthly take-home income, including that of all the family? (Average bonuses and other special income into the monthly total.) Please circle whichever place on the list you fit into:

1. Less than 30,000 yen;
2. 30-50,000 yen;
3. 50-70,000 yen;
4. 70-100,000 yen;
5. 100-150,000 yen;
6. 150-200,000 yen;
7. 200,000 yen and over.

Selected Bibliography

Selected Bibliography

Books and Articles in English

Aberbach, Joel D. "Alienation and Political Behavior." *American Political Science Review* 63:1 (March 1969), 86-99.

Abrahamson, Paul R. and Inglehart, Ronald. "The Development of Systematic Support in Four Western Democracies." *Comparative Political Studies* 2 (1970), 419-42.

Adelson, Joseph, Green, B., and O'Neill, Robert P. "The Growth of the Idea of Law in Adolescence." *Developmental Psychology* 1 (1969), 27-32.

Adelson, Joseph and O'Neill, Robert P. "Growth of Political Ideas in Adolescence: The Sense of Community." *Journal of Personality and Social Psychology* 4:3 (1966), 295-306.

Adler, Norman and Harrington, Charles. *The Learning of Political Behavior.* Glenview, Ill.: Scott, Foresman & Co., 1970.

Agger, Robert E., Goldstein, Marshall Z., and Peart, Stanley A. "Political Cynicism: Measurement and Meaning." *Journal of Politics* 23 (August 1969), 477-506.

Almond, Gabriel A. and Verba, Sidney. *The Civic Culture.* Princeton, N.J.: Princeton University Press, 1963.

Aoi, Kazuo. "A Comparative Study of Home Discipline: Rural-Urban, Sex and Age Differences." Tokyo: University of Tokyo, September 1965. (Mimeographed.)

Banfield, Edward C. *The Moral Basis of a Backward Society.* Glencoe, Ill.: Free Press, 1958.

Beardsley, Richard K. "Personality Psychology." In John W. Hall and Richard K. Beardsley, eds., *Twelve Doors to Japan.* New York: McGraw-Hill, 1965.

Beardsley, Richard K., Hall, John W., and Ward, Robert E. *Village Japan.* Chicago: University of Chicago Press, 1959.

Bell, Daniel. *The End of Ideology.* Rev. ed. New York: The Free Press, 1962.

Benedict, Ruth. *The Chrysanthemum and the Sword.* Boston: Houghton Mifflin, 1946.

Blalock, H.M., Jr., ed. *Causal Models in the Social Sciences.* Chicago: Aldine, Atherton, 1971.

Burks, Ardath. *The Government of Japan.* New York: Crowell, 1961.

Butler, David and Stokes, Donald E. *Political Change in Britain.* New York: St. Martin's Press, 1971.

Campbell, Angus et al. *The Voter Decides.* Evanston, Ill.: Row, Peterson, 1954.

Campbell, Angus, Converse, Philip E., Miller, Warren E., and Stokes, Donald E. *The American Voter.* New York: Wiley, 1960.

_____. *Elections and the Political Order.* New York: Wiley, 1966.

213

Caudill, William and Scarr, Harry A. "Japanese Value Orientations and Culture Change." *Ethnology* 1 (1962), 53-91.

Cole, Allen B. *Japanese Society and Politics.* Boston: Houghton Mifflin, 1956.

Cole, Allen B. et al. *Socialist Parties in Postwar Japan.* New Haven: Yale University Press, 1966.

Connell, R.W. *The Child's Construction of Politics.* Carlton, Victoria: Melbourne University Press, 1971.

Converse, Philip E. "The Nature of Belief Systems in Mass Politics." In David E. Apter, ed., *Ideology and Discontent.* New York: The Free Press, 1964.

Converse, Philip and Dupeux, Georges. "Participation of the Electorate in France and the United States." In Angus Campbell et al., *Elections and the Political Order.* New York: Wiley, 1966.

_____. "Politicization of the Electorate in France and the United States." *Public Opinion Quarterly* 26 (1962), 1-23.

Dahl, Robert A. *Modern Political Analysis.* 2nd ed. Englewood Cliffs, N.J.: Prentice-Hall, 1970.

_____. *Political Oppositions in Western Democracies.* New Haven, Conn.: Yale University Press, 1973.

_____. *A Preface to Democratic Theory.* Chicago: University of Chicago Press, 1963.

Davies, James C. "The Family's Role in Political Socialization." *Annals of the American Academy of Political and Social Science* 361 (September 1965), 10-19.

Dawson, Richard E. and Prewitt, Kenneth. *Political Socialization.* Boston: Little, Brown & Co., 1969.

Dennis, Jack. *Socialization to Politics: A Reader.* New York: Wiley, 1973.

Dennis, Jack et al. "Political Socialization to Democratic Orientations." *Comparative Political Studies* 1:1 (April 1968), 71-100.

Dennis, Jack, Lindberg, Leon, and McCrone, Donald. "Support for Nation and Government among English Children." *British Journal of Political Science* 1, Part 1 (January 1971), 25-48.

Dennis, Jack and McCrone, Donald. "Preadult Development of Political Party Identification in Western Democracies." *Comparative Political Studies* 3:2 (July 1970), 243-63.

Doi, Takeo. "Amae: A Key Concept for Understanding Japanese Personality Structure." In Robert J. Smith and Richard K. Beardsley, eds., *Japanese Culture: Its Development and Characteristics.* Chicago: University of Chicago Press, 1962.

Dore, Ronald P. *City Life in Japan.* Berkeley and Los Angeles: University of California Press, 1963.

Duijker, H.C.T. and Frijda, N.H. *National Character and National Stereotypes.* Amsterdam: North Holland Publishing, 1960.

Easton, David. *A Systems Analysis of Political Life.* New York: Wiley, 1965.

215

Easton, David and Dennis, Jack. *Children in the Political System.* New York: McGraw-Hill, 1969.

———. "The Child's Acquisition of Regime Norms: Political Efficacy." *American Political Science Review* 61:1 (March 1967), 25-38.

———. "The Child's Image of Government." *The Annals of the American Academy of Political and Social Science* 361 (September 1965), 40-57.

Easton, David and Hess, Robert D. "The Child's Political World." *Midwest Journal of Political Science* 6 (1962), 229-46.

Edelman, Murray. *The Symbolic Uses of Politics.* Urbana: University of Illinois Press, 1964.

Elkin, Frederick. *The Child and Society.* New York: Random House, 1960.

Erikson, Erik H., ed. *The Challenge of Youth.* Garden City, N.Y.: Anchor Books, 1965.

Erikson, Erik H. *Childhood and Society.* 2nd ed. New York: Norton, 1963.

Finifter, Ada W. "Dimensions of Political Alienation." *American Political Science Review* 64:2 (June 1970), 389-410.

Flanagan, Scott C. "Voting Behavior in Japan." *Comparative Political Studies* 1:3 (October 1968), 406.

Frager, Robert E. "Conformity and Anticonformity in Japan." *Journal of Personality and Social Psychology* 15:3 (1970), 203-10.

———. "Experimental Social Psychology in Japan: Studies in Social Conformity." *Rice University Studies* 56:4 (Fall 1970).

Fukui, Haruhiro. *Party in Power.* Berkeley and Los Angeles: University of California Press, 1970.

Fukutake, Tadashi. *Man and Society in Japan.* Tokyo: Tokyo University Press, 1960.

Gallatin, Judith and Adelson Joseph. "Individual Rights and the Public Good: A Cross-National Study of Adolescents." *Comparative Political Studies* 3:2 (July 1970), 226-42.

Gallup Opinion Index. March 1972.

Goldrich, Daniel. *Sons of the Establishment.* Chicago: Rand McNally, 1966.

Goodman, Mary Ellen. "Values, Attitudes and Social Concepts of Japanese and American Children." *American Anthropologist* 59:6 (December 1957), 979-99.

Gorer, Geoffrey. "Themes in Japanese Culture." Reprinted in B.S. Silberman, ed., *Japanese Character and Culture.* Tucson: University of Arizona Press, 1962.

Greenberg, Edward J. "Black Children and the Political System: A Study of Socialization to Support." Paper delivered at Annual Meeting of the American Political Science Association, New York, 1969.

Greenberg, Edward S., ed. *Political Socialization.* New York: Atherton, 1970.

Greenstein, Fred I. *The American Party System and the American People.* Englewood Cliffs, N.J.: Prentice-Hall, 1970.

Greenstein, Fred I. "The Benevolent Leader: Children's Images of Political Authority." *American Political Science Review* 54:2 (December 1960), 934-43.

_____ . *Children and Politics*. New Haven, Conn.: Yale University Press, 1965.

_____ . "French, British, and American Children's Images of Government and Politics." Paper delivered at Annual Meeting of the Northeastern Political Science Association, Philadelphia, 1970.

_____ . "Personality and Political Socialization: The Theories of Authoritarian and Democratic Character." *The Annals of the American Academy of Political and Social Science* 361 (September 1965), 81-95.

_____ . *Personality and Politics*. Chicago: Markham Publishing Co., 1969.

Greenstein, Fred I. et al. "Queen and Prime Minister—The Child's Eye View." *New Society* 23 (October 1969), n.p.

Greenstein, Fred I. and Tarrow, Sidney. "Political Orientations of Children: The Use of a Semi-Projective Technique in Three Nations." *Sage Professional Papers in Comparative Politics* Series 01-009, 1 (1970), 479-588.

Hall, John W. and Beardsley, Richard K., eds. *Twelve Doors to Japan*. New York: McGraw-Hill, 1965.

Haring, Douglas G. "Aspects of Personal Character in Japan." Reprinted in D.G. Haring, ed., *Personal Character and Cultural Milieu*. Syracuse, N.Y.: Syracuse University Press, 1956.

_____ . "Japanese National Character: Cultural Anthropology, Psychoanalysis, and History." Reprinted in B.S. Silberman, ed., *Japanese Character and Culture*. Tucson: University of Arizona Press, 1962.

Hess, Robert D. "The Socialization of Attitudes toward Political Authority: Some Cross-National Comparisons." *International Social Science Journal* 15 (1963), 542-59.

Hess, Robert D. et al. *Authority, Rules, and Aggression: A Cross-National Study of the Socialization of Children into Compliance Systems*. Chicago: University of Chicago, March 1969, for Bureau of Research, Office of Education, U.S. Department of Health, Education and Welfare, Part I, Part B, chapter 5, and Part C.

Hess, Robert D. and Easton, David. "The Child's Changing Image of the President." *Public Opinion Quarterly* 114 (Winter 1960), 632-44.

Hess, Robert D. and Torney, Judith V. *The Development of Basic Attitudes and Values toward Government and Citizenship during the Elementary School Years, Part I*. Chicago: University of Chicago Press, 1965.

_____ . *The Development of Political Attitudes in Children*. Garden City, N.Y.: Anchor Books, 1968.

Hyman, Herbert. *Political Socialization*. Glencoe, Ill.: Free Press, 1959.

Iga, Mamoru. "Cultural Factors in Suicide of Japanese Youth with Focus on Personality." *Sociology and Social Research* 46:1 (October 1961), 75-90.

Inkeles, Alex. "National Character and Modern Political Systems." In Nelson

Polsby et al., eds., *Politics and Social Life.* Boston: Houghton Mifflin, 1963.

Inkeles, Alex and Levinson, Daniel. "National Character: The Study of Modal Personality and Socio-cultural Systems." In G. Lindzey, ed., *Handbook of Social Psychology*, vol. 2. Cambridge, Mass.: Addison-Wesley Press, 1954.

Ishida, Takeshi. "Popular Attitudes toward the Japanese Emperor." *Asian Survey* 2 (April 1962), 29-39.

Jahoda, Gustave. "The Development of Children's Ideas about Country and Nationality. Part I: The Conceptual Framework." *British Journal of Educational Psychology* 33 (1963), 47-60; and "Part II: National Symbols and Themes," ibid., 143-53.

Jansen, Marius. "Education, Values and Politics in Japan." *Foreign Affairs* 35:4 (July 1965), 666-79.

Jaros, Dean, Hirsch, Herbert, and Fleron, Frederic J., Jr. "The Malevolent Leader: Political Socialization in an American Subculture." *American Political Science Review* 52:2 (June 1968), 564-75.

Jennings, M. Kent and Niemi, Richard G. "The Division of Political Labor Between Mothers and Fathers." *American Political Science Review* 55:1 (March 1971), 69-82.

_____. "Family Structure and the Transmission of Political Values." Paper delivered at Annual Meeting of the American Political Science Association, New York, 1966.

_____. "The Transmission of Political Values from Parent to Child." *American Political Science Review* 62:1 (March 1968), 169-84.

Kato Takakatsu. "Political Attitudes of Japanese Adolescents in Comparison with American." *Psychologia* (Kyoto) IV (December 1961), 198-200.

Kawai, Kazuo. *Japan's American Interlude.* Chicago: University of Chicago Press, 1960.

Keniston, Kenneth. *The Uncommitted: Alienated Youth in American Society.* New York: Dell Publishing, 1965.

_____. *Young Radicals.* New York: Harcourt, Brace & World, 1968.

_____. "Youth: A 'New' Stage of Life." *The American Scholar* 39:4 (Autumn 1970), 631-53.

Kenyon, Sandra J. "The Development of Political Cynicism among Negro and White Adolescents." Paper delivered at Annual Meeting of the American Political Science Association, New York, September 1969.

Kerlinger, Fred N. "Behavior and Personality in Japan: A Critique of Three Studies of Japanese Personality." Reprinted in B.S. Silberman, ed., *Japanese Character and Culture.* Tucson: University of Arizona Press, 1962.

Kiefer, Christie W. "The Psychological Interdependence of Family, School, and Bureaucracy in Japan." *American Anthropologist* 72:1 (February 1970), 66-75.

Krauss, Ellis S. *Japanese Radicals Revisited: Student Protest in Japan.* Berkeley and Los Angeles: University of California Press, 1974.

Kubota, Akira and Ward, Robert E. "Family Influences and Political Socialization in Japan." *Comparative Political Studies* 3:2 (July 1970), 140-75.

Kuroda, Yasumasa. "Agencies of Political Socialization and Political Change: Political Orientations of Japanese Law Students." *Human Organization* 24:4 (Winter 1965), 328-31.

_____. "Sociability and Political Involvement." *Midwest Journal of Political Science* 9:2 (May 1965), 133-47.

Kuroda, Yasumasa and Kuroda, Alice K. "Aspects of Community Political Participation in Japan: Influences of Education, Sex, and Political Generation." Paper delivered at Annual Meeting of the American Sociological Association, San Francisco, August 1967.

LaBarre, Weston. "Some Observations on Character Structure in the Orient." Reprinted in B.S. Silberman, ed., *Japanese Character and Culture*. Tucson: University of Arizona Press, 1962.

Lambert, William W. and Lambert, Wallace E. *Social Psychology*. Englewood Cliffs, N.J.: Prentice-Hall, Inc., 1964.

Lane, Robert E. *Political Ideology*. New York: The Free Press, 1967.

_____. *Political Life*. New York: The Free Press, 1959.

_____. *Political Thinking and Consciousness*. Chicago: Markham Publishing Co., 1969.

Langdon, Frank. *Politics in Japan*. Boston: Little, Brown & Co., 1967.

Langton, Kenneth P. *Political Socialization*. New York: Oxford University Press, 1969.

Lanham, Betty B. "Aspects of Child Care in Japan: Preliminary Reports." Reprinted in B.S. Silberman, ed., *Japanese Character and Culture*. Tucson: University of Arizona Press, 1962.

_____. "Cultural Aspects of Ethical Training in the Schools of Japan and the United States . . ." Paper delivered at Annual Meeting of the American Anthropological Association, Washington, D.C., November 1967.

La Palombara, Joseph. "Decline of Ideology: A Dissent and an Interpretation." *American Political Science Review* 50:1 (March 1966), 5-18.

Lasswell, Harold D. "Democratic Character." *The Political Writings of Harold D. Lasswell*. Glencoe, Ill.: Free Press, 1951.

_____. "Key Signs, Symbols, and Icons." In L. Bryson et al., eds., *Symbols and Values: An Initial Study*. New York and London: Cooper Square Publishers, 1954.

Leighton, Alexander and Opler, Morris. "Psychological Warfare and the Japanese Emperor." In R. Hunt, ed., *Personalities and Cultures*. Garden City, N.Y.: The Natural History Press, 1972.

Leites, Nathan. "Psychocultural Hypotheses about Political Acts." Reprinted in P.F. Lazarsfeld and M. Rosenburg, eds., *The Language of Social Research*. New York: The Free Press, 1965.

Lifton, Robert J. "Youth and History: Individual Change in Postwar Japan." In

Erik H. Erikson, ed., *The Challenge of Youth*. Garden City, N.Y.: Anchor Books, 1965.

Lipsitz, Lewis. "If as Verba says, the State Functions as a Religion, What Are We To Do Then To Save Our Souls?" *American Political Science Review* 52:2 (June 1968), 527-35.

Litt, Edgar. "Political Cynicism and Political Futility." *Journal of Politics* 25 (May 1963), 312-22.

Matsumoto Yoshiharu. "Contemporary Japan: The Individual and the Group." *Transactions of the American Philosophical Society*, New Series, 50, Part I, 1960.

McDougall, Terry E. "Local Politics and the Emergence of a Viable Political Opposition in Japan." Paper delivered at Seminar on Japan by 1980, Yale University, 1973.

McGinnies, Elliott. "Attitudes Toward Civil Liberties Among Japanese and American University Students." *Journal of Psychology* 58 (1964), 177-86.

McNelly, Theodore. *Politics and Government in Japan*. 2nd ed. Boston: Houghton Mifflin Co., 1972.

Mead, Margaret. "The Study of National Character." In D. Lerner and H.D. Lasswell, eds., *The Policy Sciences: Recent Developments in Scope and Method*. Stanford: Stanford University Press, 1965.

Merelman, Richard M. "The Development of Political Ideology: A Framework for the Analysis of Political Socialization." *American Political Science Review* 53:3 (September 1969), 750-67.

_____. "The Development of Policy Thinking in Adolescence." *American Political Science Review* 55:4 (December 1971), 1033-47.

Moloney, James C. *Understanding the Japanese Mind*. New York: Philosophical Library, 1954.

Mussen, Paul Henry, Conger, John Janeway, and Kagan, Jerome. *Readings in Child Development and Personality*. 2nd ed. New York: Harper and Row, 1970.

Niemi, Richard G. *How Family Members Perceive Each Other: Political and Social Attitudes in Two Generations*. New Haven, Conn.: Yale University Press, 1974.

Norbeck, Edward. "Common Interest Associations in Rural Japan." In Robert J. Smith and Richard K. Beardsley, eds., *Japanese Culture: Its Development and Characteristics*. Chicago: University of Chicago Press, 1962.

Okamura Tadao. "The Child's Changing Image of the Prime Minister." *The Developing Economies* 6:4 (December 1968), 566-86.

_____. "Political Socialization of Upheavals: A Case in Japan." Unpublished paper, Department of Political Science, University of Chicago, 1962.

Patman, Carole. *Participation and Democratic Theory*. Cambridge: Cambridge University Press, 1970.

Pinner, Frank A. "Parental Overprotection and Political Distrust." *The Annals of the American Academy of Political and Social Science* 361 (September 1965), 58-70.

Putnam, Robert D. "Studying Elite Political Culture: The Case of Ideology." *American Political Science Review* 55:3 (September 1971), 651-81.

Richardson, Bradley M. "Party Loyalties and Party Saliency in Japan," *Comparative Political Studies* 8:1 (April 1975), 32-57.

_____. *The Political Culture of Japan.* Berkeley and Los Angeles: University of California Press, 1974.

_____. "Urbanization and Political Participation: The Case of Japan," *American Political Science Review* 67:2 (June 1973), 433-52.

Rosenburg, Morris. "Misanthropy and Political Ideology." *American Sociological Review* 21 (1956), 650-95.

_____. *Society and the Adolescent Self-Image.* Princeton, N.J.: Princeton University Press, 1965.

Scalapino, Robert A. *The Japanese Communist Movement, 1920-1966.* Berkeley and Los Angeles: University of California Press, 1967.

Scalapino, Robert A. and Masumi Junnosuke. *Parties and Politics in Contemporary Japan.* Berkeley and Los Angeles: University of California Press, 1962.

Sebert, Susanne K. "Friend and Peer Influences on the Politics of the High School Senior." Paper delivered at Annual Meeting of the American Political Science Association, New York, September 1969.

Shimbori Michiya. "The Sociology of a Student Movement—A Japanese Case Study." *Daedalus* 97:1 (Winter 1968), 204-28.

Sigel, Roberta S., ed. *Learning about Politics: A Reader in Political Socialization.* New York: Random House, 1970.

_____. *Political Socialization: Its Role in the Political Process.* Special issue of the *Annals of the American Academy of Political and Social Science*, 361 (September 1965).

Smith, Richard J. and Beardsley, Richard K., eds. *Japanese Culture: Its Development and Characteristics.* Chicago: University of Chicago Press, 1962.

Steiner, Kurt. *Local Government in Japan.* Stanford: Stanford University Press, 1965.

Stokes, Donald E. "The Study of Political Generations." Noel Buxton Lecture, University of Essex. London: Longmans, 1969.

Sunoda, Ichiro. "The Thought and Behavior of Zengakuren." *Asian Survey* 9:6 (June 1969), 457-74.

Tarrow, Sidney, Greenstein, Fred I., and Williams, Mary F. "Associational Incapacity in French Children: Some Evidence from a Study of Political Socialization in France and England." Unpublished manuscript, Department of Political Science, Yale University, and Department of Government, Wesleyan University, 1971.

Thayer, Nathaniel. *How the Conservatives Rule Japan.* Princeton, N.J.: Princeton University Press, 1969.

Thompson, Dennis F. *The Democratic Citizen.* Cambridge: Cambridge University Press, 1970.

Titus, David A. "Emperor and Public Consciousness in Postwar Japan." *The Japan Interpreter* (Summer 1970), 189-190.

Verba, Sidney. "The Kennedy Assassination and the Nature of Political Commitment." In Bradley S. Greenberg and Edwin B. Parker, eds., *The Kennedy Assassination and the American Public.* Stanford: Stanford University Press, 1965.

Vogel, Ezra. *Japan's New Middle Class.* Berkeley and Los Angeles: University of California Press, 1963.

Ward, Robert E. "Japan: The Continuity of Modernization." In Lucian W. Pye and Sidney Verba, eds., *Political Culture and Political Development.* Princeton, N.J.: Princeton University Press, 1965.

Watanuki Joji. "Patterns of Politics in Contemporary Japan." In S.M. Lipset and Stein Rokkan, eds., *Party Systems and Voter Alignments.* New York: The Free Press, 1967.

_____. "Social Structure and Political Participation in Japan." Report No. 32, Department of Political Science, Laboratory for Political Research, University of Iowa, May 1970.

White, James. "The Political Implications of Cityward Migration in Japan." Unpublished manuscript, Department of Political Science, University of North Carolina, 1971.

_____. *The Sokagakkai and Mass Society.* Stanford: Stanford University Press, 1970.

Whitehill, Arthur and Takezawa, Shin'ichi. *The Other Worker.* Honolulu: East-West Center Press, 1965.

Wilson, Richard W. *Learning to be Chinese: The Political Socialization of Children in Taiwan.* Cambridge, Mass.: M.I.T. Press, 1970.

Wolfenstein, Martha and Kliman, Gilbert, eds. *Children and the Death of a President.* Garden City, N.Y.: Doubleday and Co., 1965.

Wylie, Laurence. *Village in the Vaucluse.* New York: Harper and Row, 1964.

Yanaga, Chitoshi. *Big Business in Japanese Politics.* New Haven, Conn.: Yale University Press, 1968.

_____. *Japanese People and Politics.* New York: Wiley, 1956.

Zax, Melvin and Takahashi, Shigeo. "Response Styles among Japanese and American Children." *Japanese Psychological Research* 9:2 (1967), 58-61.

_____. "Cultural Influences on Response Style: Comparisons of Japanese and American College Students." *The Journal of Social Psychology* 71 (1967), 3-10.

Zeigler, Harmon. *The Political Life of American Teachers.* Englewood Cliffs, N.J.: Prentice-Hall, 1967.

Zureik, Elia T. "Party Images and Partisanship Among Young Englishmen." *British Journal of Sociology* 25:2 (June 1974).

Books and Articles in Japanese

Asahi Shinbun. 1964-1972. In particular, November 17, 1968; November 24, 1968; December 27, 1968; July 9, 1969; July 23, 1969; June 26, 1971; July 9, 1971; September 18, 1972; and October 19, 1972.

Bando Satoshi and Iwai Sadao. *Seinen-ron (On Youth).* Tokyo: San'ichi Shobo, 1963.

Fujiwara Hirotatsu. *Gendai Nihon no Seiji Ishiki (Political Consciousness in Contemporary Japan).* Tokyo: Sobunsha, 1958.

Fujiwara Kietsu. *Seinen to Shakai (Youth and Society).* Tokyo: Dai Nihon Tosho, 1966.

Harada Shigeru. "Atarashii Aikokushin to wa Nani ka" (What is the New Patriotism?). *Seinen Shinri* 7:2 (February 1956).

Hatano Nobumaro and Mase Masaji, eds. *Aikokushin (Patriotism).* Tokyo: Toyokan Suppansha, 1966.

Hayashi Chikio. "Sengoha Seiji Ishiki" (Political Consciousness of the Postwar Generation). *Jiyu* 6:1 (January 1964), 57-65.

_____. "Sengo Seito Shiji no Hensen" (Changes in Postwar Political Party Support). *Jiyu* 3:8 (August 1961), 104-11.

Hayashi Chikio et al. *Zusetsu: Nihonjin no Kokuminsei (Japanese National Character, Illustrated).* Tokyo: Shiseido, 1965.

Hiratsuka Masatoku, ed. *Gendai no Kodomo—Sono Seikatsu to Ishiki (Today's Children: Their Life and Consciousness).* Tokyo: Toyokan Shuppansha, 1967.

Honda Koei. *Shakaika Rekishi Kyokasho no Hihan (A Critique of History Texts Used in Social Studies).* Tokyo: Meiji Tosho, 1967.

Ienaga Saburo. *Kyokasho Kentei (Government Approval of Textbooks).* Tokyo: Nihon Hyoronsha, 1965.

Ishida Takeshi. *Nihon no Seiji Bunka (Japanese Political Culture).* Tokyo: Tokyo Daigaku Shuppansha, 1970.

Ishido Shukuro. *Gendai no Seinenzo (An Image of Contemporary Youth).* Tokyo: NHK Books, 1965.

Kamishima Jiro. *Kindai Nihon no Seishin Kozo (The Mental Structure of Modern Japan).* Tokyo: Iwanami Shoten, 1960.

Karasawa Tomitaro. *Asu no Nihonjin (Tomorrow's Japanese).* Tokyo: Nihon Keizai Shinbunsha, 1964.

Kodama Masahide. "Seishonen no Seijiteki Kanshin: Judai no Taido" (Adolescent Political Interest: The Attitudes of Teenagers). *Seinen Shinri* 7:2 (February 1956), 151-56.

Komei Senkyo Renmei. *Komei Senkyo no Jittai—Yoron Chosa Kekka no Gaiyo (The Actual Conditions of Fair Elections; A Summary of the Results of a Public Opinion Survey).* Tokyo: Komei Senkyo Renmei, 1958.

Kyogoku Jun'ichiro. *Seiji Ishiki no Bunseki (The Analysis of Political Consciousness).* Tokyo: Tokyo Daigaku Shuppansha, 1968.

Mainichi Shinbun. 1964-1972. In particular, October 18, 1971, January 1, 1972, April 4, 1972, and June 10, 1972.

Matsubara Haruo. *Gendai no Kazoku (The Contemporary Family).* Tokyo: Nihon Keizai Shinbunsha, 1964.

Miyake Ichiro. "Seiji Ishiki Kozo-ron no Kokoromi" (Toward Constructing a Theory of the Structure of Political Consciousness). *Nenpo Seijigaku,* 1965.

_____. "Seito Shiji no Ryudosei to Anteisei" (Stability and Instability of Party Support). *Nenpo Seijigaku,* 1970.

_____, Kinoshita Tomio, and Aiba Juichi. *Kotonaru Reberu no Senkyo ni okeru Tohyo Kodo no Kenkyu (Research on Voting Behavior in Different Levels of Elections).* Tokyo: Sobunsha, 1967.

Minami Hiroshi. *Nihonjin no Shinri (Psychology of the Japanese).* Tokyo: Iwanami Shinsho, 1953.

Mita Munesuke. *Gendai no Seinenzo (An Image of Contemporary Youth).* Tokyo: Kodansha, 1968.

Munakata Seiya. *Nihon no Kyoiku to Kyokasho Saiban (Japanese Education and the Textbook Trial).* Tokyo: Roko Shinsho, 1968.

Munakata Seiya et al. *Kyoiku Kokusho (Black Paper on Education).* Tokyo: Rodo Kohosha, 1968.

Munakata Seiya and Kokubu Ichitaro, eds. *Nihon no Kyoiku (Japanese Education).* Tokyo: Iwanami Shinsho, 1962.

Murao Jiro. *Kyokasho Chosakan no Hatsugen (A Statement by a Ministry of Education Textbook Official).* Tokyo: Hara Shobo, 1969.

Nagai Yonosuke. *Seiji Ishiki no Kenkyu (Research in Political Consciousness).* Tokyo: Iwanami, 1971.

Nakane Chie. "Nihonteki Shakai Kozo no Hakken" (The Discovery of a Japanese-Style Social Structure). *Chuo Koron,* May 1964.

_____. *Tate Shakai no Ningen Kankei (Human Relations in a Vertical Society).* Tokyo: Kodansha, 1967.

Nakano Sazo, ed. *Kodomo no Seikaku Kyoiku (Children's Character Education).* Tokyo: Kaneko Shobo, 1957.

Nihon Chiiki Kaihatsu Sentaa. *Nihonjin no Kachikan (The Values of Japanese).* Tokyo: Shiseido, 1960.

Nihon Yunesko Kokunai Iinkai. *Kindai Kojo ni okeru Seisho-nen no Kachi Ishiki ni Kansuru Chosa (A Survey of Value Consciousness of Youth in Modern Factories).* Tokyo: Nihon Yunesko Kokunai Iinkai, 1959.

_____. *Noson ni okeru Seishonen no Kachi Ishiki ni Kansuru Chosa (A Survey of Value Consciousness of Youth in Farming Villages).* Tokyo: Nihon Yunesko Kokunai Iinkai, 1956.

_____. *Seishonen no Kachi Ishiki, Jinken Ishiki, Kokusai Ishiki (Consciousness of Values, Consciousness of Human Rights, and Consciousness of International [Matters] among [Japanese] Youth).* Tokyo: Nihon Yunesko Kokunai Iinkai, 1961.

Ninoseki Takami. "Junsui Sengoha no Kangaekata" (Ways of Thinking of the First Wholly Postwar Generation). *Asahi Janaru* 6:3 (January 19, 1964).

Nishihira Naoki. *Gendai Seinen no Ishiki to Kodo 1: Kyozetsu to Shakai Sanka* (*The Attitudes and Behavior of Contemporary Youth 1: Alienation and Social Participation*). Tokyo: Dai Nihon Tosho, 1970.

_____. "Oya no Ken'i no Keisei to Hokai" (The Formation and Collapse of Parental Authority). *Jido Shinri* 22:2 (February 1968), 33-40.

_____. *Seinen Bunseki* (*An Analysis of Youth*). Tokyo: Dai Nihon Tosho, 1964.

Nishihira Shigeki. *Nihonjin no Iken* (*The Opinions of the Japanese*). Tokyo: Seishin Shobo, 1963.

_____. "Seinenso no Hoshuka to wa Nani ka" (Are Young People becoming More Conservative?). *Asahi Janaru* 6:31 (July 26, 1964), 12-19.

Nishimura Saburo. "Kokosei no Seiji Katsudo" (High School Students' Political Activism). *Gekkan Jiji* 14:4 (April 1969), 64-68.

Oka Yoshitake, ed. *Gendai Nihon no Seiji Katei* (*The Political Process in Contemporary Japan*). Tokyo: Iwanami Shoten, 1958.

Okamura Tadao. "Gendai Nihon ni okeru Seijiteki Shakaika" (Political Socialization in Contemporary Japan). *Nenpo Seijigaku*, 1970.

_____. "Seiji Ishiki no Kitei to shite no Soridaijinzo" (The Prime Minister's Image as the Foundation of Political Consciousness). In Taniuchi Ken, Ari Bakuji, Ide Yoshinori, and Nishio Masaru, eds., *Gendai Gyosei to Kanryosei.* Tokyo: Tokyo Daigaku Shuppankai, 1974.

Okamura Tadao et al. "Seijiteki Shakaika ni okeru 'Minshushugi' to 'Heiwa' " ("Democracy" and "Peace" in Political Socialization). *Shakai Kagaku Janaru,* 1969.

Onishi Seiichiro et al., eds. *Gendai Seinen no Shinri* (*The Psychology of Contemporary Youth*). Nagoya: Reimei Shobo, 1966.

Owaki Kenzo. "Chugakusei no Seiji Ishiki" (The Political Consciousness of Middle-School Students). *Ide,* 77 (February 1968).

Saito Koji. *Gendai Nihon no Ishiki to Kodo 2: Seikatsu Kanjo no Tenkai* (*The Attitudes and Behavior of Contemporary Youth 2: Change in Feelings toward Life*). Tokyo: Dai Nihon Tosho, 1970.

Sawada Keisuke, ed. *Seinen Shinrigaku* (*The Psychology of Youth*). Tokyo: Tokyo Daigaku Shuppansha, 1966.

Sayama Kisaku. *Chugakusei* (*The Middle School Student*). Tokyo: Iwanami, 1963.

Shimizu Ikutaro. *Seinen* (*Youth*). Tokyo: Yuhikaku, 1959.

Shinohara Hajime. *Nihon no Seiji Fudo* (*Japanese Political Culture*). Tokyo: Iwanami Shinsho, 1968.

Sofue Takao, and Wagatsumi Hiroshi. *Kokumin no Shinri—Nihonjin to Obeijin* (National Psychology: Japanese and Westerners). Tokyo: Kodansha, 1959.

Sorifu Seishonen Taisaku Honbu. *Gendai Seishonen no Ishiki to Kodo ni Kansuru Chosa: Chosa Hokokusho* (*A Survey of the Attitudes and Behavior of Contemporary Youth: Report of the Survey*). Tokyo: Mimeographed, 1969.

_____. *Seishonen Hakusho* (*White Paper on Youth*). Tokyo: Okurasho Insatsukyoku, 1970.

Suzuki Hiro. *Gakusei Undo* (*The Student Movement*). Tokyo: Fukumura Shuppan, 1968.

_____. "Kokosei no Seiji Katsudo Hihan" (Criticism of High School Students' Political Activism). *Gekkan Jiji* 14:4 (April 1969), 74-77.

Suzuki Hiro. *Kokosei Undo* (*The High School Student Movement*). Tokyo: Fukumura Shuppan, 1969.

Takahashi Akira. "Katsudoka Gakusei: Sono Undo e no Doki" (The Activist Students: Their Motivation for Joining the Movement). *Chuo Koron* (June 1968), 170-87.

Takeda Yuzo. *Kokosei* (*The High School Student*). Tokyo: San'ichi Shinsho, 1959.

Tanaka Kunio. *Nihonjin no Shakaiteki Taido* (*Social Attitudes of the Japanese*). Tokyo: Saishin Shobo, 1964.

Tanaka Yasumasa. *Gendai Nihonjin no Ishiki* (*The Consciousness of Contemporary Japanese*). Tokyo: Chuo Koronsha, 1966.

Tokei Suri Kenkyujo. Kokuminsei Chosa Iinkai. *Nihonjin no Kokuminsei* (*Japanese National Character*). Tokyo: Shiseido, 1961.

_____. *Dai-ni Nihonjin no Kokuminsei* (*Japanese National Character: Second Study*). Tokyo: Shiseido, 1970.

Tokyo Gakugei Daigaku Shakai Kenkyushitsu. "Kodomo no Shitsuke to Dotoku Kyoiku" (Child-Rearing and Moral Education). *Kyoiku Shakaigaku Kenkyu* 18 (October 1963), 2-65.

Tokyo-to. *Chugaku, Kokosei no Seikatsu Kozo Chosa–Chosa Hokokusho* (*Survey of the Life-Structure of Middle and High School Students: A Report*). Tokyo: Tokyo-to Somukyoku Seishonen Taisakubu, 1963.

_____. *Tokyo-to ni okeru Seishonen Mondai no Genjo to Sono Taisaku* (*Present Problems of Youth in Tokyo and Policies [for Dealing with Them]*). Tokyo: Tokyo-to Somukyoku Seishonen Taisakubu, 1969.

Tsuchiya Kiyoshi. *Nihon no Howaito Karaa* (*Japanese White Collar*). Tokyo: Diamondosha, 1964.

Tsuru Hiroshi. *Kokosei no Seikatsu to Shinri* (*The Daily Life and Psychology of the High School Student*). Tokyo: Dai Nihon Tosho, 1965.

Uno Seiichi. *Rekishi Kyoiku to Kyokasho Ronso* (*Education in History and the Textbook Debate*). Tokyo: Nihon Kyobunsha, 1968.

Ushijima Yoshitomo. *Seio to Nihon no Ningen Keisei* (*Human Development in Western Europe and Japan*). Tokyo: Kaneko Shobo, 1961.

Watanuki Joji. *Gendai Seiji to Shakai Hendo* (*Contemporary Politics and Social Change*). Tokyo: Tokyo Daigaku Shuppansha, 1962.

_____. "Kyu Chukaiso no Seiji to Ishiki" (The Politics and Consciousness of the Old Middle Class). *Chuo Koron* (July 1962), 110-19.

_____. *Nihon no Seiji Shakai* (*Japan's Political Society*). Tokyo: Tokyo Daigaku Shuppansha, 1967.

Watanuki Joji. "Rodosha no Tohyo Kodo to Seito Shiji Taido" (Workers' Electoral Behavior and Party Support). *Nihon Rodo Kyokai Zasshi* (January 1969).

_____. *Seiji Ishiki to Senkyo Kodo no Jittai–Tokyo Tomin no Seiji Ishiki to Tohyo Kodo* (*Political Consciousness and the Actual State of Electoral Behavior: The Political Consciousness and Voting Behavior of Tokyo Citizens*). Tokyo: Komei Senkyo Unmei, 1967.

_____. "Tato Jokyoka no Seiji Ishiki to Tohyo Kodo" (Political Consciousness and Electoral Behavior in Multi-party Circumstances). Materials prepared for the panel on politics of the Convention of the Japan Sociological Association, October 1968.

Yoda Arata. *Kazoku no Shinri* (*Psychology of the Family*). Tokyo: Baifukan, 1958.

Yoda Arata, ed. *Gendai Seinen no Jinkaku Seikei* (*Character Formation of Modern Youth*). Tokyo: Kaneko Shobo, 1968.

_____. *Nayami to Hanko* (*Anxiety and Rebellion*). Tokyo: Kaneko Shobo, 1955.

Yoda Arata et al., eds. *Masu Komyunikashion to Kyoiku* (*Mass Communications and Education*). Tokyo: Meiji Tosho Shuppan, 1967.

Yomiuri Shinbun. 1964-1972. In particular, October 13, 1970, and December 5, 1972.

Yoshida Yoshiaki, Titus, David, and Agata Yukio. "Shocho Tennosei no Ishiki Kozo" (The Mentality of the Symbolic Emperor System). *Meiji Daigaku Hosei Kankyujo Kiyo*, n.d.

Index

Abrahamson, Paul R., 25, 29
Adelson, Joseph, 103
Adolescents, 16-17; ideology of, 101, 112, 114, 122; influence of family on, 188; and parents' politics, 163; political interest of, 144; political socialization of, 2; socializing influences on, 52. *See also* Students; Teenagers
Affection, patterns of, 18, 157; political, 46; political influence of, 170-174. *See also* Family
Affiliation. *See* Partisanship
Age, and cynicism, 39; and parental transmission of partisanship, 166; and parent-child political congruence, 170; and peer group influence, 160; and political development, 187-188; and political efficacy, 134; and political orientation, 150; of sample, 16
Alienation, 126; of student activists, xvii, 14; of urban youth, 91
Allegiance, creation of, 45; party, 96 (*see also* Partisanship); political, 21
Almond, Gabriel, 4, 6, 129, 157, 175
America, attitudes toward political leaders in, 37; attitudes toward presidency in, 27, 28; childhood political socialization in, 7, 21; images of presidency in, 183; parent-child political correspondences in, 165; political participation in, 81; political perceptions of children, 53. *See also* United States
Ancien regime, 12, 45; rejection of, 184. *See also* Emperor system
Apathy, 81
Asahi poll, 30, 78
Asahi Shinbun, 183
Asch conformity tests, 62
Attitudes, toward American presidency, 27, 28; toward capitalism, 109, 110, 112, 113, 187; constraint of, 102; toward corruption, 41, 43; toward democracy, 65, 66, 109, 114; influence of peer group on, 160; toward majority rule, 60, 62; political, 2, 5, 7, 90, 126; toward political authority figures, 6, 37; sources of, 155. *See also* Cynicism
Authority, 4; attitudes toward, 61, 190; democrat and, 9; family, 18, 174-175 (*see also* Family); Japanese youths' view of, 21-50; political influence of, 170-174; and political socialization, 7 (*see also* Socialization); skepticism toward, 39; submis-

siveness to, 156; traditional attitudes toward, 11. *See also* Emperor; Emperor system
Autonomy, student's, 174; teenagers', 173

Behavior, political, 126
Beheiren, 192
Beliefs, 16; acquisition of, 192; sources of, 155; of young Japanese, 4
Benevolent leader thesis, 21, 22, 26, 48, 157, 175, 183-184. *See also* Political leaders
Big business, 75
"Black mist" scandals, 41
Blue-collar workers, Japanese, 128
Buddhism, Soka gakkai sect of, 76, 88, 135, 151. *See also* Religion
Burks, Ardath, 24

Candidates, appeal of, 37; corrupt behavior of, 41. *See also* Political leaders
Capitalism, 13; affective reaction to, 108, 109; attitudes toward, 109, 110, 112, 113, 187; rejection of, 14; in school texts, 104; teenagers' attitudes toward, 102, 105, 115, 116
Censorship, political, 14
Change, 1; social, 190
Chauvinism, 10
Chief executives, adult popular support for, 31; images of, 35-36. *See also* Political leaders
Children, and party preference, 79. *See also* Adolescents; Family; Students; Teenagers
Communism, affective reactions to, 108; attitudes toward, 112, 113; perceptions of, 107. *See also* Japan Communist Party
Communists, SES of, 91
Competition, 9
Compliance systems, 29
Conflict, ideology of, 12; institutional basis of, 78-79; partisan, 77. *See also* Partisanship
Conformity, 11, 128
Confrontation, 9, 75-77
Consensus, 11, 12; and democracy, 69; v. majority rule, 56-64; national, 70; nuclear elements of, 73; in political culture, 185; preference for, 68; symbols of, 61-71. *See also* Dissensus
Conservatism, 75; postwar, 101. *See also* Emperor system
Conservatives, 2, 86, 146, 151; and emperor

Conservatives (cont.)
 system, 25; opposition to, 12-13; SES of,
 91; support for, 94
Constitution Memorial Day, 45
Continuity, 1
Converse, Philip, 83, 102-103, 111
Corruption, attitudes toward, 41, 43
Countercultures, political, 9-15
Cross-national comparative studies, 79, 80,
 86, 197
Crown prince, 26, 191-192
Culture, Japanese, 2; past patterns of,
 10-12; political, 4, 183, 187-188; 190; and
 politics, 127; traditional, 5, 10-12, 128
Cynicism, of Japanese youngsters, 184;
 political, 38, 142: v. support, 149; of up-
 per-status teenagers, 145. See also Atti-
 tudes

Dahl, Robert, 60
Data, for national character studies, 3
Decision making, attitudes toward, 58; consensual, 69 (see also Consensus); in family,
 170; teenagers posture toward, 190; traditional, 57; unanimity in, 51; and urban-
 rural residence, 63
de Gaulle, Charles, 30n
Democracy, acceptance of, 64; affective
 reactions to, 108; attitudes toward, 65,
 66, 109, 114; concept of, 54; consensual,
 70 (see also Consensus); formal ideal of,
 8-9; as import, 67; in Japan, 2; meaning
 of, 52-55; role of, 51; in school texts, 104;
 symbols of, 185; teenagers' attitudes
 toward, 116; values of, 54, 55-56
Democratic Party, 75. See also Democratic
 Socialist Party; Liberal Democratic Party
Democratic regime, support for, 7
Democratic Socialist Party (DSP), 74, 76,
 78; support for, 87, 88, 119
Democratic Youth League (Minsei) of JCP,
 13, 77, 145, 146
Demonstrations, mass, 170
Denmark, attitudes toward political leaders
 in, 29
Dennis, Jack, 24, 27, 29, 87, 131, 132, 134,
 197
Diet, Japanese, 6; attitudes toward, 38, 39,
 40, 42, 142; corruption in, 43; support
 for, 143, 144
Dissensus, symbols of, 185. See also Consen-
 sus
Dissent, freedom to, 61; tolerance of, 63
Doi Takeo, 177
Dupeux, Georges, 83

Easton, David, 4, 5, 6, 21, 27, 29, 45, 64,
 131, 132, 134, 197

Edelman, Murray, 64
Education, and occupational change, 8; and
 public policy, 14
Efficacy, family, 162; political, 131-136,
 164, 166, 197
Ego-Autonomy, 127-131, 140-142; scales
 for, 197
Eighth graders, 199. See also Adolescents
Eisenhower, Pres. Dwight D., 31
Elections, attitudes toward, 40, 42, 43; of
 local leaders, 37; perceptions of, 39; sup-
 port for, 143, 144. See also Diet
Elementary schools, political interest in,
 137
Emperor, 6; perceptions of, 24; as peripher-
 al monarch, 23-26; replacement of, 8; as
 symbol, 22, 184; traditional attitudes
 toward, 10
Emperor system, "family state of," 156;
 ideology of, 10-11; "organ theory" of, 44
Equality, 6; inequality, 109, 114. See also
 Democracy

Family, authoritarian, 179; and authoritarian institutions, 3; child's influence in,
 172; influence of, 17; and partisanship,
 80-90, 96, 188; political socialization of,
 189; politicization of, 169; role of, 155;
 socioeconomic status of, 145; as source of
 political attitudes, 178; stereotypes of,
 170; "writ large," 174-177, 188. See also
 Parents
Father, political influence of, 158, 159,
 160, 168, 170-174; political role of, 157,
 161-164
Flag, 25, 45. See also Symbols
Frager, Robert, 62, 128
France, attitudes toward political leaders in,
 29, 36; party identification in, 86; political participation in, 81-83
Freedom, attitudes toward, 67
Free enterprise, teenagers' perceptions of,
 106
French, family politics of, 7; national character of, 130
Friends, political influence of, 158, 159. See
 also Peers

Gallup Poll, British, 30n
Generalization, concept of, 175-176
Government, attitudes toward, 38, 39, 40,
 42, 142; corruption in, 43; support for,
 143, 144. See also Diet; Prime minister
Great Britain, attitudes toward political
 leaders in, 37; childhood political socialization in, 7, 21; images of queen in,
 23-24, 183; party affiliation in, 77; party
 identification in, 86

Greece, attitudes toward political leaders in, 29

Greenstein, Fred I., 21, 24, 38, 79, 91, 94, 118, 128, 138, 145, 159

Haring, Douglas, 3

Harmony, 11, 12, 51. *See also* Consensus

Hatoyama, Prime Minister, 31

Hero, missing, 44. *See also* Leader

High school students, 199; attitudes toward emperor of, 25; ideology of, 115; political identification of, 160. *See also* Students; Teenagers

Hiroshima, 66

Hoguchi Hideo, 46

Holland, attitudes toward political leaders in, 29, 37; childhood political socialization in, 21

Hyman, Herbert, 156

Ideal, of consensual democracy, 70

Idealism, of youth, 43

Identification, 25; party, 77-80, 103, 188 (*see also* Partisanship); political, 2, 7, 74, 75, 125; popular, 37

Identity, national, 64, 185

Ideology, 18, 102; acquisition of, 2, 122; and cognitive development, 121; of conflict, 12; democratic, 39, 131; of emperor system, 10-11; parent-student agreement on, 164, 166; and partisanship, 117 (*see also* Partisanship); role of, 101; and socialization, 94; as style of thought, 111-117; as symbol of dissensus, 185; teenagers', 120, 149

Ikeda Daisaku, 191; support for, 31

Imperial Japan, characteristics of, 47

Imperial Rule Assistance Association, 83

Inclusiveness, of political institutions, 42

India, attitudes toward political leaders in, 29

Individualism, 52, 55. *See also* Autonomy

Inequality, attitudes toward, 109, 114

Inglehart, Ronald, 25, 29

Institutions, adolescents' support for, 122; of democratic regime, 2; support for, 143; teenagers' support for, 142, 190. *See also* Government

Intellectuals, 13

Interest, political, 136-139, 162, 164, 166, 197

Interviews, 16, 198, 199. *See also* Questionnaires

Ishihara Shintaro, 192

Italians, national character of, 130

Italy, attitudes toward political leaders in, 29

Ito Hirobumi, 47

Jamaica, parent-child political correspondences in, 165

Japan, as "peace power," 67

Japan Communist Party (JCP), 13, 77, 88; student support of, 119, 135; support for, 92; youth support of, 146

Japan Socialist Party (JSP), 73, 76; children's attitudes toward, 94-95; children of rural supporters of, 167; support for, 88, 89, 92, 119

Japan Teachers Union, 13, 77

Jaros, Dean, 176

Jennings, M. Kent, 84, 156, 165, 168, 171, 197

Johnson, Pres. Lyndon B., 31

Kato Takakatsu, 61

Kazuo Kawai, 24

Kennedy, Pres. John F., 31

Kishi Nobusuke, 36, 44, 46; support for, 31

Kokutetsu (national railway), 106

Komeito (political party), 74, 76; student support of, 119; support for, 88, 135, 155; youth support of, 146

Kubota Akira, 94, 165

Kusunoki Masashige, 46

Labels, ideologically based, 186-187

Lane, Robert, 5, 128, 139

Langdon, Frank, 60, 77, 78, 84

Language, and problems of methodology, 197

Lasswell, Harold, 5, 64, 128, 129

Leader, missing, 44-47; role of, 192; theory of benevolent, 21, 22, 26, 48, 157, 175, 183-184. *See also* Political leaders

Learning, political, 5, 117

Legitimacy, emperor as source of, 6; political, 21

Liberal Democratic Party (LDP), 37, 75, 167; children's attitudes toward, 94-95; domination of, 146; identification of youth with, 81; student support of, 119; support for, 78, 87, 89, 190

Liberalism, affective reactions to, 108

Liberty, 6; attitudes toward, 109, 114. *See also* Equality

Life cycle, 189

Lifton, Robert, 170

Linguistics, 197

McCrone, Donald, 87

McGinnies, Elliott, 61

Mainichi poll, 30

Majoritarianism, 56, 60, 68

Majority rule, attitudes toward, 60, 62

Marriage, and politics, 87, 88. *See also* Family

Marxism, 73, 186
Media, government ownership of, 76; influence of, 158, 189; and political interest, 136; and student partisanship, 121
Mendelian law, of political inheritance, 84
Merelman, Richard, 103, 118, 121, 122
Methodology, 15-17, 195-199. *See also* Questionnaries
Michigan, Univ. of, project on Japanese voter, 78
Militarism, 70
Minobe Ryokichi, 32, 34, 44, 184, 191; personal style of, 36; popularity of, 33
Minsei (Democratic Youth League), of JCP, 13, 77, 145, 146
Minshushugi, 53. *See also* Democracy
Mishima Yukio, 191
Mobility, intergenerational social, 138
Monarchy, allegiance to, 45; role of, 25. *See also* Emperor
Monopoly, government, 75-76; national, 106
Morals, in curriculum 14
Mother, political influence of, 158, 159, 160, 161-164; political role of, 157; teenagers and, 178. *See also* Family; Parents
Mt. Fuji, 25
Multi-party system, 95. *See also* Party system
Mutual security treat, U.S.-Japan, 59, 76, 95

Nagasaki, 66
Nakane Chie, 130
National anthem, 45
National character, 2, 3, 127; studies of, 10, 55
National goals, 70
National identity, 64, 70
Nationalism, 10
National leaders, attitudes toward, 28-29. *See also* Political leaders
National policy, 75
National pride, 10
National Railway (Kokutetsu), 106
New Haven study, 38
Niemi, Richard G., 84, 89, 156, 165, 168, 171, 197
Ninomiya Sontoku, 46
Nixon, Pres. Richard, 30, 31
Nogi, Gen., 46
Nonconformity, tolerance of, 63. *See also* Dissensus
Norms, antidemocratic, 68; of democratic ideology, 131; subordination, 11. *See also* Values

Occupation, American, 1, 3, 45; and edu-

cational policy, 14; and emperor system, 23; purpose of, 46; reformers of, 8
Oda Makoto, 192
Okamura Tadao, 15, 17, 22, 24, 27, 29, 35, 53, 67; survey of, 79, 105, 116
Opinion polls, on political parties, 78; on youth, 43
Opposition, to tradition, 9-15
Orientations, political, 11

Pacifism, affective reactions to, 108; attitudes toward, 65, 66
Parents, agreement with students, 169; on ego-autonomy scale, 129; party identifications of, 84; on political efficacy scale, 132; political influence of, 159, 165; on political interest scale, 136; and political parties, 82; questionnaire for, 15-17, 208-210; response rates of, 196; role of, 179; on social trust scale, 130; support for institutions among, 38-44; value transmissions of, 156. *See also* Family; Father; Mother
Participant democrat, 125
Participation, political, 126, 136; measures of, 162; and political socialization, 7; support for, 143. *See also* Democracy
Partisanship, 9, 18; acquisition of, 122; in family, 173; growth of, 73-99; ideology and, 117; influence of family on, 96; inheritance of, 80-90; parental transmission of, 160, 164; social determinants of, 90; as symbol of dissensus, 185; and teenagers' support, 148; transmission of, 179
Party system, 75-77, 91; continuity of, 96; early postwar instability of, 87; roots of, 186; support for, 82, 143, 144; transmission of partisanship in, 89. *See also* Political parties
Paternal dominance hypothesis, 166
Path analysis model, 140-142; of teenagers support of governmental institutions, 147-149
Pathologies, social, 172
Patriarchy, authoritarian, 188-189; stereotypical, 178-179
Peace, attitudes toward, 67, 70, 109, 114; ideal of, 65; as right, 54; symbols of, 185
Peace Constitution, 66
Peers, influence of, 158, 159, 189. *See also* Friends
People's Republic of China, perceptions of, 107
Personality, 5; political, 143; and politics, 127. *See also* Political leaders
Policy, public educational, 14
Political efficacy, 131-136; parent-student

agreement on, 164, 166; scales for, 197
Political gravity, principle of, 88
Political interest, 136-139; parents', 162; parent-student agreement on, 164, 166; scales for, 197
Political leaders, children's attitudes toward, 33, 189; honesty of, 29; images of, 175, 189; local, 37; national v. local, 34; respect for, 46. *See also* Leader
Political parties, attitudes toward, 38, 40, 42; elections and, 37; identification with, 73-74, 77-80, and ideology, 102, 118; Komeito, 74, 76, 88, 119, 135, 155; parent-student agreement on, 164, 166; perceptions of, 39; pre-war, 83; and socialization process, 186; support for, 82
Political regimes, 1-2
Political science theory, 4
"Political senescence," 81
Political systems, linkages of, 4; and preadult socialization, 2
Political trust, 39, 142-147
Politicization, family, 168
Politicians, attitudes toward, 68; local v. national, 35. *See also* Political leaders; Prime minister
Politics, cultural, 94; foundations of, 1; national, 35; patterns of orientation toward, 11; popular input into, 44; psychocultural influences on, 127-131
Polls, *Asahi*, 30, 78; British Gallup, 30n; *Mainichi*, 30; opinion, 43, 78
Popular participation, support for, 143, 144
Popular sovereignty, 6, 24, 47, 52
Poverty, attitudes toward, 109, 114
Powerlessness, political, 11, 139
Presidency, American, 21; attitudes toward, 27, 28, 183; support for, 31
Presidential system, 23
Press, and Imperial family, 36; and popularity of leader, 31
Pretesting, 17, 198. *See also* Questionnaires
Prime minister, attitudes toward, 22, 30, 38, 39, 40, 42, 142, 184, 197; role of, 23, 27-37; students' image of, 176; support for, 143, 144; teenagers' images of, 158; younger children's attitudes toward, 28. *See also* Political leaders
Private ownership, teenagers' perception of, 106
Progressives, 2, 86
Psyche, Japanese national, 127
Psychocultural factors, 126-127

Questionnaires, administration of, 195; as data source, 15; for elementary students, 24; fixed-choice, 198; parents', 208-210;

pretesting for, 17, 198; student, 201-208; for Tokyo eighth graders, 53

Radical student movement, 14, 157, 170
Railway, 76; national, 106
Random sample, 195
Reform, of society, 3
Religion, political systems as, 21; and politics, 22, 76, 88
Research design, 15-17. *See also* Questionnaires
Residence, and political interest, 142. *See also* Urban-rural residence
Responsiveness, of political institutions, 40
Revolution, 45; heroes of, 47
Rhetoric, 101, 122; political, 186
Richardson, Bradley, 35, 83, 94, 134, 145
Rural areaa,
Rural areas, attitudes in, 63; democracy in, 56; and family authority, 176; parental transmission of partisanship in, 167; partisanship of, 75, 91; teenagers in, 121; traditional culture in, 12
Rural residence, and political development, 187-188. *See also* Urban-rural residence

Saigo Takamori, 46
Sample, demographic composition of, 196; for questionnaire, 195
Sato Eisaku, 22n, 44; personal style of, 36; support for, 31. *See also* Prime minister
Scalipino, Robert, 58, 59
Schools, 195; political impact of, 161
School texts, 104; government control of, 101
Security treaty, U.S.-Japan, 59, 76, 95
Self-Defense Forces, 95
Semantics, 197
Sex, and parental transmission of partisanship, 166; and parental transmission of political values, 178; and political development, 187-188; and political efficacy, 135, 140-141; and political interest, 138; and politics, 121, 134; and teenage attitudes, 149-150. *See also* Women
Shaming, 128
Shinohara Hajime, 55
Social change, 190
Social Darwinism, 103
Socialism, 76; affective reactions to, 108, 109; attitudes toward, 109, 110, 112, 113, 187; in school texts, 104; teenagers' attitudes toward, 116; teenagers' perceptions of, 102, 105
Socialist ideology, 13, 14
Socialists, SES of, 91
Socialization, family and, 155, 156 (*see also*

Socialization (cont.)
Family); and ideology, 94; to partisanship,
83; and party system, 186; political, 1-2,
190; resocialization, 189
Socializing agents, 125
Social theory, 2
Social trust, 127-131; and political efficacy,
140-141; scales for, 197
Society, Marxist view of, 13
Socioeconomic status (SES), and partisan-
ship, 90-94; and political development,
187-188
Soka gakkai (value creation society), 76, 88,
135, 151
Soviet Union, perceptions of, 107
Stability, political, 179
Status, and political interest, 138
Stereotypes, of Japanese family, 170-174;
political, 126, 150; of traditional Japa-
nese, 145
Stokes, Donald, 81
Student groups, leftist, 14
Student movement, 14
Students, agreement with parents of, 169;
attitudes toward emperor of, 26; on ego-
autonomy scale, 129; party identification
of, 85; party support of, 119, 120; on
political efficacy scale, 132; on political
interest scale, 136; questionnaries for,
15-17; revolutionary, 101; on social trust
scale, 130
Subordination, 128
Surveys, 15n
Symbolism, of political leader, 21
Symbols, 122; condensation, 64; emperor,
8; flag, 25, 45; ideologically based,
186-187; national anthem, 45
Systems analysis theory, 5

Takeo Miki, 30n
Takezawa Shin'ichi, 61
Tanaka Kakuei, 30
Teachers, 13, 77; political influence of, 158,
160
Teenagers, attitudes toward prime minister,
32; autonomy of, 173; and capitalism,
102, 105, 115, 116; on consensus, 57;
cynicism of, 145; ideology among, 120;
influence of family on, 166; and parents'
partisanship, 89; and partisanship, 81, 83;
political development of, 187; political
efficacy of, 133, 134, 135, 141; political
identity of, 17; political interest of, 137,
141; political role of, 161; psychocultural
influences on, 151; sample of, 15-16; support for institutions among, 38-44. See
also Adolescents; Students

Texts, school, 101, 104
Throne, support for, 25. See also Emperor
Titus, David A., 26
Tobacco, 76
Togo, Adm., 46
Tokyo, Governor of, 32
Tokyo Citizen's Party (Tomin no To), 35
Torney, Judith V., 27, 53, 91, 118, 137,
138, 145, 156
Tradition, 126; of Japanese family, 156;
opposition to, 9-15
Translation, problem of, 197
Truman, Pres. Harry S., 30, 31
Trust, political, 142-147
Twelfth graders, survey of, 26

United States, movements in, 102; party
affiliation in, 77; party identification in,
86. See also America
Upper-status groups, 138
Urban areas, attitudes in, 62; parental transmission of partisanship in, 167; teenagers
in, 121
Urban guerilla warfare, 101
Urbanization, political effects of, 190; and
political interests, 138; and politics, 74-75
Urban residence, and political development,
187-188
Urban-rural dichotomy, 186, 188
Urban-rural residence, impact of, 96; influence of, 127, 145; and parental transmission of political values, 178; and partisanship, 90-94; and political attitudes, 150;
and political efficacy, 134

Values, 55; acquisition of, 192; antidemocratic, 68; in democracy, 54, 55-56;
family transmission of, 174; influence of
peer group on, 160; parental, 190; peace,
70; political, 5, 105; sources of, 155 (see
also Socialization); testing of, 66; of
young Japanese, 4
Verba, Sidney, 21, 129, 157, 175
Village, image of, 150
Violence, of leftist students, 14
Vogel, Ezra, 61, 130

Ward, Robert, 57, 94, 165
Watanuki Joji, 91, 93, 134, 142
West Germany, party identification in, 86
Whitehill, Arthur, 61
Women, opportunities for, 131; political
interest of, 138; politics and, 162. See also
Mothers
Workers, blue-collar, 128
Work ethic, 110
World War II, 45, 66, 67

Xenophobia, 12

Yara, Gov., 191
Yoshida Shigeru, 30, 31, 47
Yoshida Yoshiaki, 26
Youth, feelings toward political leaders of, 7; influences on, 9; party identification of, 73; skepticism of, 43. *See also* Adolescents; Students

Zureik, Elia T., 83, 118

About the Author

Joseph A. Massey is Assistant Professor of Government at Dartmouth College. He received the B.A. degree in political science from Villanova University, the M.A. degrees in both Japanese studies and political science, and the Ph.D. in the latter subject from Yale University. Dr. Massey's experience includes intensive language study at the Inter-University Center for Japanese Language Training in Tokyo and survey research and data analysis at the Inter-University Consortium for Political Research. In 1974-75, he was the recipient of a Japan Foundation grant for research on the expressive aspects of political leadership in Japan. His publications include "The Missing Leader: Japanese Youths' View of Political Authority," *American Political Science Review*, March 1975, and, with Elizabeth T. Massey, "The Language Competence of American Specialists on Japan: A Quantitative Inquiry," forthcoming.